Governance and Development in India

The study of the political economy of development in India is significant as India has emerged as one of the fastest-growing countries during the last three decades and the rate of economic growth and poverty reduction have not been matched in India's subnational states. Although the Union Government has introduced and implemented several economic reforms since 1991 to enhance the economic development, the results of implantation have varied.

Governance and Development in India compares two Indian subnational states, Andhra Pradesh and Bihar. The book does not consider the state as an aggregate entity; rather, it disaggregates the state relationally and spatially. Concentrating on the micro-institutional variables and the role of regional elites, the author investigates the political roots of the divergence of development trajectories among India's subnational states since liberalization, as an essential aspect of the political economy of development in India. The book explores the black box of the multi-layered state of India and interactions among the Central Government, the states, regional leaders and other stakeholders and explains why the regional leaders have pursued divergent economic strategies using the analytical narrative research method and the subnational comparative research method.

Firmly based on the theoretical foundations of the neo-institutional rational choice model of governance, polycentric hierarchy theory and the strategies for regional elite strategy analysis, combined with empirical research, this book is a valuable contribution to the fields of comparative political economy, state politics in India, governance and development in developing countries, and South Asian comparative politics.

Seyed Hossein Zarhani is a post-doctoral research fellow and lecturer at the Department of Political Science, South Asia Institute, Heidelberg University, Germany.

Routledge Advances in South Asian Studies

Edited by Subrata K. Mitra

Institute for South Asian Studies, the National University of Singapore

South Asia, with its burgeoning, ethnically diverse population, soaring economies, and nuclear weapons, is an increasingly important region in the global context. The series, which builds on this complex, dynamic, and volatile area, features innovative and original research on the region as a whole or on the countries. Its scope extends to scholarly works drawing on history, politics, development studies, sociology, and economics of individual countries from the region as well those that take an interdisciplinary and comparative approach to the area as a whole or to a comparison of two or more countries from this region. In terms of theory and method, rather than basing itself on any one orthodoxy, the series draws broadly on the insights germane to area studies, as well as the tool kit of the social sciences in general, emphasizing comparison, the analysis of the structure and processes, and the application of qualitative and quantitative methods. The series welcomes submissions from established authors in the field as well as from young authors who have recently completed their doctoral dissertations.

32 India-China Relations
Politics of Resources, Identity and Authority in a Multipolar World Order
Jagannath P. Panda

33 Indigenous Identity in South Asia
Making Claims in the Colonial Chittagong Hill Tracts
Tamina M. Chowdhury

34 Gender Justice and Proportionality in India
Comparative Perspectives
Juliette Gregory Duara

35 Governance and Development in India
A Comparative Study on Andhra Pradesh and Bihar after Liberalization
Seyed Hossein Zarhani

For a full list of titles, please see: www.routledge.com/asianstudies/series/RASAS

Governance and Development in India

A Comparative Study on Andhra Pradesh and Bihar after Liberalization

Seyed Hossein Zarhani

Routledge
Taylor & Francis Group
LONDON AND NEW YORK

First published 2019
by Routledge
2 Park Square, Milton Park, Abingdon, Oxon OX14 4RN

and by Routledge
52 Vanderbilt Avenue, New York, NY 10017, USA

First issued in paperback 2020

Routledge is an imprint of the Taylor & Francis Group, an informa business

British Library Cataloguing-in-Publication Data
A catalogue record for this book is available from the British Library

Library of Congress Cataloging-in-Publication Data
A catalog record has been requested for this book

ISBN 13: 978-0-367-58676-8 (pbk)
ISBN 13: 978-0-8153-6831-1 (hbk)

Typeset in Times New Roman
by Wearset Ltd, Boldon, Tyne and Wear

For Samareh and Saba

Contents

Figures

Tables

Foreword

This book comparing the divergent developmental trajectories of the Indian states – Andhra Pradesh and Bihar – is an important addition to the comparative literature on the political economy of Indian states. India presents substantial subnational diversity, pregnant with possibilities for comparison. Differing developmental outcomes persist within subnational state structures in the framework of the same constitution in a country governed by one parliament. India's rich diversity presents developmental outcomes whose characteristics range from Ukraine to Sub Saharan Africa. In terms of per capita income (purchasing power parity), Tamil Nadu resembles Ukraine, Andhra Pradesh is similar to Cape Verde, and Bihar lands us in Sub Saharan Africa. Seyed Hossein Zarhani queries the substantial question: what produces this developmental diversity within the same political system.

The book presents a thoroughgoing review of the governance literature. The variety of views around which the term governance revolves, reveals that state capacity is only one of the strands in the governance literature. The central theme of this book is state capacity. It interrogates the question, what produces the capacity within the subnational state in India to grow more or less successfully?

Indian was a federation even before the economic reforms of 1991. The policy changes undertaken by the government in July 1991, constituted a watershed in the economic history of India. These reforms favoring the private sector and globalization accelerated the federalization of the economy and gave plentiful powers to chief ministers of every state. After 1991, the most significant investment decisions lay with the subnational states in India. If the state was favorable toward the private sector and engaged the global economy, it could produce globalized information technology hub in the city of Hyderabad. Special economic zones could be successfully launched in Andhra Pradesh and Tamil Nadu, whereas West Bengal struggled with acquiring industrial land for entrepreneurs. In Bihar, governance favoring growth declined in the 1990s until chief minister Nitish Kumar came to power in the new millennium.

What explains this diversity in state capacity in India's subnational states? Seyed Hossein Zarhani makes a compelling argument that executive agency matters. This book will extend the debate on subnational variation in developmental outcomes in India.

Rahul Mukherji
February 2018

Preface and acknowledgments

The study of the political economy of development in India is significant for several reasons. First, India has emerged as one of the fastest-growing countries during last three decades despite all pessimism. Second, the rate of economic growth and poverty reduction have not been similar in different subnational states in India. Although the Union Government has introduced and implemented several economic reforms since 1991 to enhance the economic development, the results of implantation have varied in different subnational states. Some states have had a disappointing economic performance, and some had better performance than average. Why?

Within the literature on the political economy of development in India, a great deal of attention is paid to the role the state. The neo-liberal perspective (pro-market approach with a minimum intervention of state), as well as the neo-statist approach (mostly based on institutionalism, rational choice or historical), recognize the 'state' as the key variable that had a positive or adverse impact on India's economic performance. However, the majority of these works have dealt mainly with the role of 'Central Government' as a unitary actor.

This book does not consider the state as an aggregate entity; rather, it *disaggregates* the state relationally and spatially. Unlike the majority of both neo-liberal and neo-statist types of research on India, considering the state as a unitary actor, this study tries to open up the black box of state and concentrates on the micro-institutional variables and the role of regional elites. This book investigates the political roots of the divergence of development trajectories among India's subnational states since the liberalization, as an essential aspect of the political economy of development in India. It opens up the black box of the multi-layered state of India and interactions among the Central Government, the states, regional leaders and other stakeholders.

This book represents an example of implementation of the subnational comparative method, comparing two Indian subnational states, Andhra Pradesh, and Bihar. As scholars like Kennedy (2004), Mitra (2011), Lloyd I. Rudolph and Rudolph (2013), and Mukherji (2014) revealed, one of the results of economic liberalization in India after the 1990s, was enhancing the autonomy of the subnational states toward the Central Government, particularly in terms of economic policymaking. Accordingly, as Lloyd I. Rudolph and Rudolph (2013) elaborated,

India moved away from 'Command and control economy' toward a 'federal market economy' in the 1990s. Accordingly, the chief ministers can be seen as the main actors in the post-liberalization drama.

However, this explanation only hints at the *possibility* of divergent developmental policy in the States based on the priorities of rational regional or national elites. Moreover, the patterns of behavior and strategic choices of these leaders in the new institutional arrangement have not been studied explicitly and separately. This book tries to explain *why* the regional leaders have pursued divergent economic strategies. Therefore, this book, using an analytical narrative research method and the subnational comparative research method, seeks to answer these questions:

- Why did Andhra Pradesh and Bihar with relatively similar initial institutional and economic conditions after independence, and with experience of strong subnational movement that ended the hegemony of the Congress Party in both states, display a significant divergence in development trajectory after the liberalization?
- Why did regional leaders in Bihar and Andhra Pradesh adopt the divergent strategies toward the Center and the responses to the reform policies in both states were entirely different?

This study does not understand the accelerated economic growth after the liberalization as the result of the simple top-down implementation of the reforms or result of the application of normative good governance principles; conversely, the book argues the spatial, as well as central–local dynamics, affects the regional developmental patterns. Accordingly, the post-liberalization divergence in regional development does not attribute merely to the historical and colonial context or initial economic condition; rather, this book argues the difference between Bihar and Andhra Pradesh are associated with the elite's strategic choices in the face of the vertical and horizontal games.

With growing acknowledgment of India's economic emergence despite the regional variations, this book is particularly relevant for those interested in the comparative political economy as well as politics of development in India. Furthermore, it should appeal to a generation of researchers and academics, applying rational choice institutionalism, and governance theory in the context of developing post-colonial countries.

This book is an adaptation of my doctoral thesis, which I completed in December 2015 at the Faculty of Economics and Social Sciences at Ruprecht Karls Universität Heidelberg, Germany. I have revised and developed the manuscript during my post-doctoral research at the department of political science, South Asia Institute, Heidelberg University. I am grateful to the SAI for providing me with the opportunities through this process.

The completion of this book would not have been possible without the help of many individuals. First, my deepest gratitude and appreciation go to my *Doktorvater*, Professor Subrata K. Mitra, for his guidance and continued confidence in my work throughout my doctoral study. I could not have reached this stage without his continuous and warm-hearted support.

I am also especially grateful to Professor Rahul Mukherji, Head of Department of Political Science, South Asia Institute, Heidelberg University, for his friendship, support, and valuable comments. The revision of the book was made possible by his guidance, insights, and suggestions.

I am thankful to my second supervisor, Professor Ditmar Rothermund, who gave me many valuable suggestions at different stages of my research. Moreover, I would also like to thank Professor Markus Pohlmann and Professor Reimut Zohlnhöfer for serving as my examination commission members.

I would like to thank of Mr. K. Raju, the Chairman of the SC Department, Indian National Congress for his time and fruitful discussions. I am also grateful to Prof. K.C. Suri, not only for hosting me at the University of Hyderabad but also for his critical comments and for helping me to conduct interviews. I am also thankful to Dr. K. Lakshminarayana and Mr. Kambhampati Rammohan from the TDP for their time and the interviews.

Special thanks also go to my dear friends and colleagues in the Department of Political Science, South Asia Institute. My research has profited much from their feedback on several occasions, and I will always remember the inspiring intellectual exchange in this interdisciplinary environment. I would like to express my gratitude to my friends and colleagues Dr. Markus Pauli, Dr. Michael Liebig, Dr. Bernhard M. Beitelmair-Berini, Dr. Jivanta Schötlli and Dr. Stefan Diederich for their comments and friendship. I would also like to thank Markus and Stefan for their remarks, critiques and suggestions during the review meeting, which proved to be very useful in the next stages of the research.

I would like to thank the editorial team, especially Dorothea Schaefter and Lily Brown at Routledge, the U.K., for their patience and support. Incredibly detailed, incisive and sustained comments and suggestions from two anonymous reviewers have transformed and improved this book immeasurably.

Of course, the acknowledgments would not be complete without giving thanks to my parents. Both have instilled many admirable qualities in me and taught me hard work, self-respect, and persistence. They have supported my academic pursuit, and I could always rely on them. I do not imagine a life without their love and blessings.

Finally, my heartiest gratitude goes to my wife, Samareh, for her love, patience, support, and her imperturbable belief in my abilities. Also, I would like to thank Samareh for her critiques and comments on my work. She has been a never-ending source of love, encouragement, and motivation. Undoubtedly, this book could not have been written without her.

Seyed Hossein Zarhani
February 2018

Abbreviations

AIADMK	All India Anna Dravida Munnetra Kazhagam
AP	Andhra Pradesh
BC	backward castes
BIMARU	Bihar, Madhya Pradesh, Rajasthan, and Uttar Pradesh
BJP	Bharatiya Janata Party
BJS	Bharatiya Jana Sangh
BLD	Bharatiya Lok Dal
BRIC	Brazil, Russia, India, China
BSP	Bahujan Samaj Party
CM	chief minister
CMO	Chief Minister Office
CPI	Communist Party of India
CPI(ML)	Communist Party of India (Marxist–Leninist) Liberation
CPM	Communist Party of India (Marxist)
DMK	Dravida Munnetra Kazhagam
EBCs	extremely backward castes
FDI	Foreign direct investment
GNP	gross national product
IAS	Indian Administrative Service
ICT	information and communication technology
IMF	International Monetary Fund
INC	Indian National Congress
IT	information technology
JD	Janata Dal
JD(S)	Janata Dal (Secular)
JD(U)	Janata Dal (United)
JMM	Jharkhand Mukti Morcha
JP	Janata Party
KCR	Kalvakuntla Chandrashekar Rao
LJP	Lok Janshakti Party
MIM	Majlis-i-Ittihad-al-Muslimeen (Association for Muslim Unity)
MLA	Member of the Legislative Assembly
MP	Member of Parliament

MPI	multi-dimensional poverty index
NDA	National Democratic Alliance
NIE	neo-institutional economics
NSDP	net state domestic product
NTR	Nandamuri Taraka Rama Rao
OBCs	other backward castes
RBI	Reserve Bank of India
RJD	Rashtriya Janata Dal
SEZ	special economic zone
RTI	right to information
Rs	rupees
SAL	structural adjustment loan
SAP	structural adjustment program
SCs	scheduled castes
SDP	state domestic product
SRC	States' Reorganization Commission, 1957
SSP	Sanghata Socialist Party
STs	scheduled tribes
TDP	Telugu Desam Party
TRS	Telangana Rashtra Samithi
UP	Uttar Pradesh
UPA	United Progressive Alliance
USAID	United States Agency for International Development
UT	union territories
WTO	World Trade Organization
YSR	Yeduguri Sandinti Rajasekhara

1 Introduction

The puzzle of divergent development trajectories within a debated (non-)developmental state

Casting the context

In the 1990s, the literature on state capacity portrayed the Indian state as a weak state that was not able to engender rapid economic growth; nor enforce the rule of law. For example Kohli in his *Democracy and Discontent: India's Growing Crisis of Governability* (1990, 1) observed India as a functioning democracy; nevertheless, "increasingly it is not well governed." Kohli explicated how the decline of Congress system[1] contributed to the crisis of governability in India. He explained the crisis of governability as the result of an 'organizational vacuum,' which took place after the decline of Congress Party's position without being replaced (Kohli 1990, 6–9). Following Huntington (1968), Kolhi tried to explain how the fraction of Indian elites at both the Center and the regional level caused destabilizing competitions and resulted in the deinstitutionalization of the political system. The increase of political instability in India in the 1980s was the symptom of the increasing deinstitutionalization of Indian state since the 1970s. Consequently, Kohli (1990) predicted more government instability, an increase in the number of caste and community conflicts, and the growth of violence as symptoms of a crisis of governability in the next decades. Kohli (1990, 6) considered the crisis of governability as the main cause for the low-level state capacity to boost economic development: "India's massive developmental problems demand the state's attention, but no problem in India is likely to be more serious than is disintegration of the major problem-solving institution, namely, an effective democratic state."

In the same way, Herring (1999) claimed 'embedded particularism' affected the state-society relations in India negatively; thus, he described India as "the most dramatic case of a failed developmental state" (Herring 1999, 306). Herring suggested the rate of economic growth and success in poverty eradication as two significant indicators to measure the success of economic performance after the independence. Accordingly, India was witness to 3.5% annual growth of GDP between 1950 and 1980, which has been branded as the 'Hindu rate of growth.'[2] This rate should be compared to the average of other developing countries – around 4.9% per annum in the same period (Herring 1999, 310). Following Johnson (1987) who worked on the institutional roots of development in East

Asian countries, Herring tried to depict the differences between India and East Asian Tigers in terms of state capacity. Herring (1999, 306) recognized several similarities in the historical context, international position, and developmental aspiration; however, despite these resemblances, the only result of India's state-led development was 'license-permit-quota raj.' He realized the characteristics of India's state as the best explanatory variable. Inspired by Johnson's developmental state theory (1982, 1987) and the neo-statist notion of 'bringing the state back in,' Herring perceived scrutinizing of the Indian state's characteristics as the best tool to analyze India's undesirable economic performance. Therefore, he described the Indian state as the soft, pluralist class, overextended, imprisoned or structurally trapped, iron frame, and contested federal state (Herring 1999, 313–315). In sum, according to these studies, post-colonial India not only was considered as a failed developmental state that could not achieve its developments goals but also gradually could not enforce the rules and became more unstable.

In contrast to these negative predictions, the political and economic scenario in India has fundamentally changed since the 1990s. Not only the level of political instability and violence decreased drastically, but also the annual rate of the GDP growth has increased sharply. As Mitra (2006) exposed, despite the consistent crises and persistent violence, post-colonial India has preserved its democratic institutions. Similar to Kohli (1990), Mitra (2006, 8) uses the *incidence of riots* and *murders* as quantitative indicators of the orderly rule as the manifestation of effective governance. Despite Kohli's prognosis, Mitra (2006) provided evidence, demonstrating the level of the orderly rule has increased since last three decades, and the number of riots and political violence declined. Likewise, after the 1990s, the Hindu rate of growth has transformed to what *The Economist* (2010) called "India's surprising economic miracle." Figure 1.1 exposes how India's GDP per capita swiftly increased after the 1990s.

The average of the annual growth rate of India's gross national income during the First to Seventh economic development plan was less than 4%. Nevertheless, it has increased to 6.5% in the Eighth Plan (1992–1997), 5.6% in the Ninth Plan (1997–2002), 7.6% in the Tenth Plan (2002–2007), and 7.8% in the Eleventh Plan (2007–2012) (see Economic Survey 2014–2015, 2015).

As Figure 1.2 portrays, while India's growth rate was less than China in the 1990s and early and mid-2000s, India could reach China's growth rate at the end of the decade. At the moment, India is growing faster than all BRIC countries.

Although, India possess considerably less GDP per capita in comparison to the East Asian so-called developmental states such as South Korea, Taiwan, and Singapore, India's economy has grown more rapidly than them since the mid-1990s. Nevertheless, as Sinha (2005, 30) noted, comparing India with the East Asian states (especially four tigers) can lead to simplistic conclusions. This kind of cross-national analysis that has become popular after the rise of 'developmental state theory' essentially neglects the differences between India and Japan, South Korea or four Asian Tigers in terms of territorial size, population, political system, and internal heterogeneity. These ranges of comparative studies are unmindful about the *internal architecture* of state in India.

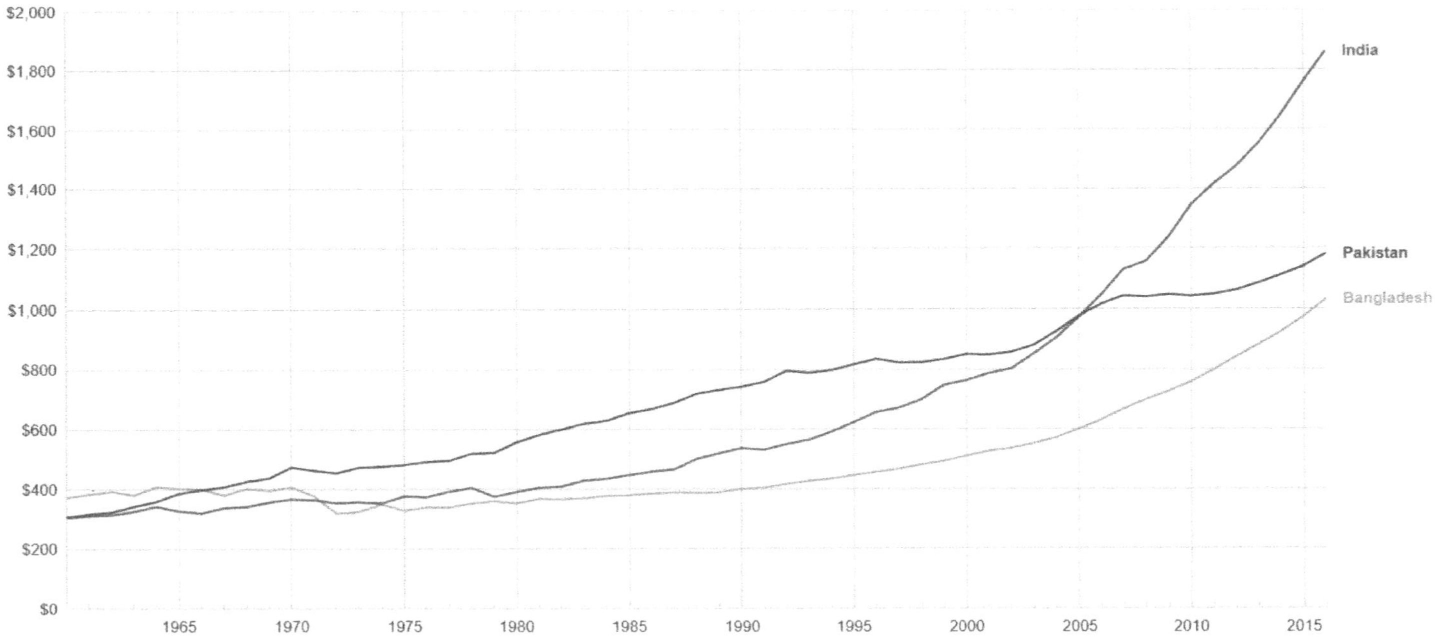

Figure 1.1 India, Pakistan, and Bangladesh's GDP per capita (constant US$), 1960–2015.

Source: World Bank (2015), drawn by the author.

Figure 1.2 Rate of GDP growth in BRICS countries, 1990–2015.

Source: World Bank (2015), drawn by the author.

Most of India's subnational s states are comparable to other independent nation-states in terms of size, GDP, and population. For example, as *The Economist* (2011) depicted, undivided Andhra Pradesh's population is equivalent to Egypt and a little bit more than Iran. Furthermore, AP's GDP is comparable to Slovakia and its GDP per capita to Nicaragua. The result of the comparison between Andhra Pradesh and these nation-states is noticeable. From 1995 to 2014, while Andhra Pradesh had average 7.05% per annum growth, Iran experienced 3.52% growth, Egypt 4.37%, Slovakia 4.04%, and Nicaragua 4.01%. Likewise, if Gujarat had been a nation-state, it would be one of the fastest growing economies in the world with its 7.96% annual growth rate during last two decades.[3]

In the same way, some of India's regional states had a better performance than others. For example, the average of Gujarat's growth rates (GSDP) at constant prices from 1995 to 2014 was 7.96%, Andhra Pradesh 7.05%, West Bengal 6.62%, and Jammu and Kashmir was 5.22%. While Bihar's disappointing rate of growth was –5.15% in the 2003–2004 financial year, Gujarat experienced the fascinating rate of 14.77%. In the same year, Andhra Pradesh with 9.35% growth had a better performance than the average of India (8.2%) and West Bengal was witness to only 6.2% growth (Planning Commission 2014, 167).

The indicators of the capability approach like the multidimensional poverty index (MPI) portray the same image.[4] Alkire and Seth (2015) analyzed the change of level of poverty in India between 1999 and 2006. Their findings show that there is a considerable reduction in the national MPI from 0.300 to 0.251, by 2.6% per annum between 1999 and 2006 (Alkire and Seth 2015, 91). However, the reduction has not been alike across different regional states. For example, Andhra Pradesh had the best performance in an absolute reduction of MPI while Bihar reduced MPI the least.

Accordingly, the critical changes in India since the last decade of the twentieth century can be summed up in two statements: (a) After a sharp decline of the orderly rule in the 1980s, this decline did not become terminal and was reversed steadily after reaching the pick in 1985, so we can see a higher level of orderly rule after the 1990s; (b) India in the last two and half decades has seen the decent rate of growth at more than 6.5%[5] and a significant reduction of mass poverty. Though per capita income in India has remained low in comparison to East Asian developing countries, the size of India's economy has become 4.5 times larger than 1990.[6] However, the rate of growth and level of poverty reduction was not similar in different subnational states. Despite common formal institutions and operating under a shared set of rules, some regional states had a better performance than India's average, and some had a meager rate of growth.

How can these changes be interpreted? Why have some of India's regional or subnational states performed better than others in terms of economic achievements? What kinds of theoretical toolbox can offer practical tools for a better explanation of these diversities? Can a neo-liberal approach and its affiliated good governance discourse explain the nature of development? Can these drastic changes and success only be attributed to the policy level and policy-makers' decisions at the Center that adopted and implemented the neo-liberal and pro-market policies? Alternatively, do neo-statist theories[7] with their emphasis on the role of the state in the development depict a more precise image? Are there any significant changes in the institutional arrangements or political process, which caused more autonomy for the subnational states in terms of policymaking and implementation?

Ongoing debate: the role of the state in development in India

First, what is the state? This book has used the word *state* with multiple implications: state, regional states, and the central state. The book uses state with a small *s* to refer to the general notion of the state. This concept denotes to "organizations claiming control over territories and people may formulate and pursue goals that are not simply reflective of the demands or interests of social groups, classes, or society" (Skocpol 1985, 9). The concept also covers institutions like bureaucracy and is used to distinguish from 'government' or 'regime.' In the literature on Indian federalism, Indian provinces are also known as states, but this book uses the term 'Indian states,' 'subnational states' or 'regional states' when it intends to refer to provinces. Most scholarship on India uses 'State' with a capital *S* to denote subnational states in India; thus, they are sometimes referred to as 'States' in this book. Moreover, the federal government in India is referred to interchangeably as the 'central government,' 'Center,' or 'Union Government,' consistent with the usage in the literature on India.

Two theoretical perspectives within the political sciences have inspired the contemporary debate on the role of the state in economic development in developing countries and particularly India: (a) neo-liberal perspective, and (b) neo-statist perspective.

Neo-liberal perspective usually understands 'India's big bang' as a result of the changes in the economic policies of the Center after 1991. The government of India's new pro-market policies such as the abolition of License-Permit-Quota Raj, ending the trade control, liberalization of the financial services and trades, reduction of tariffs, and privatization of public sector enterprises has been the engine of economic growth. This conventional narrative distinguishes mainly between two different phases of India's economic history. In the first phase, after the independence, Jawaharlal Nehru as India's first Prime Minister pursued self-resilience strategy through import substitution, centralized planning, and capital-intensive industrialization. After independence, India pursued a development strategy with two pillars: inward-looking attitudes and extremely interventionist approaches.[8] As Cerra and Saxena (2002, 3–4) illustrated, the post-independent development strategy included "import protection, complex industrial licensing requirements, financial repression, and substantial public ownership of heavy industry." The neo-liberal perspective criticized India's inward-oriented policies and mostly state-directed strategy of development. The common conclusion of neo-liberals is that the legacy of this phase was centrally economic planning, an unbelievable quantity of bureaucratic red tape and limitations, and massive inefficiency. The typical negative view on economic planning between 1950 and 1980 and the state intervention can be found in the works of scholars such as Bhagwati (1993) and Ahluwalia (1985).

According to the neo-liberal perspective, the second phase of India's post-colonial development history begins with neo-liberal economic reforms after 1991. The significant shift in the economic and financial policies was perceived as the consequence of the currency crisis of 1991. The 'BoP crisis'[9] was a turning point in the economic history of India. As the *Telegraph* (2009) reported, in 1991 India's foreign exchange reserves were around $1.2 billion, barely sufficient for three weeks' imports. Consequently, the Government of India needed emergency financial support from international financial and aid agencies like IMF and the World Bank. So, the Government of India implemented the first comprehensive economic policy reform program with the support of the $500 million structural adjustment operation (SAL). The World Bank (2012) had identified two objectives for SAL in India:

1 to help India address its immediate balance of payments crisis, and
2 to support a broad set of policy reforms aimed at liberalizing the Indian economy and opening it up to more competition both from within and abroad.

Based on the neo-liberal perspective, Prime Minister Narasimha Rao and his Finance Minister Manmohan Singh introduced a wide-range of economic reforms such as removing licensing requirements in industries, deregulation of foreign trade, and facilitation of inflow of Foreign Direct Investment (FDI), improvement of tax administration, and liberalization of the financial market. The neo-liberal perspective explains the current wave of rapid economic growth as the result of the changes in the Government of India's policies after 1991.

However, these conventional neo-liberal perspectives have been criticized in different ways. As statistics illustrate, India's real GDP growth rose from a Hindu rate of growth (3.5% per annum in the 1960s and 1970s) to over 5% per annum in the 1980s. Therefore, Kohli traces the roots of economic transformation in India in the 1980s; and writes:

> It thus can be argued that the acceleration of economic growth in India began around 1980, and not in 1991 and not in 1991, it was a product, not of liberal policies adopted in 1991, but of a growing state-capital alliance for economic growth that was initiated by Indira Gandhi, and that by now matured into central feature of India's political economy.
>
> (Kohli and Singh 2009, 9)

In the same way, McCartney (2010, 2) asserts that the period from 1950 to 1980 should not be seen as a whole. He recognized a trend of growth from 1951 to 1964 in which India's economy grew by over 4% per annum. With a neo-statist approach, he consternated on the nature of Indian state from 1950 to 1965 and its impact on the more satisfactory economic performance. McCartney (2010, 9) argued that the Indian state shares some features of developmental states in the early 1950s such as developmental elites, the autonomy of state, and more meritocratic and elitist civil services. As McCartney (2010) maintained, contrary to the much accepted neo-liberal perspective, the state's intervention has had a vital role in enhancing economic growth in India before what it is called neo-liberal reforms. His argument is the continuation of views of scholars like Reuschemeyer and Evance (1985, 44), suggesting the effective state intervention is assumed to be an integral part of successful development.

Similarly, Mukherji (2014) introduced his ideational tipping point model to open up the black box of the state, by looking at the evolution of ideas within the state and interactions between political class and technocrats. Unlike neo-liberal scholars who had highlighted the role of international financial organizations and diffusion of their neo-liberal agenda after the liberalization, Mukherji emphasized the endogenous ideational change within the state.

However, most of the academic works, discussing the role of the state in the economic success or failures (for example Bardhan 1984; Rudolph and Rudolph 1987; Herring 1999), deal mainly with the role of 'Central Government' as a unitary actor. For example, when Rudolph and Rudolph (1987) talked about *India's weak-strong state*, they perceived it as a unitary actor. Similarly, when Herring (1999) or Kumar (2008b) spoke about India as a (failed) developmental state, their perception accompanied with a unitary and top-down notion of the state.

In sum, the neo-liberal perspective (pro-market approach with a minimum intervention of state), as well as the neo-statist approach (mostly based on the East Asian authoritarian developmental state model), recognize the 'state' as the key variable that had a positive or adverse impact on India's economic performance. Nevertheless, both mostly perceive the state as 'Central Government' or 'Union Government.' This perception accompanies an aggregate, unitary and top-down notion of state.

Statement of the problem and significance of study

Studying the development in India is significant for several reasons. First, India has emerged as a fast-growing state during the last three decades despite all negativities. Second, the rate of economic growth and poverty reduction has been not alike in different India's subnational states. Although the Center has introduced and implemented several economic reforms since 1991 to enhance economic development, the results of implantation have varied in different subnational states.

Most of the studies above (both the neo-liberal and the neo-statist) explicitly or implicitly consider the state (with a focus on the aggregate level) as the core explanatory variable for analyzing development or underdevelopment in India. However, as Sinha (2005, 27) indicates, both the neo-liberal and the neo-statist approaches understand state as a "*unified actor*, which either succeeds or fails but does so coherently." Most of the debates on the necessity of the state's intervention in the economy, the impact of state's institution on development, regime type and growth, and weakness and strength of the state are almost based on this unitary and the top-down notion of the state. These studies usually consider the Center, ruling party, and elites are the primary sources for reference. These approaches look at Jawaharlal Nehru, Indira Gandhi, Rajiv Gandhi, Narasimha Rao, Vajpayee, Manmohan Singh or Modi, as the key players in politics of development; therefore, their ideas, attitudes, and decisions are the crucial determinant of development or under development. Most of the literature on the relations between the state and economy in India concentrate predominantly on nature or policies of the Center or the role of leadership in Delhi. Can this image of the state provide us an appropriate and useful theoretical framework to analyze politics of development in India after the liberalization?

Although these studies improve our understanding of the role of the Center in politics of development, the most significant problem is looking at India's state as a unified and singular entity. India's Constitution safeguarded the unity as well as diversity. Although the Center has a significant role in the Constitution, the subnational states have a significant role in policymaking and implementation of them. The Constitution, through forming an unusual federal design, balances the national interests in one hand and local and regional interests on the other hand. The interrelations between the state and development in India with the diverse political processes in the framework of complicated and multi-layered structure (from the Center to villages) and various institutions in different social and ethnolinguistic contexts cannot be comprehended in an aggregated perspective. The state in India includes complex layers of institutions, providing 'room to maneuver'[10] for the regional leaders, and empowering them for interactions with the Center and local people based on social and political context (Mitra 2006, Mitra 2008; Sinha 2005).

That is why this book keeps a distance from the traditional notion of government; rather, it employs governance discourse with its focus on complexity, diversity, and dynamics of state-society interrelations (see Kooiman 2003). Socially, India is the most heterogeneous state in the world in terms of ethnicity, language, caste, and religion. India's population as per the 2011 census is more than 1.2 billion; and it is 1.6 times more than all Europe. With 22 officially recognized languages, and diverse religions such as Hinduism, Islam (Shia and Sunni), Buddhism, Christianity, and Sikhism, India is a far more diverse and complicated entity than the whole of Europe. Politically, India adopted a federal rather than the unitary structure of government. As Mitra (2006, 65) noted, federalization has emerged as one of the "fundamental characteristics of governance in India." According to Watts (1998), federalism is a normative category, denoting the opposite of unitary rule, involving the advocacy of federal principles. A federal system a descriptive term, referring to the broad types of federal arrangements that give federalism its institutional form. According to its Constitution, India is a Union of States; it is organized institutionally in the form of a federal political system with a Center and several subnational states.[11]

Currently, India consists of 29 (subnational) States and seven Union Territories (UT). The subnational states' borders initially were drawn based on the linguistic boundaries. The states, Delhi and the UT of Pondicherry have then elected legislatures for their Legislature Assembly, with chief ministers in the executive role. The other UTs are governed directly by appointees of the Center. India's Constitution gives both Central Government (Union Government) and State Governments right for legislation. The Constitution divides the state power between the Union Government at the Center and the state governments. It divides the legislative authority between these two levels of administration through three subject lists: First, the union list contains 99 items which the Center can only legislate. Second, the state list, which has 61 items and only at the state level can be legislated. Third, the concurrent list with 52 items, which the Center, as well as States, can legislate. The Constitution gives the Center exclusive authority to act on matters of national importance; and it has a superior authority in terms of defense, foreign policy, currency, banking, and income tax.

However, the regional states have the legal power to legislate in areas such as agriculture, land, education, health, and labor. Since the subnational states have the vast areas for legislation under state list and concurrent list, they can play a significant role in the economic policymaking process. Additionally, the state governments are responsible for implantation of the Center's economic policies at the regional level. Moreover, they are the administrator of the Union Government's sponsored project and schemes; thus, they have a crucial role in the outcomes of these policies (Kennedy 2014; Panagariya, Chakraborti, and Govinda Rao 2014).

India's subnational states had different economic performances after independence. This variance becomes more visible after liberalization than the past. As Gulati (1999), Nachimuthu (2009), Hanumantha Rao (2010), and Paul and Sridhar (2015) reported, there is a growing trend of divergence among the regional states. Most economists employ indicators such as the state domestic product (SDP), net state domestic product (NSPD), per capita SPD or NSDP, and their rate of growth to depict this divergence. In 1980–1981 per capita NSDP (at constant prices, base 1980–1981) of Gujarat was Rs 1950, while that of Bihar was Rs 917 which was less than half of Gujarat's per capita product. Noticeably, per capita NSDP of Gujarat in 1997–1998 was Rs 3976, while that of Bihar was Rs1073, which now was around one-fourth of Gujarat's per capita NSDP. Historically, the range of per capita NSDP among states was wide, and there is a gap between more developed states such as Maharashtra or Gujarat with less developed states such as Bihar and Uttar Pradesh; nevertheless, it has been widening after the liberalization.

Indian policymakers in the Twelfth Five Year Plan[12] realized the inter-state inequalities in per capita income as a cause for concern. They recognize two reasons for widening this gap during the previous four Five Year Plans. First, while the rates of growth of SDP in many states like Andhra Pradesh, Gujarat, and Karnataka have been relatively high, the other States such as Uttar Pradesh (UP), Bihar and Rajasthan had a much lower rate of growth. Second, demographic changes and a higher rate of population growth in some states also played a role in the decrease of per capita SDP.

As Table 1.1 illustrates, the growth performance of India after the 1991 reforms shows a considerable contrast with what has been called the 'Hindu rate of growth'; nevertheless, this higher rate of growth does not imply all India's states have grown with the same speed. For example, some states such as Uttar Pradesh and Punjab grew slower than in India in all these years and states such as Maharashtra or Gujarat grew faster than India's average in three plans out of four. West Bengal in the first decade after liberalization grew faster than Andhra Pradesh; nevertheless, Andhra Pradesh grew faster in the tenth and eleventh programs.

As Figure 1.5 depicts, in the 1980–1981 financial year, per capita NSDP of already more developed States such as Maharashtra, West Bengal, and Gujarat[13] was more than that of BIMARU[14] states. The gap between these two kinds of states has been widening since the liberalization. The compelling case is Andhra Pradesh. Although per capita NSDP of this southern state was at the same level of BIMARU states in 1980–1981, Andhra Pradesh had a better performance, especially after liberalization. Then, it has departed from the level of BIMARU states and reached the average of Indian states. On the contrary, Bihar showed the worse growth performance in these two decades. As Figure 1.3 displays, since the end of the 1980s, all other states even other members of BIMARU club have taken off; nevertheless, the trend of economic growth in Bihar remained without any change.

As Figure 1.3 depicts, the gap between the regional states in terms of per capita NSDP has increased since the 1990s. Nevertheless, some significant

Table 1.1 Growth rates in SDP in the selected states, averages for plan periods (% per annum)

States	*Eighth Plan 1992–1997*	*Ninth Plan 1997–2002*	*Tenth Plan 2002–2007*	*Eleventh Plan 2007–2012*
Andhra Pradesh	5.5	5.4	8.2	8.2
Bihar	3.9	3.7	6.9	9.9
Goa	9.0	5.7	8.5	9.1
Gujarat	12.9	2.8	11.0	9.5
Haryana	5.2	6.1	9.0	9.0
Karnataka	6.2	5.8	7.7	7.2
Kerala	6.5	5.2	8.3	8.2
Madhya Pradesh	6.6	4.5	5.0	9.2
Maharashtra	8.9	4.1	10.1	8.6
Odisha	2.3	5.1	9.2	7.1
Punjab	4.8	4.0	6.0	6.7
Rajasthan	8.0	5.3	7.1	8.5
Tamil Nadu	7.0	4.7	9.7	7.7
Uttar Pradesh	5.0	2.5	5.8	7.1
West Bengal	6.3	6.5	6.2	7.3
All India	6.5	5.7	7.6	8.0

Source: Twelfth Five Year Plan (2013, 35), drawn by the author.

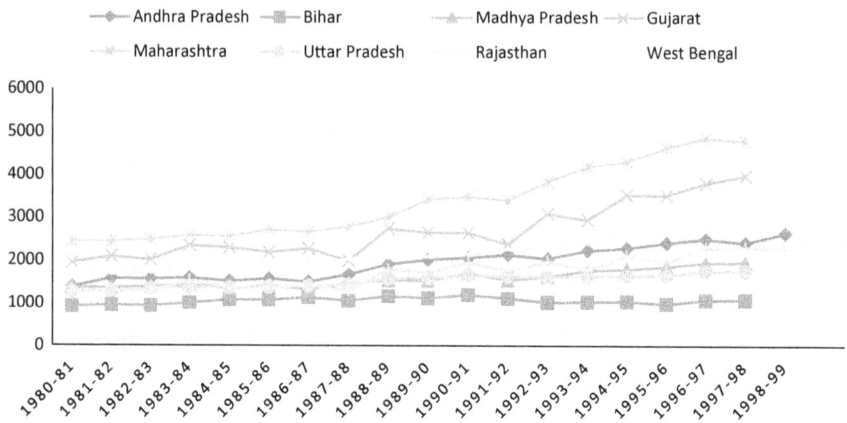

Figure 1.3 Per capita NSDP at factor cost in selected States (at constant prices, the base year 1980–1981) from 1980–1981 to 1998–1999.

Source: *Handbook of Statistics on Indian Economy 2005–06* (2006), drawn by the author.

changes in the pattern of regional development took place. While Maharashtra and Gujarat as two previously more advanced states kept their rate of growth, West Bengal could not grow at the same pace. In contrast, Andhra Pradesh, which had a lower level of infrastructure, development, and income, has performed better than West Bengal; therefore, its per capita NSDP has become more than the national average and States like West Bengal. Also, Bihar, who was reluctant to growth for more than two decades, has been increasing its rate

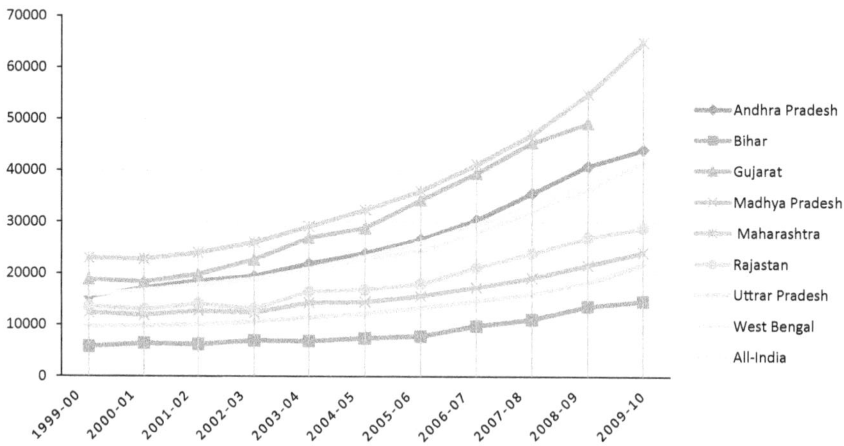

Figure 1.4 Per capita NSDP at factor cost in selected States (at constant prices, the base 1993–1994) from 1999–2000 to 2009–2010.

Source: *Handbook of Statistics on Indian Economy 2009–10* (2010), drawn by the author.

of growth swiftly since 2005–2006, but the gap still exists. Ahluwalia (2002) also depicted there was variation in growth performance across States in pre and post liberalization eras; however, the degree of dispersion in growth rates has increased significantly since the 1990s.

At first glance, it can be concluded that economic growth in India is a spatial phenomenon. Consequently, when we talk about India's economic performance or the economic miracle of India, we should be aware of these regional variations. These dissimilar economic performances are the crucial puzzles for the comparative political economy. How can these variations and divergence of economic performances in a nation-state be interpreted and explained? Why did Bihar remain relatively stagnant; contrariwise, Andhra Pradesh developed faster than the national average?

Despite operating under a shared set of formal institutions and political structure, these regional differences in economic performances of subnational states suggest we should move away from the unitary and top-down notation of the state. While both neo-liberal and neo-statist approaches perceive the state as a unitary actor or organization, this book perceives the Indian state as the multilayered framework and ensemble of intuitions, allows subnational states and regional elites room to maneuver (Mitra 1991). Dreze and Sen (1997, 3–4) observe these vast diversities and disparities in regional developments and suggest that scholars should examine India's development experiences in a disaggregated form:

> Given the extremely heterogeneous character of the Indian economy and society, India's achievements and failures cannot be understood in composite terms, and it is essential to examine the experiences in the disaggregated form … The internal diversities in India offer a great opportunity to learn from each other.

Therefore, unlike most of the comparative political economy models, constructed on a unitary and top-down notion of state, this study argues that analyzing development in India as a federal and multilevel political system is not possible with a mere aggregate notion of state. As Kohli (1987, 3) argues, "the federal nature of the Indian polity allows for a disaggregated and comparative analysis within India." Following Snyder (2001, 100), this book argues the 'Center-centered' perspectives that "treat the national level as an autonomous, separate sphere and obscures the connections between actors in the periphery and the Center" cannot explain disparities, divergences and different trajectories of development within India. Disaggregating state, this book concentrates on the micro-institutional variables as well as interactions between the various levels of the political system. This study uses the neo-institutional model of governance based on rational choice theory (see Mitra 2006) and elaborates how the regional politics, as well as external and exogenous variables, shape the developmental policies of regional leaders. Based on rational choice perspective, these regional political leaders are driven by human rationality, self-interest, and tendency to maximize their interests from the games, rather than only influenced by tradition, and their local context.

In sum, most of the previous studies, concentrating on the role, structure, and nature of India's state in its economic performance mostly neglected its federal characteristics and its developmental implications. This study argues that using good governance approach, as well as the implementation of the conventional developmental state models, cannot address the dynamics and process of development in India. Unlike the majority of both neo-liberal and neo-statist approaches, considering the state as a unitary actor, this study tries to open up the black box of state and concentrates on the micro-institutional variables and the role of regional elites. This study opens up the black box of the multi-layered state of India and interactions among the Central Government, the states, regional leaders and other stakeholders based on a neo-intuitional model of governance.

Gaps in the existing literature

Needless to say, employing the prominent theoretical toolkits such as modernization theory or developmental authoritarian state theory to analyze the interrelations between governance and development in India cannot provide a satisfactory explanation about politics of development in India and political roots of the developmental variation among States.

For example, the famous claim of modernization theory is that "democratic development is an evolutionary phenomenon;" therefore, democracy is the result of "socioeconomic development, not a condition of it" (Leftwich 1996, 7). As Lipset points out, "economic development involving industrialization, urbanization, high educational standards, and a steady increase in the overall wealth of the society, is a fundamental condition sustaining democracy, and it is a mark of the efficiency of the total system" (Lipset 1959, 76–79). In the face of the modernization theory's assumptions, India has been the most populous democratic country in the world since the 1950s; however, a considerable percentage of Indian citizens are still living in rural areas, and the level of poverty even with of all efforts is relatively high. Interestingly, the rapid economic growth emerged several decades after the establishment of democratic institutions in India; therefore, the democratic political structure is not the product of industrialization and urbanization.

Oppositely, some scholars observe a strong correlation between an orderly rule, imposed by authoritarian regimes, and development. From the mid-1980s onwards, a new body of literature has emerged, arguing the economic performance of the 'late industrializers' in East Asia was largely attributable to government intervention and the synergistic relationship between the state and the private sector (see Johnson 1987). Following Johnson's argument, authoritarian developmental states are defined as the strong state regimes, engaging in facilitating fast capitalist growth. Authoritarian developmental states have characteristics such as centralized power structure and a strong drive to eliminate or subordinate all potential centers of countervailing power. Although an authoritarian developmental paradigm can be implemented to scrutinize development in countries such as Singapore or Japan, except for a short period of emergency (1975–1977), there is no example of explicit centralization of power in India.

In sum, unlike claims of modernization theory, neither historical context of urbanization nor massive industrialization have shaped Indian democracy after independence. Moreover, despite the expectations of the scholars, followed Huntington (1968), the social and structural changes after independence did not cause a significant political disorder, threatening the existence of democratic political system. Furthermore, economic development in India is not the product of a centralized authoritarian political structure that imposed rules on society. That is why India has been perceived as an outlier in theories of democracy and development; thus, this 'exception' requires a special explanation. The idea of 'Indian exceptionalism' became popular, which has been interpreted as the uniqueness of India; therefore, some scholars conclude that India as an 'exception' cannot be compared with other nation-states (Tillin 2013).

Remarkably, scholars like Harriss (1999) Jenkins (1999), Mitra (2006), Tillin (2013) concentrating on the State level studies, have criticized the notion of exceptionalism. Tillin (2013, 236) defined 'false' universalism as the opposite of 'false' exceptionalism, and proposed that looking beyond single country or region case studies can help to prevent 'false' exceptionalism as well as universalism. By solving the problem of many variables and small N problem (Snyder 2001), the subnational comparative method provides an opportunity to identify similarities and differences by with pinpointing the significant explanatory variables in a given case. Referring to political studies on India, Tillin (2013, 235) suggested that there are four primary reasons why (cross-states and within the state) comparisons are significant:

> (a) it helps to challenge false exceptionalism; (b) it helps to challenge false universalism; (c) it can contribute to theory development better than single case studies; and (d) it helps to disaggregate the all-India picture in order to generate theories that are better able to capture the variation that exists within India without getting too lost in the detail of individual subnational cases.

More significantly, by comparing the regional states within India's federal system, there are 'control variables' that are constant for all India's States. The fact that the country has several states with completely different politics, but they operate within the framework of one nation-state, which creates conditions for, controlled experiments (Harriss 1999). All these States are under the set of common condition, including Central Government's foreign and economic policy and structural and institutional design of subnational states. That is why Kohli (1987) indicated that India constitutes a 'laboratory for comparative politics.' As Jenkins (2004, 3) noted, political scientists are not able to control institutional characteristics or the external environment when they conduct the cross-national comparison. Consequently, he realizes that India's federal environment is the best framework for assessing the cause of changes; thus, he asserts that India's federal system provides "a laboratory of democracy." In the same way, India's federal system provides a "laboratory of development studies and comparative political economy" (Jenkins 2004, 3), with apparent control variables, which enable us to conduct the controlled comparisons that give the possibility of finding the valid causal relations in Small-N research.

Diverse economic performances of India's subnational states especially after the 'Big Bang' present an opportunity for scholars of comparative politics to compare these diversities in the framework of one nation-state. Surprisingly, much of research on the role of India's state in economic performance has been conducted based on an aggregated notion of state.

There are two types of literature looking at the economic development at the state level in India. At first glance, statistical and econometric comparisons do exist; nevertheless, there are few in-depth regional comparative political economy studies, testing, comparing, and analyzing the relationships between political and institutional variables and economic outcomes.

In the first type of literature, two trends can be recognized. In the first trend, scholars with the lenses of development economics look mainly at economic disparities in India. Some of them are mostly descriptive, including detailed economic statistics and data such as Khan and Vivek (2007) and Panagariya, Chakraborti, and Govinda Rao (2014). The second trend can be named, 'divergence/convergence literature,' and is the major trend in academic works on development in India's States. In works such as Paul and Sridhar (2015), Gulati (1999), Nachimuthu (2009), Hanumantha Rao (2010), Misra (2000), Banerjee and Kuri (2015) and Gangadharan (2007), the big question mark is raised by the economic variables, affecting the divergence or convergence in the economic performances of the regional states.

Despite the existence of such a laboratory setting to conduct the comparative political economy studies, it is surprising how a few inter-States comparative studies on the trajectory of development exist. While there are many edited volumes on politics of development in the Indian regional states, concentrated on case studies, there are few examples of real comparative works. For example, in the recent 'The making of Miracle in Indian States' edited by Panagariya and Govinda Rao (2015), which provided the enlightening explanations on the trajectories of development in Andhra Pradesh, Gujarat, and Bihar, each chapter exclusively dealt with one state as a case study. While the editorial introduction to this volume provided valuable reflection on the need for State-level analysis, and the final chapter offered a lesson from each state, the comparative perspective is lacking in the whole work. In this pattern, the single-state chapters in the volume try to discuss the specific issues, reflected in the introduction, but they seldom talk to each other (Kailash 2011). In this pattern, the detailed case studies with an introduction have become a norm in the study of India's political economy at the State-level.

Kohli's work (1987) was the pioneer of the comparative subnational political economy in India. Kohli (1987, 2012), Harriss (1999, 2005), Sinha (2003, 2005), Jenkins (1999, 2003, 2004), Kennedy (2004, 2014), and Deshpande, Kailash and Tillin (2017) are the main exceptions to that pattern. They have conducted the subnational inter-states comparative studies, focusing on the role of political variables on economic performances. For example, Sinha in *The Regional Roots of Developmental Politics in India: A Divided Leviathan* (2005) based on the multilevel hierarchy model focuses on the regional elite's strategies and the subnational institution variation and their impact on flow and inflow of investment in three historically more developed States: Gujarat, Tamil Nadu, and West Bengal. For her, the puzzle of divergence between East and West after independence can be addressed via analysis of the vertical and horizontal strategies of the regional elites and the regional institutional and political context. Along with Kohli (1987), Kennedy (2004), Sinha (2005) and Mitra (2006), this study argues that India's subnational states can be seen as an ideal environment to conduct comparative analysis in the context of a complicated and multilayered political system. The present book supports Subrata Mitra, Assema Sinha and Rob Jenkins's intellectual effort to conduct subnational comparative analysis and concentrate on the local context and the regional elite's agency.

However, the current book instead of studying more advanced States such as Gujarat, Maharashtra or Tamil Nadu, selected its cases from historically less developed regions: Bihar in the north and Andhra Pradesh in the south. In addition, while the current study does not neglect the historical context of both states, it seeks to shed light on recent developments especially after the 1990s reforms.

Selection of the cases

First of all, a critical problem that should be addressed is the choice of the selected states. Why Andhra Pradesh and Bihar?

As Lijphart (1971) specified, the focus of the comparative analysis is on the key variables. The 'subnational comparisons' provide better conditions for the assessment of causal inferences through more controlled experiments (Snyder 2001), and India's subnational states offer an advantageous environment for examining the different trajectory of development under a shared set of the formal institutions and foreign environment. Given the scarce resources and objective of the study, the current book rather than a limited comparison of all Indian subnational states try to present a detailed analysis on the interplays of governance and economic performance and trajectory of development in a small number of states.

As Mitra (2006, 43) noted, for a subnational comparison, the random selection of cases is unsuitable in view of the limited number of states (29 at the final stage of this study). Therefore, as Mitra (2006) and Sinha (2005) suggest, for such subnational comparative studies the strategy of 'purposive selection' is a more efficient option.

Next, this study prefers to deal with relatively the larger states. On account of the fact that any conclusion, derived from a comparative study on smaller states can confront the problem of generalization, the current book decides to concentrate on larger States to be more relevant to the bulk of India. Hence, the sample should be narrowed down to the most populous and vast subnational states: Uttar Pradesh, Maharashtra, Andhra Pradesh, Madhya Pradesh, West Bengal, Tamil Nadu, Rajasthan, Karnataka, Gujarat, and Bihar.

Moreover, the selected cases must have clear different economic performances after the reforms. One State should represent the sustaining of low economic growth and dysfunctional economic development, and the next one should represent the change. Although most of the BIMARU states can be seen as suitable samples for weak economic performance, the case of Bihar is an extreme example of the divergence between national averages and state performance. According to most of the statistical data sources, Bihar had a feeble economic performance after liberalization until 2005, but it has become one the fastest-growing states in terms of the rate of economic growth after 2005. In contrast, subnational states such as Gujarat, Maharashtra, Tamil Nadu, and Andhra Pradesh had better economic performance than the national average.

Furthermore, economically and politically, selected states should have a relatively similar initial condition before the 1990s. Since the focus of this book is analyzing the divergence in the trajectory of development and politics, the comparison between the historically more advanced states with the traditionally backward or less developed states cannot lead to a satisfying result. Therefore, the comparison between Gujarat and Bihar with the historically different level of development cannot create a framework for testing of relations of variables. Therefore, the current book mainly deals with less historically developed states.

In a significant subnational comparative study, Sinha (2005) highlighted a sharp contrast between eastern India, southern India, and western India. She selected three major India's subnational states, namely West Bengal, Tamil Nadu, and Gujarat, which were relatively more developed states after the independence. For her, the significant changes in the level of the investment were the point of focus and the contrasts in performance over the time was the chief puzzle for inquiry. Noticeably, in Rao's research on regional economic disparities in India (1973) based on six indicators, he classified West Bengal, Gujarat, and Maharashtra as the 'most developed' and Tamil Nadu as 'not so developed.' The rest of subnational states such as Andhra Pradesh, Bihar, Uttar Pradesh, Assam, and Orissa were classified as 'least developed' states.

The current study does not concentrate on the development path of already more developed states like Gujarat; rather, it focuses on the least developed states and the divergence in economic development level over the time. Therefore, again, our cases are narrowed down, and Gujarat, Maharashtra, and Tamil Nadu are removed from the list. Although there are evident differences between Andhra Pradesh and Bihar in terms of population, language, colonial experience, and social structure, there are some features that make the comparison between them very attractive. While Andhra Pradesh had a slightly better economic performance than Bihar in pre-1991 reforms, they share several socio-economic aspects. Unlike West Bengal, Tamil Nadu or Maharashtra with the trade centers such as Calcutta, Madras, and Bombay, which had been under the direct control of colonial rulers, contemporary Andhra Pradesh, and Bihar experienced a different historical background. Bihar had been a part of Bengal Presidency of the British Raj until 1912; however, Bihar was not in the heartland of the presidency. After 1912, the province of Bihar and Orissa was created as a separate province. The coastal Andhra region in Andhra Pradesh (united from 1956 to 2014) had been part of the Madras presidency; on the other hand, the Telangana region was part of the 'Princely State of Hyderabad' under the rule of Nizam. Consequently, although both states were partially a part of the colonial presidencies, they did not experience the same level of industrialization and urbanization as Maharashtra, West Bengal, and Tamil Nadu. In addition, for a long time after the independence, the two states had been the stronghold of the Congress Party and part of the 'Congress System.'

Moreover, the dominant castes had dominated the Congress after the independence in both States. Andhra Pradesh had been witness to the rise of political power of '*Reddy* caste' as the dominant agricultural caste, creating 'Reddy-Raj' more than three decades after the independence (Bernstorff 1973, Reddi and Ram 1994). In a similar pattern, *Bhumihars* and *Rajputs* as two significant upper castes organized themselves as the primary and dominant actors within the Congress in Bihar (Roy 1966).

Remarkably, in both states, the power of the Congress declined in the late 1970s, and early 1980s; then, the regional parties with the support of subnational movements challenged the authority of the Congress. In Bihar, for the first time, Janata Party (JP) defeated the Congress in 1977 Assembly Election. Although the Congress came back to power for one more decade in the 1980s, Janata Dal party (JD) and later Rashtriya Janata Dal (RJD) with the leadership of Lalu Prasad Yadav terminated the dominance of the Congress in Bihar in the 1990s in the context of caste-based politics. In a comparable pattern, Telugu Desam Party (TDP) with the leadership of charismatic N.T. Rama Rao (NTR) emerged in 1983 as the manifestation of Telugu subnational movement. The TDP challenged the power of the Congress in Andhra Pradesh in Legislative Assembly as well as Lok Sabha elections. Despite all efforts for the implementation of President's rule by Indira Gandhi, N.T. Rama Rao ruled Andhra Pradesh from 1984 to1989. TDP came back to the power again in the 1994 election and kept the Congress as an opposition party in the Legislative Assembly for the next ten years.

Furthermore, both states were witness to the separatist movements based on the regional identity. Not only the Jharkhand region of Bihar was carved out as a separate state in 2000, but also the regional identity movement in Andhra Pradesh finally created the new separate state of Telangana in 2014.

Economically, the growth rate of both states before the reforms are a crucial factor to justify the current comparison. As the Planning Commission reported (2002, 36), while the average growth rate in NSDP of India was 3.0% from 1961 to 1969, Andhra Pradesh and Bihar had a lower rate of growth, respectively 1.7% and 0.7% in the same period. In the 1970s, this rate accelerated in both states (Andhra Pradesh 3.2% and Bihar 2.8%); however, it remained lower than the national average of 3.6%. In the 1980s, India with 5.6% grew faster than Andhra Pradesh and Bihar respectively with 4.7% and 4.3%. Similarly, per capita NSDP of Andhra Pradesh in 1980–1981 was Rs 1358, and that of Bihar was Rs917 lower than most of the Indian states (Thakur 2014).

Likewise, the constituents of human development index as a symbol of the ability of the States to deliver services displays a resemblance before the 1990s. For example, literacy rates of Andhra Pradesh in 1961, 1971, 1981, and 1991 were 13.20%, 24.60%, 24.60%, 29.90%, and 44.10%. The rates in the same periods in Bihar were 12.20%, 21.80%, 19.90%, 26.20%, and 38.50%.

Therefore, both states had comparable initial situations; however, both states represent two completely different development trajectories after the 1990s that make them compelling cases for comparison.

Locating puzzle

Although these two States have the similar formal political structure, comparable formal institutions, constant foreign environment, and relatively similar political and economic trajectories before the 1990s, they had an utterly different economic performance after the liberalization, which led to more regional economic disparities. Neither developmental state theory nor modernization theory can explain this divergence.

As Figure 1.5 displays, Andhra Pradesh and Bihar had a similar NSDP in the 1980s. Conversely, after the liberalization and since the 1990s, a considerable regional divergence emerged, and the economy of Andhra Pradesh grew faster than Bihar's.

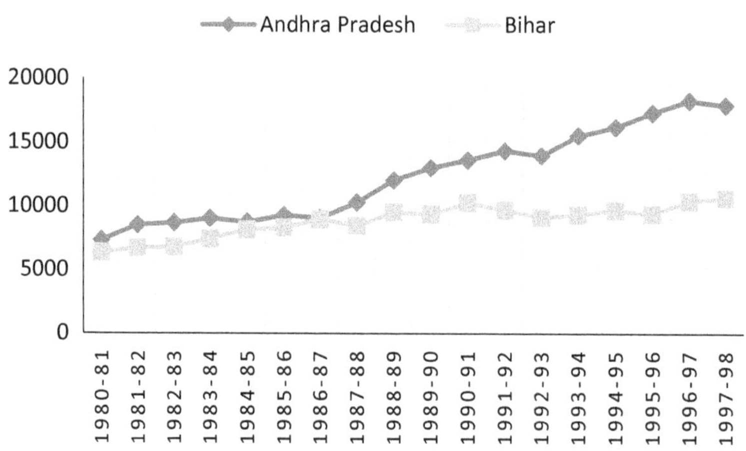

Figure 1.5 NSDP of Andhra Pradesh and Bihar in crore rupees (at constant prices, the base year 1980–1981.

Source: *Handbook of Statistics on Indian Economy 2005–06* (2006), drawn by the author.

This research does not assume the NSDP of subnational states as the primary indicator of the regional divergence in economic performance. This indicator should be translated into the everyday life of ordinary people. In the first step, the per capita NSDP at the constant price illustrates fluctuations in income level. As Figure 1.6 portrays, although both Andhra Pradesh and Bihar had a per capita NSDP lower than the national average at the beginning of the 1980s, Andhra Pradesh grew faster, and Bihar remained relatively stagnant during the 1990s.

Figure 1.7 illustrates an accelerating trend of per capita NSDP growth in Andhra Pradesh in the first decade of the twenty-first century; thus, per capita,

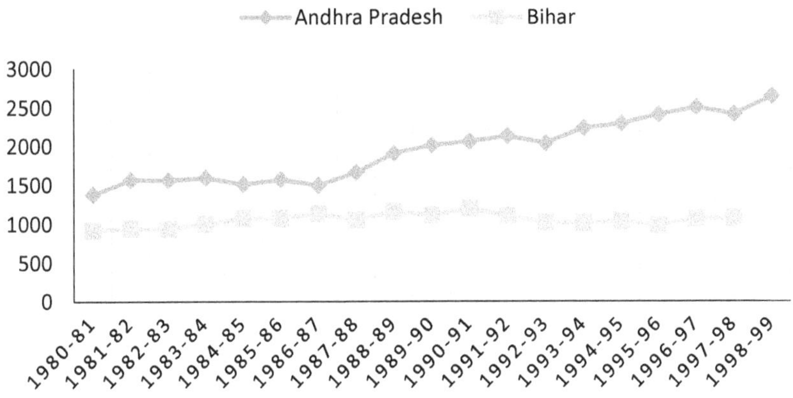

Figure 1.6 Per capita NSDP of Andhra Pradesh and Bihar (at constant prices, the base year 1980–1981) from 1980–1981 to 1998–1999.

Source: *Handbook of Statistics on Indian Economy 2005–06* (2006), drawn by the author.

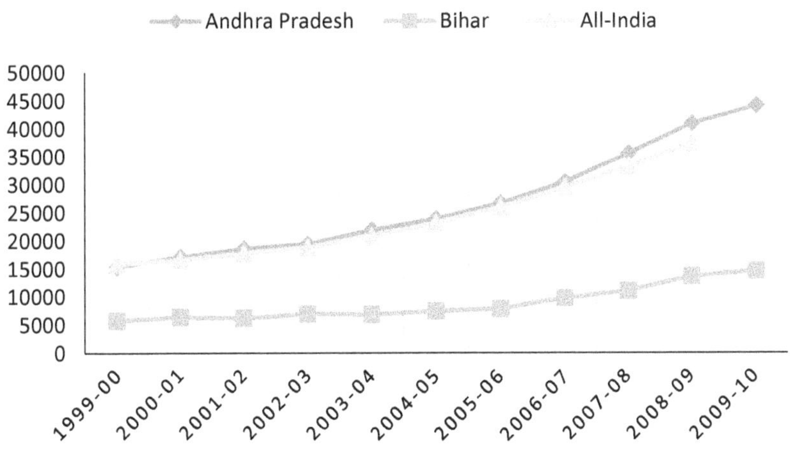

Figure 1.7 Per capita NSDP of Andhra Pradesh and Bihar (at constant prices, the base year 1999–2000) from 1999–2000 to 2009–2010.

Source: *Handbook of Statistics on Indian Economy 2009–10* (2010), drawn by the author.

NSDP in Andhra Pradesh reached the national average. In contrast, Bihar continued its low rate of growth, but after 2005, the trend has become more favorable. Therefore, as we can see, the gap between Bihar and the national average has widened since India's Economic Big Bang.

Moreover, Panagariya, Chakraborti, and Govinda Rao (2014) also calculated the real per capita GSDP in constant price (2004/2005 rupees) based on the sector-wise GDPS data. Their data also portrays the same image. Nevertheless, they used an average of 15 more populous states instead of the national average. Figure 1.8 displays how both Bihar and Andhra Pradesh had a lower level of real per capita GSDP than 15 Indian States at the beginning of the 1980s, but Andhra Pradesh could overtake the national average, and Bihar remained stagnated.

Not only the trends of economic indicators confirm this divergence, but also the capability approach and its indicators verifies the significant divergence. By using the MPI, Alkire, and Seth (2015, 91) illustrates that reduction of poverty has not been uniform across the different Indian states, and Andhra Pradesh had the best performance in an absolute reduction of MPI while Bihar reduced MPI the least.

How can this divergence be interpreted? The mono-causal explanation of development or underdevelopment such as causality between the democratic regime and development, or political stability and development are too simple for analyzing the political dynamics of development within India. The current study along with Sinha (2005, 9) assumes it is relatively difficult to establish the cause of regional growth rate of India's subnational states decisively. In the account the fact that many independent variables may cause growth in the subnational states, it would be tough to consider all of them and test the causality. Instead, this book attempts to investigate and explain the variables that had impacts on this regional divergence. In the current book, many factors that play

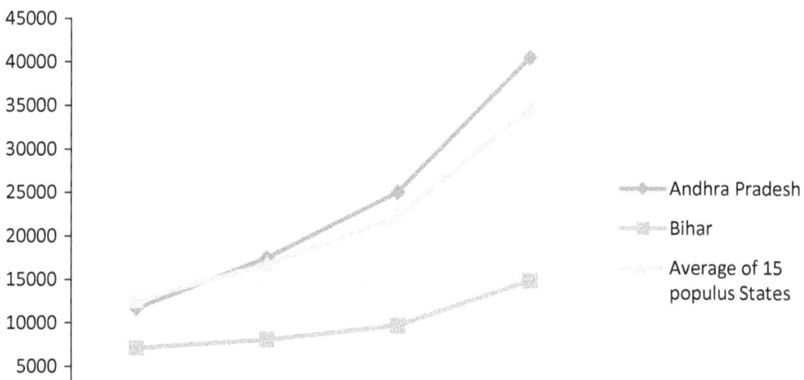

Figure 1.8 Real per capita GSDP of Andhra Pradesh, Bihar, and an average of 15 major states.

Source: Panagariya et al. (2014, 28), drawn by the author.

a role in making development possible, such as the laws of property, fundamental rights, the structure of formal institutions, and foreign environment, can be kept constant. These kinds of control variables make it easier to analyze the impact of the experimental variables that form the core of this research.

Arguments and hypotheses

First, the mono-causal explanation of development such as causality between democratic regime and development, or political stability and development are too simple for analyzing the dynamics of development within Indian subnational states. The central claim of this book is despite the similarities in initial institutional arrangement and economic conditions between two selected cases, the strategic choices of regional leaders in a two and later multilevel game created the different development trajectories with varying results.

In the context of comparative political economy, governance refers to "how institutions for economic policymaking and implementation are set up, and what their consequences are" (Kjær 2004, 194). Moreover, economic governance is defined as the "institutions and actors who shape the economic and process that coordinate the economic activities" (Kennedy 2014, 138). Can we identify the characteristics of this institutional arrangement in India and their transformations over time to reflect on the puzzle of this study?

This first institutional aspect of Indian multi-layered and dynamic political system is the existence of the 'room to maneuver' for the political leaders at different levels of the system. Mitra's study (2006), the foundation of the current study, examines how the democratic governance and orderly rule sustained as the result of "neo-institutional rational choice model of governance" (Mitra 2006, 16). Mitra suggested that while India was witness to the subnational movements and the Congress system, therefore, became dysfunctional, the mixture of federal and consociational institutional arrangements, which created a balance between self-rule and shared rule, has sustained democratic governance in India. Focusing on the institutional design that explains how the subnational movement has been accommodated, Mitra and Singh (2009, 33) referred to the flexible and multi-layer political structure of India:

The state structure in India has institutionalized these ideological and social changes from below in the form of institutional innovations. Federalism, consociationalism, and elite policy initiatives, linking social power to political and economic change, have created in the hands of national, regional and local elites useful room to maneuver in the middle.

Consequently, the national elites possess room to maneuver, enabling them to adopt strategies such as "law and order management, reform, and constitutional incorporation of values" to reduce the perceived inequality and accommodate the normative issues such as group identity (see Mitra 2006, 16). Similar to the national elites, local elites in the neo-institutional model of governance as the rational actors have an important position. Mitra (2006, 180) recognizes the role of local elites as intermediates of a traditional society and the modern state:

> The perceptions and attitudes of these regional elites are important links in the national chain of governance, joining the modern state and traditional society. Their symbiosis holds the key to the variance of governance across India's regions.

Although Mitra highlighted the political role of regional elites in his model, he rarely discussed the economic implications of the proposed model. While Mitra in his *Power, Protest and Participation* (1992) highlighted the role of *gaon ka netas* or local elites in the rural setting in India, the role of more potent elites and regional leaders at the state level, possessing the room to maneuver, had been less discussed.

The second critical institutional feature is the emergence of a complicated party politics at the Center and state level (see Chhibber 2001, Wyatt 2009, Mitra and Singh 1999). The shift in India's party system has transformed 'one dominant party system' period (1952–1977) to a multi-party system (1977–now). These profound changes not only influenced the political scene at the Center but also paved the road for the emergence of regional parties in the states. In the era of one dominant party, the Congress leadership articulated the developmental policy at the Center, and these policies and should be implemented by regional leaders. However, in the era of a multi-party system, the regional ruling elites have not necessarily obeyed the policies of the Center; thus, several patterns of interactions emerged such as modification, resistance, confrontation, coexistence, or cooperation. Therefore, the role of the regional leaders has increased drastically since the end of one dominant party era.

Therefore, neither leaders and elites at the Center nor the rural and local level are the primary focus of this study. The present book argues the rooms to maneuver for regional leaders at the *State level*, are the primary factor for an explanation of different responses to the economic reforms in India. After the rise of subnational political parties, representing a subnational or caste identity and the consequent transformation of rebels to stakeholders (Mitra and Singh 2009), the regional leaders as the rational actors have found an eminent position in economic policymaking in the State and implementation of the Center's economic policies.

Furthermore, as Kennedy (2004, 29), Mitra (2011), Rudolph and Rudolph (2013), and Wyatt (2017) asserted, one of the results of economic liberalization in India after the 1990s, was enhancing the autonomy of the subnational states, particularly in terms of economic policymaking and implementing. This significant change also contributed to the increase in the role of regional leaders in economic policymaking. As Rudolph and Rudolph (2013) maintain, in the 1990s, India moved away from 'Command and control economy' toward a 'federal market economy.' In the new circumstances, the states possess more economic autonomy and sovereignty than they did earlier in the previous institutional arrangements, called 'centrally planned economy.' Along with Rudolph and Rudolph (2013) and Wyatt (2017), this book considers the strategic choices of rational political elites at the State level, possessing room to maneuver, as the main explanatory variable in order to explain the divergence in the post-reform economic performance of states. Rudolph and Rudolph (2013, 315–316) describe the chief ministers as the 'marquee players' in 'India's federal market economy' and write:

> Whether they [States] do well or badly economically depends more on what they do for themselves. States can act in ways that transform their initial economic situation; the agency can modify the structure.

This book argues that the divergence in development trajectories in Andhra Pradesh and Bihar can be interpreted through analyzing the strategic choices of regional elites in both states. This book postulates that the regional elites are rational actors; nevertheless, their rationality is bounded by local context and embedded values (see Mitra 2006, 10–12). Following the rational choice perspective, this study assumes that regional leaders in the games model interactions stick with rules when they perceive that obeying the rules yields more than they could expect to gain by breaking the rules. This study analyzes the strategic choices of regional elites in a rational two-level game (based on Rapoport and Chammah 1965 and Putnam 1988) and their *vertical* and *horizontal* choices. As Sinha (2005, 15–16) explains, India's regional leader as rational actors faced with two-level games choices in the vertical and horizontal games and "trade-off between central transfer and regional reelection chance."

Regional leaders as the rational player and expected-utility maximizers should have strategic choices toward the central rules and vertical institutions as well as regional rules and horizontal institutions. These two-level games engender various kinds of choices for the empowered regional leaders. In the vertical game, they can adopt the anti-Center strategy, resist the reforms, cooperate with the Center, or even enhance the economic reforms in their state. The selection of these strategic choices is based on the anticipated *rewards* from the regional level in the form of reelection or more shares of power at the Center. In the horizontal game, the rational regional leaders interact with the voters, the regional institutions (formal and informal) and other political actors. At the horizontal level, domestic groups pursue their interests by pressuring the government to adopt favorable policies, and politicians seek power by constructing coalitions among those groups. The strategic choices of the chief ministers in both games are interconnected. The state-center relations and horizontal relations are often inextricably entangled, but existing theories (particularly "state-centric" theories) do not adequately account for these linkages.

In sum, in the aftermath of the end one dominant party system and the rise of the regional parties, and the breakdown of the centrally planned economy, the role of subnational states has increased. I argue thus the strategic choices of the empowered regional leaders based on the vertical and horizontal games are the primary explanatory variable for different trajectories of development in the regional states.

Therefore, this book does not understand the accelerated economic growth after the 1991 Big Bang as the result of the simple top-down implementation of the reforms or the result of the application of normative good governance principles; conversely, this book argues that the spatial, as well as central-local dynamics, affect the regional developmental patterns. Accordingly, the post-reform divergence in regional development does not attribute merely to the historical and colonial context or initial economic condition; rather, this book argues the differences between Bihar and Andhra Pradesh are associated with elite strategic choices in the face of the vertical and horizontal games. This book argues that after liberalization, the state governments gained more autonomy; as a result, their response to the reform varies. This book will illustrate that the divergence in the post-reform economic outcome in both states is associated with the strategic choices of democratically elected leaders in both States.

By employing an analytic narrative approach, and in the framework of the subnational comparative method, this book concentrates on two kinds of strategic choices of the chief ministers: their choices in the Center–State interactions (vertical analysis) and their interactions with regional institutions and other players (horizontal analysis). An analysis of political factor in each state, mostly the nature of competitive politics and social mobilization as well as the role of ruling elites, suggests hypotheses to explain the variations observed in these two states. Accordingly, this study suggests four hypotheses:

H1: If the political power of the dominant political party at the Center declines, the new room to maneuver of regional political elites makes their strategic choices (in order to gain reelection) the core determents of economic policies in the states.

> < Political power of dominant party at Centre → > importance of strategic choices of regional political elites

H2: If regional political elites expect the most gain (reelection) from confrontational rhetoric and behavior against the Central Government, they will opt for populist economic policies (handouts) – rather than implementing the reform agenda of the Central Government.

> If the expectation of reelection based on confrontation with the Center → populist economic policies and confrontation with (reform-oriented) Center

H3: If regional political elites do not expect to gain reelection through confrontational behavior against the Center but expect to be rewarded by the voter if their economic performance is convincing, they will opt for gaining access to funds from the Center and international agents and adopt reform-oriented policies.

> If the expectation of reelection based on economic growth → economic reform policies and cooperation with (reform-oriented) Center

H4: If regional political leaders opt for confrontational rhetoric and behavior against the Central Government, the share of State in financial transfers from the

Center (such as approved plan outlay) will decrease. On the other hand, if regional political leaders opt for cooperationist rhetoric and behavior toward the Central Government and implement the reform agenda of the Central Government, the share of State in financial transfers from the Center (such as approved plan outlay) will increase.

Methodological approaches and their implications

The goal of this book is not to develop a new theory of either comparative political economy or governance. Rather, elements of existing theories are integrated and applied in a new context of governance and development in India after the liberalization. To address this goal, a multi-method approach, combining two qualitative research methods, are employed.

Since the primary research focus of this thesis is the Indian states, this study uses the subnational comparative method and provides an in-depth comparison as opposed to cross-national comparisons. Moreover, this study concentrates on the strategic choices of the regional leaders and its interactions with the institutional setup. Therefore, the analytic narrative approach is used as the proper research methodology.

Analytic narrative approach

The current research employs analytic narrative approach, combining rational choice and particular case studies. This method tries to bring together the use of comparative and historical research with rational choice models (see Bates et al. 1998, 2000; Levi 2004). Bates et al. (1998) called their approach an analytic narrative because this approach mixes analytic tools, used in economics and political science with the narrative, used in history. Noticeably, the term narrative is not employed "in the post-modern sense of a master- or meta-narrative; rather it refers to research grounded in traditional historical methods" (Levi 2004, 208).

As Bates et al. (1998, 10) assert, their approach is narrative because it pays close attention to "stories, accounts, and context"; in addition, it is analytic because of analytic narrative extracts "explicit and formal lines of reasoning." Levi (2004, 204) introduces the various stages of analytic narrative respectively and states:

> Analytic narratives involve choosing a problem or puzzle, then building a model to explicate the logic of the explanation and to elucidate the key decision points and possibilities, and finally evaluating the model through comparative statics and the testable implications the model generates.

Since the current study highlights the role of institutions as well as the agency; the analytic narrative approach can shed light on the silent aspects of the games. For the analytic narrative, analyzing games is significant, because it is a useful tool to create and evaluate explanations of particular outcomes. Analytic narrative identifies agents such as elites, nations, electorates, or legislatures. This approach tries to understand actors' perceptions, information, preferences, alternative options, and the way of evaluation of alternatives (Bates et al. 1998). The analytic narrative approach uses methods such as reading documents, interviewing, surveying the secondary literature, and laboring archives seek to grasp more data about the agents.

In the current book, the method of analytic narrative, based on an analysis of the regional leaders' interviews, their public statements, published documents including regional economic plans, policy or visions, the Legislative Assembly debates, and official reports, helps to highlight the strategic choices of leaders with regard to the Center's policies and regional political and economic context. As such, rather than mechanically applying the framework of good governance or weak and strong state, it presents the dynamics and diversities in a multi-layer political system with different nodes of decision-making.

In the historical chapters, two narratives about the trajectory of development in Andhra Pradesh and Bihar will be presented; in addition, the impacts of inter-relations of the state-society and the Center-region on the economic performance of the States will be explored. Like a drama, in the current study, the narratives consist mainly of background or setting, a beginning, a sequence of scenes, and an ending. Nonetheless, the narratives are not mere historical narrative but an analytic one. This book, by modeling the processes that shaped the outcomes, tries to depict the 'essence of stories.' Following Bates et al. (1998, 12), if the current study possesses a valid representation of the story, then "the equilibrium of the model should imply the outcome we describe and seek to explain." Additionally, the current study employs rational choice and game theory, which converts the historical narratives into analytic narratives.

The subnational comparative method

More than a decade ago, Snyder (2001) defined the subnational comparative method as a systematic and comparative analysis of a small number of territorially defined subnational cases, such as states, provinces, cities, and regions. The subnational comparative method provides a useful tool for comparative politics scholars, dealing with ethnic conflict, economic policy reform, and democratization at the subnational level. This method creates an analytical framework and breaks 'whole nation bias' in the field of comparative politics and comparative political economy. Therefore, it has opened a new horizon in the field of comparative politics. The subnational comparative method, similar to the cross-national comparative method, tests the causal hypotheses; nevertheless, the emphasis is on regional variation within one state instead of national variation across states.

As Snyder (2001, 94) emphasized, the subnational comparative method provides numerous advantages in comparative politics. Not only can it help to manage some of the typical limitations of Small-N research design,[15] but also, employing subnational units is a useful tool "for increasing the number of observations and thus mitigating the problem of many variables, small N." Furthermore, a concentration on the subnational level can make it easier to construct controlled comparisons, increasing the possibility of finding 'valid causal relations in small-N research.'

According to Snyder (2001, 103),

> subnational comparisons provide a firm foundation for building theories that explain spatially uneven processes of political and economic transformation. In addition to these methodological benefits, the subnational comparative analysis offers an indispensable tool for understanding the decentralizing political and economic trends of the contemporary era.

In the same way, Mitra (2006) compared India's subnational state in terms of governance and stability. As he (Mitra 2006, 43) indicates, the 'one nation, many units' sampling frame has a significant advantage over comparing nations.

Source of data

The questions about the role of regional leaders and the impact of their strategic choices on economic performances are hard to address in any political system. Although conducting interviews with these leaders was desirable, it was, however, not possible to meet and conduct an interview with them. Two of them passed away (N.T. Rama Rao and Y.S. Reddy), and two of them are serving chief ministers (Chandrababu Naidu and Nitish Kumar) now. Therefore, this book uses several public statements, election manifestos, government documents, vision papers, interviews, the legislative assembly proceedings, biographies, and speeches as the primary source of data for analyzing the elite strategies. However, some biographies and autobiographies can be seen as the primary sources of data.

Furthermore, the shortage of reliable subnational economic data in India is another problem. Most of the subnational economic data have different methods and cannot be compared both by time and by space. Despite all these problems and limitations, the current study used data and statistics published in *Handbook of Statistics on Indian Economy* and 'State Finances: A Study of Budgets,' provided by Reserve Bank of India. Moreover, this study used the 'Crime in India series,' published by National Crime Records Bureau (NCRB) as the main source for crime statistics. Finally, the current thesis used the 'Statistical Report on General Elections, and The Legislative Assembly Elections' series, published by the Election Commission of India as the primary source for the election results.

Chapter outline

The book has been organized thematically. The second chapter deals with state of the art. The chapter provides a detailed discussion on definitions and various perspectives on governance and elaborates two main areas of governance theory, dealing with development studies. The chapter underlines the 'good governance' approaches and 'governance in comparative politics' as two areas, discussing interrelations between governance and the development. The chapter introduces the works, written on development in India based on both approaches. Furthermore, the chapter elucidates why the current book does not employ good governance approach. The third chapter reveals the theoretical foundations of the book. After introducing the alternative approaches in governance theory, the chapter presents the neo-institutional rational choice model of governance (Mitra 2006), polycentric hierarchy theory (Sinha 2005) as the theoretical foundations of the book. Finally, the third chapter introduces the strategies for the analysis of the regional elites' strategies.

Through an analytic narrative approach, the book in the fourth and fifth chapters investigates the strategic economic choices of the regional leaders in Andhra Pradesh. The fourth chapter begins with the State profile, including geography, population, demography, and economy. In the next step, Chapter 4 deals with pre-1990s politics in Andhra Pradesh. After a detailed discussion on the pre-1990s politics in Andhra Pradesh, the role of Congress, rivalries between Reddy and Kamma castes and its political implications, the chapter focuses on the rise of the TRS and charismatic leadership of N.T. Rama Rao in the 1980s. In the fifth chapter the book concentrates on the strategic choices of two significant chief ministers in AP toward economic reforms and economic liberalization. The chapter examines the strategic choices of Chandrababu Naidu from the TDP and Y.S. Reddy from the Congress. The main goal of this chapter is to understand the political roots of the policy shift in AP that has engendered what Panagariya and Govinda Rao (2015) call the 'economic miracle of Andhra Pradesh.' This chapter focuses on the shifts in the strategic choice of regional leaders in a relatively underdeveloped State and attempts to address this question: Why did the ruling elites in Andhra Pradesh especially in TDP despite a long historical background of political and economic populism decide to adopt the economic reforms that have accelerated economic development? Also, what was the political outcome of these shifts?

In parallel, Chapters 6 and 7 examine the strategic economic choices of the regional leaders in Bihar after liberalization under the rule of Lalu Yadav and Nitish Kumar. Like Chapter 4, Chapter 6 begins with the state profile and delineates the historical process, which led to the decline of the Congress in the State. Furthermore, the chapter underlines the emergence of lower-caste politics with an emphasis on the role of the Congress in pre-1990s politics, rivalries among upper castes, and the emergence of the JD and the RJD. This chapter tries to answer this question: Why did the ruling elites in Bihar, especially in RJD resist the reform policies and economic liberalization in the 1990s and early 2000s? The seventh chapter concentrates on the post-2005 scenario in Bihar under Nitish Kumar. This chapter compares the strategic choices of two chief ministers, Lalu Prasad Yadav, and Nitish Kumar, toward economic reforms and their impact on the trajectory of development in the State. This chapter examines the shifts in the strategic choices of the regional leaders in an underdeveloped State.

This chapter attempts to address this question: Despite a long historical background of political and economic populism, why did the new leaders in Bihar decide to accept the economic reforms after 2005? Also, what was the political outcome of these shifts?

The final chapter will be a combination of comparison, analysis, and a conclusion. The empirical findings of the book confirm that there is an overall tendency for the Central government to reward or punish States based on their relations with the Center and their willingness to implement the Center's recommended policies by developmental transfers to the States. Moreover, the decision of the chief ministers to accept, reject or partially implement are the result of their rational calculation in the horizontal and vertical interactions. The chapter recognizes the strategic choices of the regional leaders as the primary explanatory variable that can explain the difference in the regional development trajectories.

Notes

1 Kohli's definition of *Congress System* is based on Kothari's conceptualization. Kothari (1964, 1162) with a focus on the role and position of the Congress Party, depicted the Indian system as "a system of one party dominance which, it may be noted, is very different from what is generally known as a one-party system." The Congress system not only dominated the Center for quite some time but also dominated in all subnational states. As Rothermund (2008, 15) notes, after introducing universal adult suffrage by The Representation of People Act 1951, which reconfirmed the majority election system, the Congress won the general elections of 1952, 1957 and 1962. In this era, the Congress Party was very active in the parliament, and there was no strong opposition, who could challenge the Congress.

2 For the first time, the famous Indian economist Raj Krishna described India's disappointing trend growth as the 'Hindu rate of growth.' As Ganguly and Mukherji (2011, 60) noted, this term was employed with a secular point of view and referred to traditional characteristics of India that were considered to be a barrier to economic growth.

3 This calculation was done based on the data of World Bank development indicators (2015) and statistics of Government of India's Planning Commission (2014).

4 As Alkire et al. (2015) defined and constructed, the Multidimensional Poverty Index (MPI) is based on ten indicators grouped into three dimensions: Education, Health, and Standard of Living. The education dimension includes years of schooling and school attendance. The health dimension of the MPI includes nutrition and child mortality. Finally, the standard of living dimension consists of electricity, sanitation, water, flooring material, cooking fuel, and asset ownership.

5 According to my calculation based on the World Bank development indicators, India's average GDP growth between 1990 and 2014 is 6.51%.

6 India's GDP (constant price 2005) in 1990 was US$350,241,409,728.75. It increased to US$1,600,268,265,249.33 in 2014.

7 During the 1980s, scholars ranging from comparative historical sociology to specialists in the economics of development concentrated on the role of the state and its impact on the economy. The widely cited *Bringing the State Back In* (Evans, Rueschemeyer, and Skocpol 1985) was a turning point in the comparative political economy. The book mainly asserts that the character of political institutions in a society significantly determined economic development of society. This idea had a direct influence on the next generation of researchers. The fundamental assumption of

this approach is that institutions matter for political as well as economic outcomes. Moreover, this approach deals with the quality of institutions as a crucial element of governance. The neo-statist scholars assert that the market cannot be self-regulating and the state should have some interventions. The Theory of Developmental State is the main manifestation of this approach. This theory tries to offer an explanation for the East Asian industrialization and with a focus on the role of capitalist developmental goes beyond the contrast between the liberal-capitalist and centrally planned economies.

8 The neo-liberal perspective mostly neglects the short-lived liberalization in 1966 and the causes of its emergence and downfall (see Mukherji 2014, 38–59).

9 The World Bank summarized factors such as years of macroeconomic imbalance, political instability, internal conflicts, and the oil shock resulting from developments in the Persian Gulf in 1990 as the reasons that caused tremendous difficulties in managing India's balance of payments.

10 Mitra (1991) for the first time used this term to analyze the remarkable political stability in India's democratic system and its institutional flexibility in the Constitution. According to him (Mitra 1991, 391), "room to manoeuvre is created when bureaucrats, political decision makers, and the law of the land accept the legitimacy of multiple modes of participation from below."

11 As Mitra (2011, 87) noted, India's federal design is an unusual kind and cannot be seen as the same as other federal systems. This federal design mixes the classic characteristics of federal government, with some unique features born out of the Indian context.

12 The 12th Five Year Plan of the Government of India (2012–2017) is a principal document, which illustrates the developmental goals and policies of government of India.

13 During the colonial rule, Maharashtra (called Bombay state before 1960), West Bengal (Bengal before 1947), Tamil Nadu (Madras before 1969)., and Gujarat were economically and industrially the most developed regions in India. Bharadwaj's Study (1982) revealed that during colonial rule only a few regions such as Bombay, Bengal and Madras, which had import-export, based industries developed more than other regions.

14 BIMARU is an acronym formed from the first letters of the names of Bihar, Madhya Pradesh, Rajasthan, and Uttar Pradesh. BIMARU refers to a Hindi word 'Bimar,' which means sick. The term was used to refer to the poor economic conditions in these backward states.

15 Small-N studies examine a small number of cases in depth.

2 State of art

Governance and comparative political economy

Introduction

This book arises from a significant puzzle: Two subnational states with a comparable initial political and economic condition and the divergent economic trajectories. The variables like the Union Government and its policies, the institutional arrangements, and the foreign policy of India were constant for both cases; thus, they created a suitable environment for making a controlled comparison. As this chapter elaborates, the governance paradigm with its focus on the state–society interactions, the state capacity and the complexities and dynamism of interactions between different actors is the most beneficial approach to address the puzzle.[1]

At the start, this chapter deals with various usages of governance as an emerging term in political science. After an introduction to the concept, this chapter differentiates different usages of the term in different subfields of political science. Then, the chapter focuses on two relevant conceptualizations of this term for the current book. The first conceptualization is 'good governance.' Although this study does not use the good governance and indicators as the theoretical foundation, the regional leaders, whose strategic choices are important for us, have employed the term good governance frequently. Under the influence of the neo-liberal notion of good governance, Chandrababu Naidu introduced the *SMART governance* agenda in AP; similarly, Nitish Kumar concentrated on the implementation of principles of *Sushasan* (good governance) in Bihar. The second conceptualization of governance related to the comparative political economy that provides our operational definition of the term for the current book. Therefore, while this book does not employ good governance as the theoretical base, it elaborates it to understand regional elites' strategies in both States.

Defining governance: complexities and diversities

As Van Kersbergen and Van Waarden (2004, 165) indicated "there is no consensus on which set of phenomena can properly be grouped under the title governance." Likewise, as Kooiman (1999) asserted, governance has different types of usages in social sciences. This lack of terminological clarity and broad scope of its applications is a motivation for conceptualization and categorization of its various applications by different scholars.[2] Despite the diffusion of the concept, there is no shared understanding of governance as a concept and its definition, implications, and characterizations. As Torfing et al. (2012, 9) pointed out "the lack of a precise definition of governance has made it easy for people to attach all kinds of positive meanings and expectations to governance." In comparative politics, political economy, international relations, and public policy as the subfields of political science as well as public administration, economics, sociology or management, scholars used governance with different meanings and implications. Because of diverse interpretations of this concept by the scholars, governance becomes a 'contested concept' in political science (Richards and Smith 2002, 14; Peters 2011, 78).

One of the critical reasons for this impreciseness and the diverse uses of the term is its newness. That is why Kooiman (2003, 5) reminds us "we are still in a period of creative disorder concerning governance."

Consequently, political science and its subfields were witnesses to a profound debate on governance and its definitions and characteristics (for an overview see Bevir 2012; Chhotray and Stoker 2009; Hirst 2000; Kjær 2004; Peters 2000; Robichau 2011; Van Kersbergen and Van Waarden 2004). However, the current literature on governance covers a broad range of meaning and connotations ranging from the state or government capacity[3] to different kinds of process,[4] normative values or institutions. In the next sections, after a short discussion on the etymology, the origins of emergence, the debates and different usages of the term, the book elucidates the operational definition of governance and its implications for this study.

Origins of governance

Scholars trace the etymology of the term 'governance' to the ancient Greek.[5] This term is derived from the Greek verb *kubernan* that means to steer or to pilot[6] (Plattner 2013, 1312). Some sources traced back this term to a metaphor in *The Republic*, in which Plato compared the governing of a polis to the piloting of a ship[7] (Plattner 2013, 18). Traditionally, governance was defined as a synonym for government. The old dictionaries entries are the example of this trend (Stoker 1998, 17). According to Lynn (2012, 49) for a long time governance has been used as a "generic descriptive term."

In the emerging political science after World War II, scholars extensively had not used governance as a scientific term. That is why there is no entry on governance in the *International Encyclopedia of the Social Sciences* (Sills 1968). According to Levi-Faur (2012, 5), one of the rare examples of usage of this term is related to studies in higher education or urban governance. Moreover, as Frederickson (2007) illustrates, Herlan Cleveland (1972) was the person who used governance as an alternative to public administration for the first time. However, these rare examples never transformed into the mainstream of the discipline. The real shift and rise of governance in the academic literature happened after the 1980s.

Governance as symbol of the shift

Marinetto (2003), based on Thomas Kuhn's post-empiricist book *The Structure of Scientific Revolutions* (1970), distinguished a paradigm shift from the government – as a "dominant intellectual paradigm during the formative development of politics as a distinct academic discipline in Britain" – to governance (Marinetto 2003, 593). He recognized two paradigms of "government as an autonomous institution" in the first half of the twentieth century and the 'overloaded state' during the 1960s to 1980s (Marinetto 2003, 605). Accordingly, Marinetto argued because of the external (globalization) and internal pressures (market-style reforms), the British Government entered a new phase of intuitional configuration, in which it was "less reliant on bureaucratic hierarchies and more dependent on the networks of agencies beyond the central state" (Marinetto 2003, 605). Likewise, Sørensen (2002, 693) considers several reasons for the popularity of governance as an academic keyword such as the "increased significance of international political institutions, new administrative techniques, promoting institutional self-regulation within the political systems and intensified cooperation between public authorities and private actors like market actors or actors within civil society." These developments are the primary cause of the paradigm shift to governance. Similarly, Rhodes (2012) attributes the attractiveness of governance to the contemporary transformations in the characteristics of the government. For him, "Governance signifies a change in the meaning of government, referring to a new process of governing, or changed the condition of the ordered rule; or new method by which society is governed" (Rhodes 2012, 34).

Therefore, during the last decades of the twentieth century, the distinction between govern*ment*, govern*ing*, and govern*ance* has become more visible than past, and for the first time, the new understanding of governance entered the academic literature. After differentiating between governing and governance, Kooiman (1993, 2) defines governing as "all those activities of social, political and administrative actors that can be seen as purposeful efforts to guide, steer, control or manage (sectors or facet of) societies. " Kooiman accordingly defines governance as "the patterns that emerge from governing activities of social, political and administrative actors."

Most current scholarship on governance in political science, international relations, public administration, public policy, and development studies is the result of the transformation of the nature of the state during the last decades of the twentieth century. That is why Daly (2003) sees governance as a concept that is fundamentally 'about the change.' Levi-Faur (2012, 7) calls the emerging scholarship on governance the "the science of shiftology."[8] Comparably, Richards and Smith (2002, 14) describe governance as a term that "tries to make sense the changing nature of the state in the last thirty years." Jose (2004) attempted to depict the genealogy of discourse of governance. His study on the dominance of governance approach in Australian political discourse is based on this idea that the domination of a 'neo-liberal economic paradigm' and its 'associated politics' created substantial changes in political culture and language. He shows that how governance as a term has become widespread in everyday life and academic literature by domination neo-liberalism as the political discourse.

Similarly, Chakrabarty and Bhattacharaya (2008, 2) discussed the neo-liberal views as the dominant approach in the last decades of twentieth century overvalued market and devalued the role of the state. These changes created a trend to decenter the state from its monopoly status in steering and social control. Neo-liberals frequently recommend that the state should focus on policymaking rather than delivering services (Bevir 2009, 5). These developments led to the prominence of the governance approach as a substitute for government. In this recent observable shift from a government-centric notion of steering to a more plural approach to governance, some significant domains of social action become more highlighted: the state as well as the market and the civil society.

In another trend, after the 'institutional turn' in political science, and also the prominence of 'neo-institutional economics' in development studies, scholars mainly focused on the institutional arrangements, quality of public policy, and their effect on the economic performance of state (Ahrens 2002, 118). Therefore, governance is also a keyword, developed by comparative political economists as a theoretical tool, for analyzing the impacts of politico-institutional structure and the state capacity on the economic performance of the state.[9]

These two theoretical foundations of the current governance approach in political science had different manifestations in the definitions of governance. Sometimes, in some of the theories of governance, the state and its institutions became the central point of focus (see Bell and Hindmoor 2009; Fukuyama 2014). On the contrary, sometimes scholars talk about 'the hollowing out of the state' (Rhodes 1994). However, for more clarification at least we can define what government is not. The *acontrario* definition identifies what the concept is not and does not denote. This definition is reflected in the following quotation from Levi-Faur (2012, 9):

> Governance is not a unified, homogeneous and hierarchal approach to the study of politics, economics, and society. Indeed the very notion of homogeneity stands in contrast to the basic underlying belief of a large group of governance scholars who tend to see themselves as (neo) pluralists and pragmatists. Second, governance, so far, is not a theory of causal relations. There is no need to explain governance structures, processes, mechanism, or strategies with new theories. Still, governance and governancing can force and revitalize some explanatory strategies at the expense of others.

Governance: categorizing the definitions and approaches

As Jordan, Wurzel, and Zito (2005, 478) indicate, "there is no universally accepted definition of governance." The various connotations and implications of the term even led to some uncertainties about the position of the notion in the contemporary political science. Chhotray and Stoker (2009, 26) point out "there is no one theory of governance in political science and public administration." That is why Jose (2009, 2) in his exploration of governance as a concept, talks about the ambiguity that emerged "between concept and practice, idea and reality, and ambiguity that raises questions about the ontological commitments arising from the use of the concept."

This diversity has led to different connotations and conceptualizations in different contexts. Therefore, various scholars have tried to classify the usages of the term since the mid-1990s. For example, Rhodes in his well-known and influential article "The New Governance: Governing without Government" (1996, 652) introduced the "minimal state, corporate governance, the new public management, good governance, socio-cybernetic systems, and self-organizing networks" as six definitions and uses of governance. Likewise, Hyden, Mease, and Court (2004) identified the diverse applications of the governance concept in public administration, international relations, international development agencies and comparative politics. In another categorization, Kjær (2004) differentiated various uses of governance in public administration and public policy, International relations, European governance, comparative politics and the World Bank.

This book needs to define the most relevant literature on governance according to the research questions. Consequently, the capability for investigating the interactions between governance and development is the most critical criteria for selecting a proper analytical tool for the current research. It is so evident that some of these categories have the clear implications for the current research whereas others indirectly touch upon the critical issues or even entirely are irrelevant to the current study. Governance in the context of international relations with a focus on the notion of global governance is not a proper theoretical foundation for the current book, which deals with variables at the national or subnational levels. Equally, corporate governance theory cannot provide a suitable theoretical toolkit for the current book because it principally deals with transparency and accountability in the only private sector. As a result, this book cannot consider these two theories (corporate governance and global governance) as the analytical foundation.

Conversely, the possibility of application of the network governance approach as a theoretical framework for the current research needs more clarification. The socio-political developments such as the reforms in the public sector during the last decades of the twentieth century, increasing Europeanization, and globalization have changed the structure and functions of the state in the context of Western societies and governance paradigm (see Marinetto 2003). Scholars like Rhodes (1994, 1996, 1997, 2000) employed the term governance to depict the changes within the state in the context of neo-liberal reforms in Britain and other similar experiences in the West. Consequently, the new governance research predominantly has concentrated on Western nation-states. Theories like network governance theory can be perceived as the direct outcome of these changes, and they attempt to describe, explain and analyze these transformations. For instance, Rhodes (1996, 655) asserts that "the transformation of public sector involves 'less government' (or less rowing) but 'more governance' (or more steering)." Governance in the context of public administration and public policy is mostly influenced by what is known as Anglo-governance school or works of scholars.

Nevertheless, it can be difficult to operationalize this concept in the context of post-colonial developing states. Have we been witness to the same process of changes and developments in the structure and function of the state in non-western countries? Have the networks as the central element for the study of Anglo-governance school emerged in South Asian states like India; and if yes, do they possess same extent and influence that they have in the UK or Western Europe? Although governance theory in the field of public administration tries to investigate and explain any changes and the shifts in the structure and function of both the state and government in the context of Western nation-states, there are some serious doubts and uncertainties about its merits and applicability for studying developing non-Western nation states. Nevertheless, network governance theory can have indirect implications for the current book. Its theoretical assumptions like the plurality of actors, blurring the borders between the public and private sector and state and civil society, and a clear differentiation between government and governance, are also ratified by the current book.

Hence, only two last categories of definitions of governance deal visibly with the interactions of governance and development as their primary purposes. First, the international financial and aid organizations and development agencies with a focus on good governance created a framework for analyzing the interactions of governance and development. Second, in the framework of comparative politics and comparative political economy, based on neo-institutionalism there is a growing literature on governance that concentrates on the interplays of governance as the institutional arrangements and economic performance of developing countries. Along with this perspective, scholars like McCarney (2000) or Kjær (2014a) differentiate broadly between two streams of the definition of governance, one a *policy-oriented one* that is mainly used by the international organizations and second, a *more academic one*. This section briefly introduces both streams and presents noteworthy definitions.

The World Bank, neo-liberalism, and good governance

In development studies, different theories and approaches discuss the appropriate economic development and transition strategies in less developed countries, post-colonial countries, and post-socialist countries. One of the most significant and current approaches in this field is a 'good governance' approach, mostly used by the international financial organizations like the IMF,[10] World Bank[11] as well as United Nations[12] and United Nations Development Program (UNDP)[13] since the 1990s. Moreover, Western countries' aid and development agencies[14] consider good governance as a significant prerequisite for the allocation of aid to developing countries. That is why Grindle (2012, 261) describes good governance as 'the new kid in development discourse.' International aid agencies not only consider promoting of good governance in developing countries as an *objective* for development assistance but also as a *condition* for it (Santiso 2001, 2). Noticeably, good governance also has manifested in the development discourse of developing countries like India both as a goal and a strategy.[15]

Roots and context of good governance

The fundamental question is how good governance has become a significant factor in the contemporary development discourse. To answer this question, the roots of the emergence of the neo-liberal economy and its impacts on the development discourse should be investigated. As Chang (2002) indicated, because of the practical failure of laissez-faire doctrine between World War I and II, this doctrine had been marginalized and rejected. Hence, as he discusses (Chang 2002, 540), a range of interventionist theories like Keynesianism, welfare economics, and the early development economics emerged after World War II. Market failure was the fundamental issue that these interventionist theories dealt with it, and they prescribed an active state involvement to solve this problem.

Conversely, neo-liberalism has emerged as the leading challenger of the Keynesian welfare state since the 1970s. Gamble (2001, 127) describes neo-liberalism as the extraordinary "revival of doctrines of the free market." Neo-liberals saw state inefficient when compared it with the market. Moreover, they argued that post-war Keynesian welfare state in crisis and cannot be continued (Bevir 2009, 4). Neo-liberal economists like Milton Friedman and Friedrich von Hayek were the pioneers of this significant shift. These scholars were perceived as neo-liberal because their works are the recent adoption of liberal or laissez-faire doctrine. Consequently, as McGuigan (2005, 230) remarks, neo-liberalism can be seen as a return to the nineteenth-century liberalism in political economy, advocating "laissez-faire economics for free trade in an international division of labor and minimal state intervention within the nation." Liberal economists mainly assume that the capitalist economy can do its best performance when left to its own devices and unconstrained by government regulation (Manzetti 2009, 7). For this reason, neo-liberal economists also have a negative attitude toward the role of the state in the economy. As Chang (2002, 540) specifies, they considered the state as "an organization run by self-seeking politicians and bureaucrats." These politicians and bureaucrats are under the influences of interest groups as well as limited in collecting information and executing policies. They elucidated those government failures and their symptoms such as corruption and rent-seeking was the result of the 'imperfect nature of the state.' The neo-liberal economists assumed that the state should mostly be involved in policymaking rather than service delivery. Thus, they tried to 'roll back the state' and put emphasis on 'bringing civil society back in.' Therefore, as Leftwich (1993, 608) remarks, neo-liberalism simply cannot be seen as an economic theory. Rather, it has substantial political dimensions. These political dimensions include normative as well as functionalist theories that are related to politics and the state.

This 'neo-liberal counter-revolution' or 'neo-classical counter-revolution' played a key role in the shift in development programs in the developing countries. During the 1980s, international financial organizations faced with the threat of widespread default or partial payment of debts by developing countries especially in Latin America. So, they tried to find a strategy by which their assets would be preserved. This strategy came to be called the 'Washington Consensus' (Weeks and Stein 2006, 676). Williamson (1990) introduces the set of policy reforms that most of the officials in Washington believed would be beneficial to Latin American states:

- Fiscal discipline;
- Redirection of public expenditure priorities toward fields offering both high economic returns and the potential to improve income distribution, such as primary health care, primary education, and infrastructure;
- Tax reform (to lower marginal rates and broaden the tax base);
- Interest rate liberalization;
- A competitive exchange rate;
- Trade liberalization;
- Liberalization of inflows of foreign direct investment;
- Privatization;
- Deregulation (to abolish barriers to entry and exit);
- Secure property rights.

The neo-liberal agenda of the World Bank and IMF for the developing countries ascended in the context of Washington consensus. Accordingly, the foremost emphasis of them was rolling the state back and market-oriented policies (Bevir 2009, 94). Therefore, the World Bank and IMF have implemented new conditions for loans to developing countries and asked them to apply new policies to revise the role of the state in the economy.

As Bhattacharya (2008, 90) clarifies, the World Bank and IMF recommended two policies of 'privatization' and 'deregulation' to make markets more efficient and restrict the role of the state in economic regulation and intervention. Therefore, during the 1980s, the development assistance shifted fundamentally from financing investments in infrastructures to promoting policy reform in the framework of Structural Adjustment Program (SAP). This strategy advocates the 'adjustment trinity,' including stabilization, liberalization, and privatization that enhance growth and development (Stein 2006, 597). As Rodrik (1990, 933) elaborates, structural adjustment includes several macroeconomic and institutional reforms like trade liberalization, price deregulation, financial liberalization, and privatization.

According to Stein (2006, 597–598), stabilization involves decreasing trade deficits, limiting monetary growth, and cutting government spending, The objective of stabilization was control of inflation and decrease of imbalances in the current account and government budgets. Liberalization mostly includes policies like reducing government regulations and freeing up prices by removing government controls or subsidies on prices. Finally, based on the neo-liberal perspective, assuming private property ownership would increase the levels of efficiency and enhance the investment and growth; privatization contains policies like selling state properties (like banks or companies) to the private sector and limiting state intervention in the market activities. Therefore, the SAP can be seen as the manifestation of this neo-liberal turn of development literature in the policy context. The first aim of SAP is eliminating inefficiencies and guarantee adequate growth rates.

For the first time, the good governance emerged in the debates on development in the Sub-Saharan African countries throughout the 1990s (see Leftwich 1993; Kjær 2004). At the beginning of the 1980s, the World Bank tried to implement SAP in the Sub-Saharan African countries to enhance economic growth. Despite all the optimism, the SAP had not led to the expected results. According to Stein (2006, 597), 37 Sub-Saharan African countries had received SAP loans until 1995; nonetheless, by 2001, the GNP per capita of the region had decreased by 43% since 1980 when the first programs were initiated. Therefore, the World Bank tried to solve this crucial dilemma: Why did the neo-liberal policy packages such as structural adjustment not enhance economic growth in Africa? In *Sub-Saharan Africa: From Crisis to Sustainable Growth* (1989, 60–61) the World Bank indicated, "a crisis of governance" underlay "the litany of Africa's development problems." The report recognized factors such as self-serving public officials and corruption as the main causes of bad governance. In this report, the World Bank defined governance as "the exercise of political power to manage a nation's affairs." In this framework, the report introduced corruption, bad policies, and nepotism as the negative factors that hampered development in African countries. In contrast, the report (World Bank 1989, xii) postulated that although the private sector's initiative and market mechanisms as the neo-classic and neo-liberal economic assumptions are significant for development; nonetheless, they "must go hand-in-hand with good governance." In this sense, good governance was understood in terms of "public service that is efficient, a judicial system that is reliable, and administration that is accountable to its public." So, the first use of "good governance" was initially articulated in this World Bank's publication. From this time, the key postulation of the World Bank and IMF was that only loans and the SAP do not enhance economic growth. Therefore, good governance should accompany them. As Epstein and Gang (2009, 12) indicate, international financial and aid organizations postulated that the aids and loan would be effective if there is an "appropriate policy environment." Alternatively, the corrupt bureaucrats and self-interested politicians can divert aids and loan. Therefore, the World Bank has considered good governance as the main criteria for its lending to developing countries since 1992. The World Bank in *Governance and Development* (1992, 1) defined good governance as "sound management of a country's economic and social resources for development policy" and introduced it as "central to creating and sustaining an enabling environment for development" (World Bank 1992, 47).

In addition, as Leftwich (1993, 609) specifies, it seems that other factors more than a reassessment of implementation of the SAP in Sub-Saharan African countries played a role in the popularity of good governance. The collapse of the Berlin Wall, the disintegration of the Soviet Union, and the decay of communism provided freedom for the liberal Western states and the international financial and aid institutions to attach political conditionalities to aid and loans without anxiety of losing "its Third World allies or clients to communism in a competitive bipolar world." Similarly, as Doornbos (2001) specifies, after the collapse of the Soviet Union and end of the Cold War, there is no serious strategic need for the Western states to get the support from or give support to authoritarian regimes in developing countries. So "A new chapter of conditionalities, that is, of *internally* directed political conditionalities concerned with the structuring and operation of recipient countries' institutions, was being opened" (Doornbos 2001, 97). Mitra (2006, 236) also highlights the influence of 9/11 terrorist attacks on the good governance approach and notes "from its earlier emphasis on process, governance, particularly in the wake of 9/11, has moved on to the more loaded concept of *good governance* with a focus on electoral democracy, promoted by armed liberal governments."

Therefore, as Nanda (2006, 270) remarks, the international financial organizations and Western countries give the debt relief, debt forgiveness and increases in aid only to countries, implementing governance reform to guarantee transparency, the rule of law, human rights and accountability. After the emergence of good governance during the 1990s, the Western donor community not only insisted on economic conditionalities such as keeping inflation below 7% per year, or cutting subsidies on fertilizers, but also added a new variety of political conditionalities such as establishing a democratic political system, supporting multi-party system and safeguarding freedom of the press and expression (Chhotray and Hulme 2009, 37). The first aim of these institutional and policy reforms was enhancing the economic growth. Another noteworthy example of attachment of good governance conditionality to aid is the U.S. MCC or Millennium Challenge Corporation (earlier Millennium Challenge Account).

Bevir (2009) and Bhattacharya (2008) see roots of the good governance approach in the main ideas of neo-liberalism. According to Bevir (2009, 93) the notion of good governance is mostly associated with the neo-liberal reforms in the public sector like marketization, privatization, and the new public management. McCarney (2000, 2) construes good governance as "another element of a global hegemonic neo-liberal discourse." Similarly, Kjær (2004, 139) suggests that the good governance model, recommended by the international financial and development organizations, was constructed based on the 'Anglo-American liberal-democratic model.'

Despite all neo-liberal inspirations, good governance was not constructed based on those ideas merely. Apparently, some elements of neo-institutional economics (NIE) gradually influenced good governance as an emerging concept (Pomerantz 2011, 163). After the publication of *Institutions, Institutional Change and Economic Performance* (North 1990) and popularity of NIE, institutions were understood as the "underlying determinant of long-term performance of economies" (North 1990, 107). The NIE highlights the role of institutions in the creation of variant economic performance throughout history and across the world. Moreover, the efforts of scholars like March and Olsen (1983, 1989) and Skocpol (1985) that led to the rise of neo-institutionalism in political science with more attention to the role of the paved the path for the emergence of good governance as a hybrid concept. Hence, we can see the influence of NIE and the idea of 'bringing the state back in' in *World Development Report 1997: The State in a Changing World* (World Bank 1997b), which acknowledges the decisive role of the state as central to economic development. The World Bank, with a particular focus on the role of the state in development, pointed out that "An effective state is vital for the provision of the goods and services and the rules and institutions that allow markets to flourish and people to lead healthier, happier lives" (World Bank 1997b, 1).

Defining good governance: efforts and ambiguities

With a hybrid attitude, both the neo-liberal and neo-institutional, the World Bank has published several studies on good governance since 1997. In a very explicit statement, the World Bank in *World Development Report 2002: Building Institutions for Markets* (2002, 99) defined good governance as "the ability of the state to provide institutions that support markets such as property rights and regulatory regime that support competition." Thus, according to this report, good governance matters for economic growth and poverty reduction. Eventually, this institutional trend was highlighted by Kaufmann, Kraay, and Mastruzzi (2011, 222), defining governance as

> the traditions and institutions by which authority in a country is exercised. Good governance includes (a) the process by which governments are selected, monitored and replaced; (b) the capacity of the government to effectively formulate and implement sound policies; and (c) the respect of citizens and the state for the institutions that govern economic and social interactions among them.

While 'governance' as a key concept was rarely used in the context of development before the 1990s, governance, particularly good governance, has become predominant in development debates since the last two decades. So Grindle (2007, 553) describes good governance as a '*Mantra*' for current development organizations and professionals. Nevertheless, good governance like governance has not an agreed or single definition. As Holmberg, Rothstein, and Nasiritousi (2009, 136) indicate, "because good governance is such a broad concept and encompasses a range of issues, empirical analyses hinge on the definition of the term." Furthermore, as Börzel, Pamuk, and Stahn (2008, 5) specify, some development studies scholars or international organizations tend to define good governance as a synonym of governance without providing a clear definition of either term. Ten years after the popularity of the term, Doornbos (2001, 94) describe good governance as a 'policy metaphor' and asserted that a consensus on the core meaning of the term hardly could be achieved. Some definitions concentrate on performance and the result; others underline the process. Some of them deal with the institutional structure and some with the elite agency. Some of them consider governance as a synonym of government and some focus on the roles of civil society and NGOs. Some of the definitions see good governance as the capacity of the state to implement policies, and some consider it as policy (Pomerantz 2011, 164). That is why Bevir (2009, 92), describes good governance definitions critically as "wish-list of reforms, practices, and outcomes, usually with a particular eye on developing states."

Good governance as a theoretical tool: assessments and critiques

Question about the causality assumption

Good governance approach hypothesizes that there is a linear causality between good governance and economic development. Nevertheless, several scholars have raised questions about the linear causality between the quality of governance and economic outcomes, particularly economic growth. For instance, Kurtz and Schrank (2007) remind that the empirical foundations of correlation between quality of governance and growth are weaker than it has been claimed. As they suggest, although clean and effective governance is desirable; nevertheless, it is not so clear whether it is a crucial or even significant originator of economic growth or not (Kurtz and Schrank 2007, 541). Looking at corruption and unstable political system in post-World War Italy, the rapid economic growth for them is clear evidence for the independence of economic performance. Correspondingly, as Holmberg, Rothstein, and Nasiritousi (2008, 4) point out, in the studies, aiming to prove a correlation between good governance and economic growth; scholars sometimes have used the definitions that serve to confirm their hypothesis. For instance, some scholars emphasize regulatory quality over other aspects of quality of governance. Likewise, as Baird (2012, 265) indicates, the World Bank, as well as some scholars "include elements of democracy among measures of governance and elements of governance among measures of democracy, respectively." Therefore, it would be problematic – if not impossible – to find out which institutions matter for development, how and when they matter, or if they matter at all.

Normative roots of good governance

The normative foundation of the good governance approach can also weaken the scientific solidity of the approach. This deep normative foundation keeps scholars uncertain about its ability to serve as a proper academic theory in development studies. For instance, as Gregory (2014, 16) points out, "good governance and bad governance are rhetorical categories rather than scientific ones." Grindle (2004, 527) describes good governance as "an outcome of 'advocacy' by dedicated supporters of the democratic government, universal human rights, sustainable development, empowerment of the poor, free trade, participatory development, and other desirable conditions."

Zanotti (2005, 468) identifies neo-liberalism as the main normative foundation of and states "good governance doctrines originated within the Anglo-American neo-liberal critique of the interventionist welfare state." Similarly, Mitra (2006, 52) distinguishes between three perspectives on governance: (i) realist-rational perspective (governance as *order*), (ii) the liberal (governance as a *process*) and (iii) the normative (*good* governance) perspectives. He concludes that governance with its great analytical power has been changed to a political slogan. According to Mitra (2006, 236),

> as a concept, good governance, loaded with liberal values, privileges those who have the ontological control over the definition of these categories. In real-life situations, this method privileges the specialist and the observer of governance as compared to the actors who are part of the context.

Khan (2012) observes this normative basis as an obstacle for more objective analysis on governance and development and describe this approach as part of a much wider tradition within modern liberal economics. According to him, this liberal tradition "develops economic models from a minimal set of 'plausible' first principles and then looks to cross-country or historical evidence using regression analysis on relatively large data sets to see if particular hypotheses are rejected or supported" (Khan 2012, 52). Bevir (2009, 93) compares the normative origins of good governance definitions by the World Bank and UNDP. In the World Bank's liberal perspective, the notion of good governance as a strategy for development associated with democratic political institutions as well as the market economy, free trade, and reduced public sector. Alternatively, in the definition of good governance by the UNDP the principal focus is on the social and political condition because economic liberalism has fewer influences on this international organization.

Not only definitions of good governance were perceived as mostly normative, but also the good governance indicators are characterized as normative. For example, Rotberg (2014, 513) criticizes the World Governance Indicators, developed by the World Bank experts (see Kaufmann, Kraay, and Mastruzzi 2011) and states, "The indicators are largely normative, encompassing policy preferences rather than measuring the satisfaction of citizen-request priorities."

Neglecting different contexts

Western donor community and international financial organizations attempt to provide a universal definition of good governance and indicators for measuring its quality. These standard universal conceptualizations have neo-liberal roots. As Doornbos (2001, 100) indicates, "If donor-conceptualized standards of 'good governance' were to be more fully elaborated and insisted upon, it would thus almost certainly imply an insistence on Western-derived standards of conduct to be adopted in nonwestern politico-cultural contexts."

According to Zanotti (2005, 472), it was assumed that the principles and proposed way for good governance are effective across borders and in all circumstances. Thus, institutional and public management reforms can find suitable implementation in all states, regardless of their local contexts. Therefore, good governance approach proposes the standardized solutions to the full range of contexts with different problems. That is why Mitra (2006, 236) concludes that "being exogenous to their life world, the categories of good governance lack legitimacy for the same reason that an earlier generation of scholars became skeptical of modernization theories."

Considering diverse institutional contexts, Andrews (2010, 28) observes that countries with satisfactory economic performance and outcomes can have very different governance structures. As he concludes, "Countries that come out reflecting 'good government' according to the influential good governance indicators look very different, varying on the very dimensions that indicators imply are central to good government." Therefore, this evidence challenges the current predomination for a one-best-way model of good or effective governance. Khan (2012) similarly concentrates on dissimilar historical contexts of development in different countries. As he asserts, sustaining growth and development need

> a major transformation of pre-capitalist and largely agrarian societies into modern productive ones. These processes involve interlinked strategies of accumulation, technology acquisition, and the management of deeply conflictual processes of social and class transformation. Given that society starts with different political, social and economic histories, it is hardly surprising that there is no blueprint of transformation that we can discern in actual history.
>
> (Khan 2012, 55)

Good governance and the study of interrelations of governance and development in India

Most works, discussing and examining the interrelations between governance and development in India used 'good governance' discourse. For example, R.N. Ghosh, Rony Gabbay and Abu Siddique (1999) edited a book, consisting of articles presented at an international seminar held in 1996 that emphasized good governance and sustainable development in the Indian Ocean region. Good governance discourse profoundly influenced the book, its introduction, and each chapter. Another example is R.B. Jain (2003), presenting a detailed view of the quality of governance, and he focused on control of corruption as an indicator of good governance. In the same way, E. Vayunandan and Dolly Mathew (2004) focused on the issues and strategies of good governance in India. Their study deals with issues such as accountability, transparency, equity, efficiency, effectiveness, participation responsiveness, decentralization.

Not only good governance has influenced several academic works on governance and development in India, but also even the significant economic planning documents such as 'Five Years Plans' applied the term good governance. For the first time, the Planning Commission introduced the concept of governance to the planning literature in India with a specific chapter titled, 'Governance and

Implementation' in the *Tenth Five-Year Plan* (2002, 177) and consider good governance as one of the most crucial prerequisites of successful implementation of the plan. It defines governance as

> The management of all such processes that, in any society, define the environment which permits and enables individuals to raise their capability levels, on the one hand, and provide opportunities to realize their potential and enlarge the set of available choices, on the other. These processes, covering the political, social and economic aspects of life impact every level of the human enterprise, be it the individual, the household, the village, the region or the national level. It covers the State, civil society and the market, each of which is critical for sustaining human development. The state is responsible for creating a conducive political, legal and economic environment for building individual capabilities and encouraging private initiative. The market is expected to create opportunities for people. Civil society facilitates the mobilization of public opinion and peoples' participation in economic, social and political activities.

Congruently, the *Eleventh Five-Year Plan* (Planning Commission 2008, 223) considers improving the quality of governance as the precondition for inclusive growth:

> The Eleventh Plan vision of inclusive growth, reducing poverty and bridging the various divides that continue to fragment our society can only be achieved if there is a significant improvement in the quality of governance. There are many different definitions of good governance, but it is agreed that good governance must be broadly defined to cover all aspects of the interface between individuals and businesses on the one hand and government on the other.

Neo-institutionalism, governance, and comparative political economy

In this section, the book focuses on the application of the term governance in the context of the comparative political economy. As McCarney (2000) indicates, two flows of the definition of governance have been emerging, 'one a policy-oriented' one like good governance and second, 'a more academic one.' The rise of 'neo-statism' in the social sciences played a significant role in the emergence of governance as a scientific keyword in political science. In the period before World War II, the focus of political science was studying the legal aspects and formal institutions of the state (Kjær 2004, 124). Barkey and Parikh (1991, 523) illustrate how in post-World War II political science, approaches such as structural functionalism, Marxism, and pluralism had become more significance with underlying social variables like class or human behavior. According to Rothstein and Teorell (2012, 16), approaches like pluralism, elitism, and Marxism claim, "variables like economic power configurations, systems of social stratifications or the structure of class divisions were central in explaining political and thereby social and economic outcomes." Nevertheless, the institutional turn in political science returned the emphasis of the subject to the state. Scholars ranging from comparative historical sociology to specialists in the economics of development concentrated on the role of the state in the 1980s. The widely cited and influential book *Bringing the State Back In* (Evans, Rueschemeyer, and Skocpol 1985) was a turning point. In the introduction to the book, Theda Skocpol (1985, 4) described approaches like structure–functionalist or pluralist that were predominant in political science and sociology in the US during the 1950s and 1960s as the 'society-centered theories.' As Skocpol delineated, there has been a rising tendency in political science since the 1980s that represents a shift from society centered theories to the state-centered theories. The new approach reconsiders and focuses on the role of the state in relation to the economy and society. Thus, Skocpol argues for "a fundamental rethinking of the role of states in relation to economies and societies" (1985, 7). The book had a clear message: the characteristics and configurations of political institutions affect the economic performances.

Whereas the society-centered theories suggest that the state is so overwhelmingly influenced by powerful social actors such dominant classes, castes or interest groups, the neo-statist approach perceive the state is a more autonomous actor. Hence, the interests of powerful social actors are not the only determinant of the state's actions. Accordingly, the institutionalists argue that political institutions are the fundamental factor in analyzing the social and economic outcomes. Noticeably, the 'state-centered theories' also paid attention to the state-society relations; because the nature of these relationships would be the critical determinant for types of states that emerge (Barkey and Parikh 1991). In a parallel path, economists such as Knack and Keefer (1995) or Mauro (1995) investigated the cross-national data that suggested the importance of the institutional organization of the state. These studies also proposed that 'quality of government' has a positive effect on the economic growth.

The institutional approach not only in political science but also in economics and sociology has become popular since the 1980s. In these disciplines, in order to distinguish between new approaches and the pre-world war approach with its concentration on the formal institutions of the state, scholars like March and Olsen (1983), Peters (1999), Powell and DiMaggio (2012) refer to this revived approach as 'new institutionalism.' Around 1990, two major institutionalist works were published, that played a significant role in the second approaches for understanding interrelations between governance and development. Not only March and Olsen with a concentration on the institution in the political science in their work *Rediscovering Institutions (*1989) represented the 'institutional turn' in political science, but also North as a leading figure in the institutional economics in his *Institutions, Institutional Change, and Economic Performance* (North 1990) concentrated on the institutions (both formal and informal) in the state and their impact on economic performance. He described institutions as the "the rules of the game in society, or more formally, the humanly devised constraints that shape human interaction" (North 1990, 3). Moreover, as he points out, institutions are "underlying determinant of long-run performance of economies" (North 1990, 107). Similarly, Peter Hall (1986, 20) defines institutions as "formal rules, compliance procedures, and standard operating practices that structure relationships between individuals in various units of the polity and the economy." The institutions as the rules of the games can be formal or informal. Formal institutions are mostly the rules, openly codified and enforced by a state actor. In contrast, the informal institutions involve unwritten and socially shared rules of the game like caste in the Indian context.

The fundamental assumption of this new institutional approach is that institutions matter for political as well as economic outcomes. Moreover, this approach deals with the quality of institutions as a crucial element of governance. Correspondingly, we are witness to a growing interest in governance in political science as a reflection of the institutional debate on capacity or incapacity to govern. Therefore, we can see how increasing interest in governance in political science and particularly in comparative politics, represents a return to interest in organizations and institutions, in contrast to the methodological individualism of behavioralism or marginalization of the state by the society centered theories. Since the 1990s, governance theory has become an integrated part of research in most subfields of comparative politics. Whether cross-national or cross-sectorial, it is evident that research areas like comparative political economy, institutional analysis as well as public sector reform analysis have been influenced vastly by the growing governance theory (see Peters 2000, Kjær 2004).

With a neo-institutional perspective, governance enables us to conceptualize the complex arrangement of relationships between the institutions (the rules of the game) that play a significant role in policymaking and distributing resources in the transformed nation-states, where the traditional top-down process of command and control are no longer sufficient. Thus, institutions and governance are interlinked, and institutionalists attempt to explain the divergent performances and trajectories by reference to transformation in the institutions, institutional arrangements, and their implications. Accordingly, with an institutionalist approach, Kjær (2004, 12) conceptualizes governance with a focus on rules of the game:

> We have defined governance as the setting, application, and enforcement of the rules of the game.

In sum, growing literature has appeared that deals with the governance as the traditions and institutions that form the pattern of the exercise of power in society and its impact on the economic development. Therefore, scholars like Goodin and Klingemann (1996, 25) call this new institutional approach as "the next revolution in the discipline of social science."

Developmental state theory

Kjær (2004, 194) conceptualizes governance as "how institutions for economic policymaking and implementation are set up, and what their consequences are." She defined this area of study as the *comparative political economy*, and she states that this approach overlaps with the area, discussing governance in public policy and administration. This approach rejects the neo-liberal assumption that claims that the state should not have the role in development and market itself is the central factor. This approach rooted in the idea of *Bringing the State Back In* (Skocpol 1985) and neo-statist approach of the 1980s and 1990s. They do not believe in self-regulation of the market and assert that there is the need for some interventions. Kjær (2004) considers 'developmental state theory' as one of the significant theories of governance in comparative politics. In the 1980s, the concept of the 'developmental state' (DS) emerged to explain East Asian states' growth, concentrating on synergetic interactions between state and economic agents and their role in economic growth. Developmental state theory seeks to conceptualize the role of the state in economic development where governments' economic strategies (for example, industrial policies) have been associated with political motives (for example, the strengthening of legitimacy). The first manifestation of this approach can be seen in the developmental state theory that was conceptualized by Johnson (1982, 1987). While neo-liberal scholars considered the remarkable economic growth of four East Asian countries (Hong Kong, Taiwan, Singapore, and South Korea) during the 1960s and 1970s as the result of the unguided market, developmental state theory highlighted the synergetic interactions between state, ruling elite and political institutions, and economic agents. Whereas the neo-liberal theories advocate the minimum intervention of the state in the economy and try to explain economic success or failure by success or failure of the market, developmental state theory with its institutional approach argues that the state of development of a nation or society hinges on its political purpose and institutional structures. Also, developmental state theory criticizes good governance approach for its normative preferences and imposing its neo-liberal values on the developing countries.

Adrain Leftwich (1995, 401), the eminent political scientist, defines developmental state and elaborates its characteristics as follows:

> The developmental states may be defined as states whose politics have concentrated sufficient power, autonomy and capacity at the Centre to shape, pursue and encourage the achievement of explicit developmental objectives, whether by establishing and promoting the conditions and direction of economic growth, or by organizing it directly, or a varying combination of both.

Leftwich (1995, 405) defined six significant components of developmental state model:

- A determined developmental elite;
- Relative autonomy;
- A powerful, competent and insulated economic bureaucracy;
- A weak and subordinated civil society;
- The effective management of non-state economic interests; and
- Repression, legitimacy, and performance.

Neo-statism and study of development in India

The institutional turn in political science and developmental studies and emergence of 'neo-statism' inspired scholars whose interest was political economy of development in India. The role of the state in the economic success or failures has emerged as the main research question in the field (Rudolph and Rudolph 1987; Herring 1999; Ahluwalia 2002; Harriss 2005; Kennedy 2004, Mukherji 2009, 2014; Naseemullah 2017). When Rudolph and Rudolph (1987) talked about *India's weak-strong state* or Herring (1999) spoke about India as a *(failed) developmental state*, they remarked on the limited autonomy of the Indian state due to the dominance of social actors as the main obstacle for independent pro-development policymaking. These perceptions are close to Bardhan's (1984) society-centric view that considered the dominant coalition of industrialists, farmers, and professionals as the primary cause of the persistence of the import substitution in India during the 1980s.

Accordingly, some scholars (for example see Brass 1994; Platteau 1995; Chandra 2007; Markussen 2011; Bardhan and Mookherjee 2012; Wyatt 2013, Srivastava 2017) highlighted the significance of the patron-client relations when they were depicting the nature of the state society-relation in India. These clientelism-based approaches dominate scholarship on the state-society relations and their effects even at the State level (See Elliott 2011, 2016). According to these perspectives, the state has been so penetrated by the vested interests of dominant castes, wealthy farmers, and industrialists that cannot be autonomous in terms of economic policymaking.

Since the institutional turn in political science, the role of the Indian state in development has emerged as one of the primary debates in the political economy of India. Scholars like Herring, Kohli, and Chandra had pessimistic views on the capacity state to enhance economic development. The keywords such as 'embedded particularism,' 'weak state,' 'a failed developmental state,' 'institutional vacuum,' 'dominant coalition' or 'patronage politics' had been used to designate the political roots of the 'Hindu rate of growth' and India's unsatisfactory economic performance after the independence.

Nevertheless, the economic emergence of India after the 1990s and rapid growth in manufacturing sector despite the absence of the fundamental characteristics of the developmental state model has puzzled the scholars, scrutinizing the role of state and its institution in development. In the recent institutional reactions to India's emergence, scholars like Mukherji (2009, 2014) revisited the role of the state in development. Highlighting and analyzing the homegrown ideas within state bureaucracy and political class, Mukherji tried to open up the black box of the Indian state, which led to a significant policy shift in favor of economic reforms in India. Unlike Mukherji who argued that ideas within the Indian state are significant for establishing an institutional and policy trajectory in the foundational moments that led to economic success, Naseemullah (2017) looks at the empty half of the Indian state. He considers the Indian state as an unable markets regulator who cannot provide a predictable macroeconomic environment within which to invest, manage capital-labor relations, or advocate and efficiently mediate on behalf of Indian industry to the world market.

Nonetheless, most of the works based on the statist approach look at the state as an actor or as an organization as an aggregated entity. This perception accompanies with an aggregate, unitary and top-down notion of state. This understanding is reflected in the majority of works that analyze the role of the state in the economic performance. Moreover, other examples of academic work, discussing the role of the state in the economic success or failures (for example Bardhan 1984; Rudolph and Rudolph 1987; Herring 1999), deal mainly with the role of 'Central Government.' When Rudolph and Rudolph (1987) talk about *India's weak-strong state*, it was perceived as a unitary actor. Similarly, when Herring (1999) or Kumar (2008b) spoke about India as a (failed) developmental state, their perception accompanied with a unitary and top-down notion of state. Similarly, when Ahluwalia (2002) investigated the causes for variation in growth performance across States before and after the liberalization, beyond the economic variables such as private investment, industrial, fiscal, and financial policies affected the growth of states; he highlighted the role of the central government. His work is silent about the regional institutional (formal and informal) variations across the States.

The recent democratization in Latin America presented a rich context for the subnational comparative studies in comparative politics. As Tillin (2013, 237) indicates,

> as yet reflecting the possibility of conducting reasonably controlled comparisons within a federal setting and the importance of capturing within-country variation, the subnational comparative method has been steadily embraced by researchers in a number of federal countries over the last few decades.

This trend also finds its way in the study of the political economy of India. Kohli's work (1987) was the pioneer of the comparative subnational political economy in India. Kohli (1987) suggested India constitutes a laboratory for comparative political analysis. Kholi (1987) suggested the nature of political mobilization of classes and castes engenders particular political regimes. These different regimes across the States pave the path for different policy regimes and developmental outcomes. Following Kohli, Harriss (1999, 2005) differentiated political regimes in the different States based on the balance of caste or class relations and the nature of party organization within those States. According to Harriss (1999), Kerala, Tamil Nadu, and West Bengal are states with political regimes dominated by lower castes and classes; nevertheless, in different ways. Jenkins (1999 2003, 2004), Kohli (2012), Kalaiyarasan (2017) are other examples of subnational inter-States comparative studies, focusing on the role of political variables on economic performances in the states. Deshpande, Kailash, and Tillin (2017) scrutinize the role of the States in shaping the implementation and framing of social policy. Their finding suggests that three critical variables can explain different performances: First, the role of policy legacies in shaping policy frames; second, social coalitions supporting the political parties, and finally the role of political leaders in strengthening state capacity Correspondingly, Sinha (2005) – based on the theory of multilevel hierarchy – focuses on regional elite strategies and subnational institutional variations and their impact on flow and inflow of investment in three historically more developed States: Gujarat, Tamil Nadu, and West Bengal. For her, the puzzle divergence between East and West after the independence can be addressed via analysis of the vertical and horizontal strategies of the regional elites and the regional institutional and political context.

Final remarks: governance beyond good governance in the Indian context

This chapter reviews the different approaches, discussed the linkage between governance and development. Understanding this linkage is essential for this book because the term governance has various applications in the different fields of social sciences. The chapter recognized good governance and governance in the context of a comparative political economy with an institutionalist approach as two relevant approaches for the current study. According to international aid agencies, 'good governance' is not only a critical condition for the achievement of development but it is also a goal. The book does not employ the governance indicators to measure the quality of governance, but rather pays attention to good governance as it has been perceived by the regional leaders such as Chandrababu Naidu or Nitish Kumar.

Beyond good governance rhetoric, governance as an academic keyword also has manifested in the studies on India's political economy and inter-States comparison. This perspective highlights the role of the state but recognizes the significance of state–society and state–market interactions. For instance, Jenkins (2002, 485) conceptualized governance as "the prevailing patterns by which public power is exercised in a given social context." Mitra (2006, 21) delineates governance as "as the overlap of the thin norms of the state and the thick perceptions of social groups is the interface of societies and institutions." Governance for him deals with the capacity of the state to enforce orderly rule: "…Governance understood as orderly political transactions, consistent with the highest law of the land" (Mitra 2008, 1).

With an institutionalist perspective as well as by underlying the agency, Kennedy (2014, 138) conceptualized the governance in the context of the political economy of India as "the institutions and actors who shape the economic and process that coordinate the economic activities." The current book follows Kennedy's conceptualization that highlights institutions and actor simultaneously. Both shape the economic and political processes that coordinate economic activities. Governance is about not only the democratic process, sound policies or the state capacity to enforce the orderly rule; rather it depicts the complex and multi-layered interactions within the state including bureaucracies, associations, parties, leaders, and informal institutions as well state–society and state–market interactions. The concept of governance signifies the multiple actors, state and non-state. Moreover, it implies the multilevel actors, national, regional and supranational, participating in the political process with economic outcomes. In the process of institutional transformations, emerging institutional arrangements affect outcomes both at national and subnational levels.

Notes

1 The governance approach is not merely about the state and the formal institutions; rather it deals with the state–society interactions, public–private relations, formal as well as informal institutions. As Wachhaus (2014, 588) indicates

> Governance is shifting our notions of government: Moving outside governmental walls; shifting the flow of resources, power, and accountability much closer to the citizenry; altering that flow from a top-down to a two-way flow; and de-centering the locus of power, resources, and accountability.

2 Rhodes (2000) proposed seven kinds of definitions of governance. He summarizes different definitions to following categories:

   1 Governance as corporate governance
   2 Governance as the new public management
   3 Governance as 'good governance.'
   4 Governance as international interdependence
   5 Governance as socio-cybernetic system
   6 Governance as new political economy
   7 Governance as networks.

3 For instance, Fukuyama (2013, 350) conceptualizes governance as "a government's ability to make and enforce rules, and to deliver services, regardless of whether that government is democratic or not."

4 For example Ebner (2009, 218) defines governance as "the process of designing, formulating and implementing policy goals and instruments in line with the diverse institutional carriers of these policies, involving agents from the private and public sectors."

5 Scholars like Kaufmann and Kraay (2008, 3) assert that governance as a concept is not new and early discussions about it can be traced to Arthashastra, the great work of Kautilya (*c*.350–283 BCE) who was the advisor of Emperor of India. They even translated Arthashastra as 'art of governance.'

6 As we can see, the root of the word governance as well as of government is a word meaning to steer a boat. Peters (2012, 64) describes 'steering metaphor' as a right way to approach governance in contemporary societies.

7 Remarkably, governance and cybernetics have the same roots. The Greek verb *kubernan*, was the root of *kubernētikos*, as an adjective form that means skilled in steering.

8 Interestingly, some scholars have identified shifts even in the new uses of governance. For example, Pierre and Peters (2000, 36–53) detect two dissimilar views of governance and call them the 'old governance' and 'new governance.' The first approach or old governance deals with the steering and rulemaking. This view discusses how the state steers the society and economy. In the old governance approach, the traditional concept of steering is the focus of analysis, and it is top-down. In particular, old governance deals with identifying "the capacity of the center of government to exert control over the rest of government, and over the economy and society" (Peters 2000, 38). In contrast, new governance refers to state–society interactions and focuses on self-organizing networks for steering. The main issues here are the role of networks, public and private interactions and self-governance.

9 For example, Ahrens (2002, 129) defines "Governance as the capacity of country's institutional matrix (in which individual actors, firms, social groups, civic organizations and policymakers interacts with each other) to implement and enforce public policies and to improve private-sector coordination."

10 The IMF defines good governance as "ensuring the rule of law, improving the efficiency and accountability of the public sector, and tackling corruption" (International Monetary Fund 1997).

11 At the beginning of the 1990s, the World Bank introduced "Good governance, as synonymous with sound development management" (World Bank 1992, 1). In the next step the World Bank defined it as

> epitomized by predictable; open, and enlightened policymaking (that is, transparent processes); a bureaucracy imbued with a professional ethos; an executive arm of government accountable for its actions, and a strong civil society participating in public affairs; and all behaving under the rule of law.
>
> (World Bank 1994, vii)

Finally, with a more institutionalist tone, the World Bank pointed out,

> Good governance includes the creation, protection, and enforcement of property rights, without which the scope for market transactions is limited. It includes the provision of a regulatory regime that works with the market to promote competition. And it includes the provision of sound macroeconomic policies that create a stable environment for market activity. Good governance also means the absence of corruption, which can subvert the goals of policy and undermine the legitimacy of the public institutions that support markets.
>
> (World Bank 1997b, 99)

12 The UN considers good and democratic governance almost as the synonyms:

> In the community of nations, governance is considered good and democratic to the degree in which a country's institutions and processes are transparent. Its institutions refer to such bodies as parliament and its various ministries. Its processes include such key activities as elections and legal procedures, which must be seen to be free of corruption and accountable to the people. A country's success in achieving this standard has become a key measure of its credibility and respect in the world.
>
> (United Nations 2009)

13 The UNDP characterized good governance as

> participatory, transparent … accountable … effective and equitable … promotes the rule of law … ensures that political, social and economic priorities are based on broad consensus in society and that the voices of the poorest and the most vulnerable are heard in decision-making over the allocation of development resources.
>
> (UNDP 1997)

Later, the UNDP emphasized more on the political dimension of the term and referred to it

> governing systems which are capable, responsive, inclusive, and transparent. All countries, developed and developing, need to work continuously towards better governance. Good, or democratic governance as we call it at UNDP, entails meaningful and inclusive political participation. Improving governance should include more people having more of a say in the decisions which shape their lives.
>
> (UNDP 2011)

14 For example, U.S. Millennium Challenge Corporation (MCC) defines "Good governance is a critical component of promoting economic growth. Policies that respect the rule of law protect civil liberties and fight corruption help lay the foundation for a society to thrive" (Millennium Challenge Corporation 2013, 9). Similarly, the U.K. Department for International Development (DFID) points out,

> Good governance requires capability – the extent to which government has the money, people, will and legitimacy to get things done; responsiveness – the degree to which government listens to what people want and acts on it; and accountability – the process by which people are able to hold government to account.
>
> (DFID 2006, ix)

15 For Instance, the twelfth five-year plan (2012–2017) introduces good governance as a critical factor "to translating Plan outlays into significant outcomes on the ground." The plan assumes good governance as a key that "ensures effective use of resources and deliverance of services to citizens and also provides social legitimacy to the system."

3 Theoretical framework

Introduction

This chapter builds the theoretical foundations of the book and discusses their methodological implications. The theoretical assumptions of this study have two roots. First, based on rational choice institutionalism[1] (see Shepsle 1989, 2008), this study assumes the rationality of actors[2] and their game model behavior (see Tsebelis 1990) at and between different levels. Moreover, this approach postulates 'institutions matter.'[3] This book, along with the mainstream of rational choice approaches in political science, assumes that human activity is goal oriented and instrumental and that individual and institutional actors try to maximize their goal achievement. Rationality assumption[4] is the fundamental assumption throughout the book. The rational choice institutionalism discusses how institutions shape the behavior of the rational actors.[5] As Weyland (2002, 60) remarks, rational choice institutionalism is methodologically an individualist analysis. It discusses

> (I) the creation, preservation, and modification of the sets of rules governing behavior, which are conceptualized as products of utility-maximizing individual action and strategic interaction, and (II) the impact of those rules on utility-maximizing individual action and strategic interaction.[6] Thus, investigations of institutions and their effects that explicitly start from interest calculations by individual actors.

Second, based on governance theory, the current book assumes the diversity of actors (the Union Government, subnational actors, the private sector, and civil society) and diversity, complexity, and dynamism of the interactions. Moreover, this study considers the arrangement of the political institution (formal as well as informal) and the agency of rational actors at the different levels of the game as a crucial factor in adopting and implementing of economic policy. Governance has multiple usages. In this book, 'institutional design for development' (not to be confused with governance in IR or public administration, as argued in the previous chapter) and 'good governance' (as perceived by the regional leaders in their economic reform agenda) are two main usages of the term.

Scholars like Mitra (2006) perceived governance as an orderly rule that depends on whether or not people choose to follow or rebel against the *transaction rules*; thus, governance is 'high' when people follow the transaction rules. However, this book transcends the borders of Mitra's neo-institutional model of governance to an institutional arrangement. In the context of comparative political economy, "governance refers to the study of different institutional models and processes that are relevant to economic development and discusses how institutions for economic policymaking and implementation are set up, and what their consequences are" (Kjær 2004, 194). In the context of India, the neo-institutional rational choice model of governance (Mitra 2006, 2008) and theory of polycentric hierarchy (Sinha 2005), are the best examples of implementations of those theoretical lenses.

This study examines the role of the state (as multi-layered institutions with the complex and dynamic interaction between different layers) in the development and opens up the black box of the state through analyzing determinants of policy choices of regional leaders. This book employs the subnational comparative method (Snyder 2001) and regional institutional analysis method (Sinha 2005; Mitra 2006) to depict a more transparent image of interrelations of governance and development India.

Neo-institutional rational choice model of governance

As Mitra points out (2006, 1), "India belongs to a minority of changing societies that have achieved the distinction of having durability, adaptability, and innovativeness as characteristics of their institutions." He argues that the elasticity and durability of India's institutions are the results of strategic thinking of her elites, reflected in the constitution. Accordingly, the main explanatory variable, explaining the sustainability of India's democracy is 'room to maneuver' (see Mitra 1991), provided by constitutional and institutional arrangements for the political elites. In his model, elite agency plays a significant role in the law and order management. Mitra (2008) considers 'the room to maneuver' as a crucial factor for the neo-institutionalist model. The room to maneuver allows the political elite to involve meaningful political and social intervention to sustain orderly rule. As Mitra explains,

> crucial to the neo-institutional model is the room to maneuver that the constitution permits the political elite (a democratic regime, as opposed to military rule, offers more scope for negotiation and bargaining) and the political accountability of the elites, which makes it necessary for them to engage in purposeful social intervention.
>
> (Mitra 2006; 16)

As Mitra (1991, 2006) discussed, the room to maneuver enables political elites to sustain orderly rule via being accountable to their local and regional context and initiating reform and interventions. These agencies aim at the improvement in the level of welfare and accommodating identity. These reforms can enhance political order and hence resilience of the system. As we can see, Mitra constructed his model based on the central role of the political elites in India's political system. As Mitra states,

> the response of the decision-making elites to crises through law and order management, strategic reform and redistributive policy and constitutional change in order to give legitimacy to contested, embedded values, acts as a feedback loop that affects the perceptions of crucial variables ... by people at the local and regional level.
>
> (Mitra 2006, 16)

Another significant aspect of conceptualization of governance in Mitra's model is the parameters. Mitra (2006, 19) proposed security, welfare, and trust as hypothetical parameters of governance. Based on the neo-institutional model of governance, Mitra (2006, 2008) argues that the strategic mixture of policing and reform, which simultaneously raises the stakes for rule violators and removes the incentives to riot and rebel by improving the level of welfare and accommodating identity, enhance the governance (orderly rule).

According to Mitra (1991, 2006), in the complex nodes of governance in India, the political elites perform as 'nodal points of political actions.' These political elites connect the Central Government and national level institutions to the regional and local actors and institutions. In the framework of rational choice institutionalism, the rationality of actors plays a significant role in the strategic choices of players. That is why Mitra (2006, 16) remarks,

> in a case of successful transaction, competing elites choose their options in a manner that maximizes benefits and minimizes transaction costs, and negotiate on the basis of a complex repertoire that combines instruments of rational protests with elements of participation such as contacts with high-level decision-makers, lobbying, voting and sending petitions.

Mitra's neo-institutional model of governance has more capabilities and merits for an objective analysis of governance in India than good governance perspective. However, the significant question is what would be implications of the dynamic neo-institutional model of governance for understanding the nature of development in India?

Polycentric hierarchy theory

Sinha (2005) criticizes the conventional idea, interpreting the Hindu rate of growth before liberalization as the result of centralized control and policies of the Union Government. Her study (2005) proves that there were different patterns of interactions between the Center and States before the liberalization, which led to various levels of inflows of private investments to States and consequently a divergence in their development trajectory.

Sinha introduces the polycentric hierarchy model as the substitute for the top-down unitary of state, providing an analytical framework for disaggregation of the interactions between various nodes at different levels in a seemingly aggregate system.

The polycentric hierarchy model does not concentrate on the Central Governments; on the contrary, it focuses on both national and subnational levels. As the theory suggests, the subnational states in India are not entirely autonomous and thus cannot be considered like nation-states; however, they are located within a polycentric hierarchy, and they respond to and evolve strategies toward the Central Government in diverse ways. As Sinha (2005, 27) proposes, the model of polycentric hierarchy postulates that the policy framework of growth in most countries "may not be centrally guided but is a joint product of central rules, provincial strategic choice, and subnational institutional variation." Sinha (2005, 27) considers the interaction between different levels of government as a significant factor for the ways in which central policy is receipted and implemented. She identifies the interaction between the various levels of government as a consequential factor which had influences on political conflict or central–local relations as well as the ways in which central policy is implemented, and developmental states are created and sustained.

In her model, the Central Government is not a single actor that imposes the rules of the game in a top-down way; on the contrary, there are several interactions between the central states, provincial actors, and private market. These complex, diverse, and dynamic interactions within and between different levels cannot be analyzed with conventional institutionalist or neo-statist theories.

Sinha (2005) introduces the capability to disaggregate the multilevel political system as a distinctive element of polycentric hierarchy theory that lets us realize how diverse actors located at spatially separable levels of the system evolve and react to economic policies.

Sinha (2005) does not consider the states (nation-states) as hierarchies with a unitary decision-maker. She perceives the states as polyarchies, identified by multi-leveled actors and institutions. For her, polyarchy is a concept to understand 'the territorial character of an internal heterogeneity in large states.' Therefore, she recognizes a combination of horizontal (within subnational units) and vertical (across levels of governments) interactions within polyarchies. As Sinha (2005, 34) indicates, the fundamental idea behind such interconnected games is crucial:

> Political actors act and live in two different arenas simultaneously. While actors face different pressures and constraints from these different domains, the goals, choices, and actions of these political actors are shaped by the interconnectedness of these various arenas.

The horizontal interactions, which include interactions with the social, political factors in the regional environment and vertical strategies toward the Central Government, which includes strategies such as bargaining and confrontation. She (2005, 35) highlights the importance of regional leaders in the game model interactions:

In the case of India, while economic games are played by regional states with the Central Government in the hope of obtaining central resources, political games primarily reside in the regional arena where regional elites must be elected and reelected. Regional rulers hold the key to both games as they are the intermediate hinge points responding to regional constituents as well as evolving vertical political strategies toward the Center in the hope of greater resources. The nested game depends on three variables: strategic political choices of regional elites, regional political institutions, and central institutions. In this framework, the strategic political choices of the elites are themselves a function of their policy preferences and regional electoral incentives.

Regional elite strategy analysis

This book assumes that not only national level institutions and national elites matter, but also the regional institutions and regional elites matter. The book takes its shape in the style and substance of the attitudes and political discourse of regional leaders in the Indian States. These regional elites, operating as the intermediaries between the society at the regional level and the Central Government, are the catalysts of social and economic change. The process of their strategic choices in the nested two-level games are the substantial variables in the creation and implementation of economic policies in India's States.

Following Mitra (2006) and Sinha (2005), the current book focuses on the role of regional institutions in the strategic choices of regional leaders. Sinha (2005, 14) defines regional institutions as "decision-making structure, bureaucratic agencies, formal and informal rules that are responsible for translating national policies." In a multi-layer political system such as India, the regional institution can play a significant role in the implementation of both regional and the Center's policies in different ways. Not only does the current book considers the role of modern institutions such as bureaucracy but it also analyzes the impacts of the traditional institutions like caste and its variations.

By employing rational choice-neo institutionalism, this study highlights the role of rational actors, maximizing their interest[7] in the game model behavior. Following Sinha (2005) and Mitra (2006), this study focuses on the role of regional leaders at the State level. The study deals primarily with the elite strategies, adopted by regional elites in the face of rules of the game. As mentioned, Mitra's framework (2006, 10) is "rational choice neo-institutionalism whereby all interactions between social actors ultimately be represented as two-player games that are hierarchically ordered and with outcomes that depend on the information available to the actors."

This study considers these players as self-interest actors; however, the contents of these interests are driven by the incentives and constraints set by two game levels with the Central actors and institutions as well as local and regional actors and institutions. Based on the assumptions of rational choice institutionalism about the actor interests, this study observed variations in the political behavior of regional leaders in Andhra Pradesh and Bihar by emphasizing the variations of incentives and constraints, created by the specific institutional rules.

Two types of constraints bound regional leaders' economic choices and developmental strategies: first, central rules and second, regional context. The regional leaders stick with rules from the Center when they perceive that orderly transactions yield more than they could expect to gain by breaking the rules. Their social and political background, political visions, the composition and position of their vote bank are essential factors for a detailed analysis. The goals, interests, and perceptions of regional elites and leaders and national ruling elites may vary.

Moreover, regional leaders' strategic choices have also been influenced by the intensives. In the context of India's democratic federal system, regional political actors at the State level are driven mostly by self-interest in improving their political positions, mainly by winning elections at the State level or finding a better position at the Central level.

In the context of India's States politics, the reelection in regional, as well as national elections is the leading intensive for the regional elites' behavior, also bounded by regional and central constraints. Accordingly, the variations in terms of strategic choices of economic policies, as well as the relations with the Center, should be addressed with reference to these incentives and constraints.

Based on this model and in the framework of India's democratic and federal system, the chief ministers' strategic choices are the result of a trade-off between interests at two distinct levels: the regional level and the central level. Therefore, the strategic decisions of chief ministers for implementation or rejection of the national policies (like economic liberalization) is based on a rational calculation of chief ministers, looking at the incentives created by central and by regional institutions.

As a result, following Mitra (2006) and Sinha (2005), this study uses a two-level game model for analyzing strategic choices of regional leaders (the chief ministers) toward the economic reforms.

Regional leaders are involved in a two-level game. In the horizontal game, they interact with other regional political actors (political parties, interest groups, and other actors), regional institutions, and voters. In the vertical game, regional leaders interact with the Union Government in Delhi. Figure 3.1 depicts the two-level interactive model, exposing the interactions between a regional leader at the State level and Central Government as well as regional political actors, regional institutions, and voters.

This two-level interactive model is constructed based on the notion of 'room to maneuver,' elaborating how regional elites are involved in meaningful political and social intervention and connect a traditional society to the modern state, and 'polycentric hierarchy,' opening up the black box of state in India. This multilevel interactive model provides a framework, delineating the State–Center relations (the vertical interactions) along with interactions within subnational states (horizontal interactions).

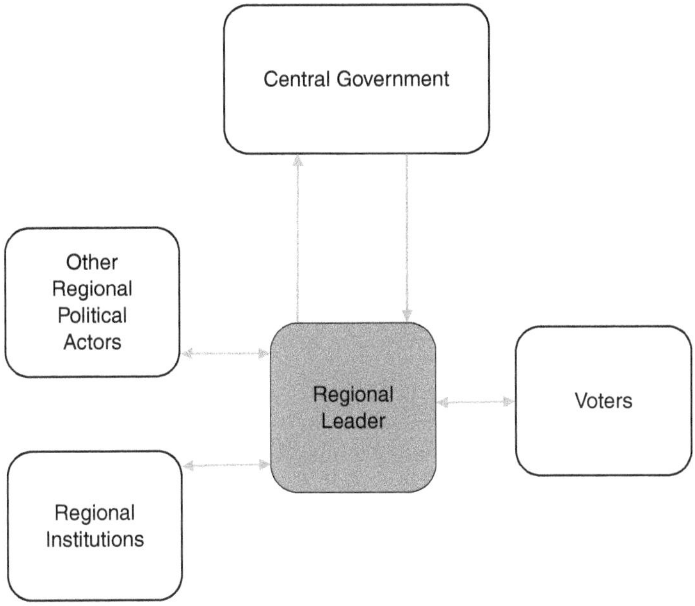

Figure 3.1 Two-level game of regional elites before the 1991 reforms.

Source: Drawn by the author.

This study delineates how these variations in the strategic choices of regional leaders had a different impact on the economy of the selected cases. According to this multilevel interactive model, chief ministers are not rulers of a nation-state; therefore, they are not entirely free in their choices of policies. The regional institutions, regional constituents, and central rules bound them.

In this model, regional leaders could adopt strategies such as confrontation, cooperation or mixed strategy toward the Center. These choices were made based on the rewards of constituents in the horizontal game, regional institutional variations and the incentives in the vertical interactions. The Center also rewarded or punished the State Governments by the different level political support and allocation of the financial resources. Figure 3.2 depicts the various hypothetical relations between strategic choices of chief minister in the vertical and horizontal games.

After the independence, chief ministers interacted with the Central Government in the vertical interactions. Nevertheless, in the Congress era, this interaction included more obedience and less autonomy. However, first after the decline of the Congress and emergence of regional parties and second after the liberalization, the new pattern of relations has emerged, and other actors entered in the game model interactions.

As Rudolph and Rudolph (2013) elucidate, with the emergence of 'federal market economy' and decline of 'the command economy' the chief ministers

		Leaders' strategic choices at the horizontal level	
		Populist economic policies (Handout)	Economic Reform Agenda Reform
Leaders' strategic choices at the vertical level interactions	Confrontation with the Center	?	?
	Cooperation with the Center	?	?

Figure 3.2 Hypothetical relations between strategic choices of chief minister in the vertical and horizontal games.

Source: Drawn by the author.

became actively involved in the economic policymaking, and they attained more autonomy than previous decades. While, in the 1950s and 1960s, the Center with the crucial role of the Prime Minister, the Planning Commission and the Five-Year Plans pursued economic modernization and development, after the liberalization, the chief ministers at the State level have played primary roles in India's emergent federal market economy.

Furthermore, after the dismantling of the 'licence-permit raj,' the domestic private sector companies, as well as international companies, emerged as the new source of investment in the State. In addition, international financial organizations and aid agencies such the World Bank could allocate financial support, aid, and loan to the State. These developments could decrease the level dependency of the States to the Center in terms of financial resources. In the new institutional arrangements, the new actors in the vertical game emerged and made it more complicated. Figure 3.3 portrays the multilevel game of regional elites after the 1991 liberalization.

As a result, the multilevel interactive model has become more complex, and the nested nature of a multilevel and complex game shaped the incentives and constraints of the game.

Conclusion

Based on the primary assumptions of rational choice institutionalism and governance theory and following Mitra (2006) and Sinha (2005), this chapter suggest a simple game model for delineating the behavior of the regional leaders and their response toward the economic policies, introduced by the Center in the framework of a pluralist and federal democracy. The model illustrates the

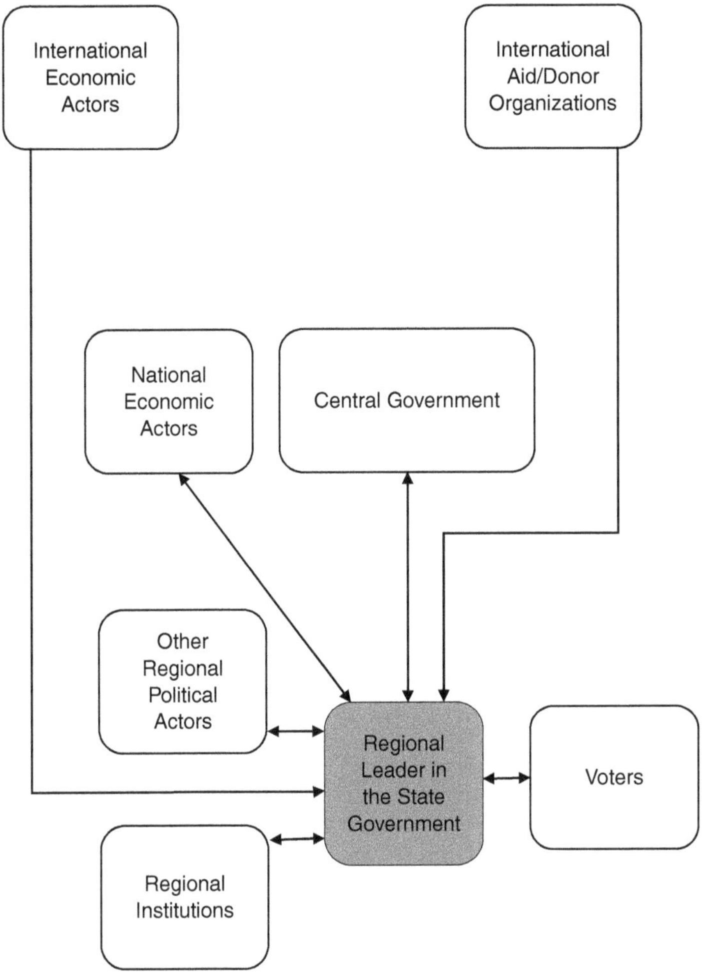

Figure 3.3 Multilevel game of regional elites after the 1991 reforms.

Source: Drawn by the author.

evolving nature of the interaction between the Center and the regional leaders when the central government needs the States to implement the reforms, and regional leaders seek reelection. The model is based on some categorized choices in the vertical and horizontal interactions:

> In the vertical game, the Center can reward the State by financial transfer to the State and political incentive in the framework of coalition politics. The Center also can punish the State by a reduction in the central transfers or implementation of the article 365 as an extension to emergency powers of

President. In the vertical game, the regional leaders also have two main choices: First, it can cooperate with the Center in terms of implementation of the policies, introduced and pursuit by the Center or reject them. Of course, a mixed response is also imaginable. Second, the leader of State can become a part of governing coalition at the Center or opt for being an opposition, trying to destabilize the dominant coalition.

Notes

1 Rational choice institutionalism (RCI) is a theoretical approach in political science that focuses on institutions and argues that actors use institutions to maximize their interests (based on instrumental rationality). Nevertheless, actors face rule-based constraints shaped by the institutional environment (see Weingast 1998).

2 As Calvert (1995, 73–74) points out,

> There is, strictly speaking, no separate animal that we can identify as an institution. There is only rational behaviour, conditioned on expectations about the behaviour and reactions of others. When these expectations about others' behaviour take on a particularly clear and concrete form across individuals, when they apply to situations that recur over a long period of time, and especially when they involve highly variegated and specific expectations about the different roles of different actors in determining what actions others should take, we often collect these expectations and strategies under the heading institution.

3 As Shepsle (2008, 23) specifies, an institution is a 'script' and consist of the "*actors*, their *strategies*, the *sequence* in which the actors choose from them, the information they possess when they make their selections, and the *outcome* resulting from the combination of actor choices."

4 Rationality, as defined by Tsebelis (1990, 18) is nothing more than an optimal correspondence between ends and means.

5 In the context of the current book, my stress on the instrumental rationality of the chief ministers – rather than policy goals or cultural determinants – is justified because political actors stand in competition. The ultimate goal of every chief minister and other regional leaders are election, reelection and upward mobility in the political hierarchy.

6 The rational choice approach to institutions deals with a group of individuals who possess well-defined preferences. The strategic interaction between these actors within a clear context is the main characteristics of the approach (Weingast 1998, 169).

7 In India, the regional leaders face electoral challengers both at regional and national level. Thus, the victory in the elections is the only way that guarantees their interests. Competition determinants force the leaders to pursue the instrumental rationality. Of course, we can imagine individual regional leaders may deviate from the commands of instrumental rationality, but larger numbers are unlikely to do so (see Tsebelis 1990, 34–38).

4 Elite agency and development in Andhra Pradesh (I)

Confrontation and populism in the age of Tollywood superstar

Introduction

The South Indian State of Andhra Pradesh (AP) is a remarkable example for scholars who want to study the politics of economic reforms in India. The trajectory of interactions between politics and development in the State makes Andhra Pradesh an attractive case for comparative political economy scholars. Although Andhra Pradesh was one of the less developed States in India three decades ago, it has experienced fast economic growth after liberalization. Andhra Pradesh as a less developed State in India could be compared with the BIMARU at the beginning of the 1980s. Moreover, Andhra Pradesh was famous for its populist politics and economic policies. The rise of N.T. Rama Rao (also known as NTR), a famous Tollywood[1] film star, the founder and charismatic leader of Telugu Desam Party[2] or the TDP, terminated the long-standing predominance of Congress Party in the State. Moreover, he introduced several populist schemes such as Rs 2 for a kilo of rice. However, in the next decade, Chandrababu Naidu, his successor, and son-in-law, as the chief minister of AP (1995–2004) adopted entirely opposing policies and implemented the pro-liberalization reforms in the State. These reforms were mostly based on the World Bank neo-liberal policy recommendations. In the framework of *Andhra 2020 vision* and by the implementation of a set of policies such as privatization, liberalization, and deregulation, Naidu tried to improve the business environment, attract foreign direct investments, and create more jobs and enhance economic development. He played a significant role in the considerable flow of foreign direct investment into State especially its capital city Hyderabad. These policies targeted the development of the IT sector in the State. Consequently, economic growth speeds up, and Naidu as the CEO of Andhra Pradesh became the role model for the chief ministers of other states.

Despite all the optimism, Andhra's 2020 dream did not come true, and the Congress (I)-led coalition (2004), defeated the reformist government of Naidu. However, it was not the end of story.

Gradually, ethnic sentiments based on the regional identity became the dominant feature of politics in the state. The old demand for the creation of a separate State of Telangana after decades again attracted attention; therefore, it led to enormous political mobilization. Finally, after a long political movement in the Telangana region of Andhra Pradesh, the Government of India decided that the new State of Telangana would come into existence on 2 June 2014.

The primary goal of this chapter and the next one is to investigate the political roots of the policy shift in the State that created what Panagariya and Govinda Rao (2015) call the 'economic miracle of Andhra Pradesh.' This chapter and the next one focus on the shifts in the strategic choice of regional leaders in a relatively underdeveloped State. These chapters rotate around this critical question: Why did the ruling elites in Andhra Pradesh especially in the TDP despite a long historical background of political and economic populism decide to adopt the economic reforms in AP, which have accelerated economic development? In addition, what was the political outcome of these shifts?

State profile

The current study deals with Andhra Pradesh in its pre-bifurcation form; hence, when this study discusses Andhra Pradesh, it refers to the State, as it existed before the formation of Telangana as a new state in 2014. However, this study has some implications for post-bifurcation States of Andhra Pradesh and Telangana. Before the bifurcation, Andhra Pradesh was one of the most highly populated States in India. Andhra Pradesh was India's fifth largest State by population (estimated at 84 million in 2011) and fourth largest by area.

Geography

Andhra Pradesh can be seen as the significant geographical and cultural link between north India and south India. Located in the southern region of India, the State had shared borders with Tamil Nadu, Karnataka, Orissa, Chhattisgarh, and Maharashtra. The State was also bounded by the Bay of Bengal. Andhra Pradesh was formed in 1956 by merging Telugu-speaking regions of the Madras Presidency and Telugu-speaking regions of Princely State of Hyderabad.[3] The united Andhra Pradesh was divided into three main regions, namely, Telangana,[4] coastal Andhra[5] and Rayalaseema[6] (Suri 2002).

On account of the fact that the coastal districts under British administration benefited from a higher level of industrialization and the large-scale irrigation works for agriculture, the Andhra region developed more than the Telangana region, which suffered from Nizam rule and the *jagirdar* system of landholding (Forrester 1970, 8). The capital city of AP is the vibrant city of Hyderabad, established by the Qutb Shahi dynasty in the sixteenth century. From 1724 until 1948, Hyderabad had been under the rule of Nizams, the descendants of Nizam-ul-Mulk Asif Jah, viceroy of Deccan and vizier of Moghul Emperor, who left Delhi and established a quasi-independent state at Hyderabad (Kulke and Rothermund 2004, 380).

Population and demography

According to the 2011 Census, the total population of Andhra Pradesh was 84,580,777. The population of Andhra Pradesh as per the census of 2001 was 76,210,007 while it was 66,508,008 according to the 1991 Census. The population of Andhra Pradesh contributed 6.99% of India's total population.

The languages spoken are Telugu followed by Urdu, Hindi, and Tamil. The literacy rate in Andhra Pradesh increased from 44.1% in 1991 to 67.7% in 2011; nevertheless, it was lower than the all-India average of 74.04%. As the *Census of India* (2011) elaborates, there is a significant gap in literacy rate between males and female, rural and urban people, tribal and non-tribal population, and socially backward castes and the upper castes. With 33.49% of the population living in urban areas in 2011, the level of urbanization in AP is almost similar to the national average (31.16%).

According to the census of India (2011), the Hindus, including the scheduled castes (SCs), constitute 89.01% of the total population. Muslims have the second rank with 9.16%, of the state population. The majority of AP's Muslims are Sunnis; nevertheless, because of the historical background of a Shia dynasty in the region (Qutb Shahi dynasty), there is a considerable number of Shias in Hyderabad city. Hyderabad has approximately 26% Muslims, mostly living in the 'old city.' Christians constitute about 1.8% of the State.

Economy

AP has a multi-structured economy. AP's economy includes a broad range of activities, from traditional agriculture in the rural areas to the IT industry in Hyderabad. Andhra Pradesh had been an important agricultural State; nevertheless, the State's service sector is the major contributor to NSDP over the years. Although the share of agriculture in the NSDP was about 60% at the time of the State formation (Suri 2002, 7), according to *Handbook of Statistics on Indian Economy 2005–2006* (2006), it fell to about 45% in 1980–1981.

However, the significant changes took place after the reforms. As Figure 4.1 illustrates, while the share of agriculture in NSDP decreased from 45.59% in 1980–1981 to 21.68% in 2010–2011, services have become the leading contributor in NSDP over last three decades. The share of the service sector as a whole has increased from 42.12% in 1980–1981 to 47.57% in 1990–1991, 54.07% in 2000–2001, and 65.20% in 2010–2011.

Moreover, as we can see in Figure 4.1, Andhra Pradesh has not transformed to an industrial State. The share of manufacturing sector in the NSDP has increased from 12.29% in 1980–1981 to 18.66% in 1990–1991; nevertheless, this proportion has decreased to 15.03% and 13.12% in 2000–2001 and 2010–2011 respectively. AP has reported a total NSDP of 4054.82 crores, which work out to be Rs 46,788 per capita for the year 2013–2014 at constant prices. Although AP's per capita income was below the national average at the beginning of the 1990s, Andhra Pradesh has transformed into the fourth most

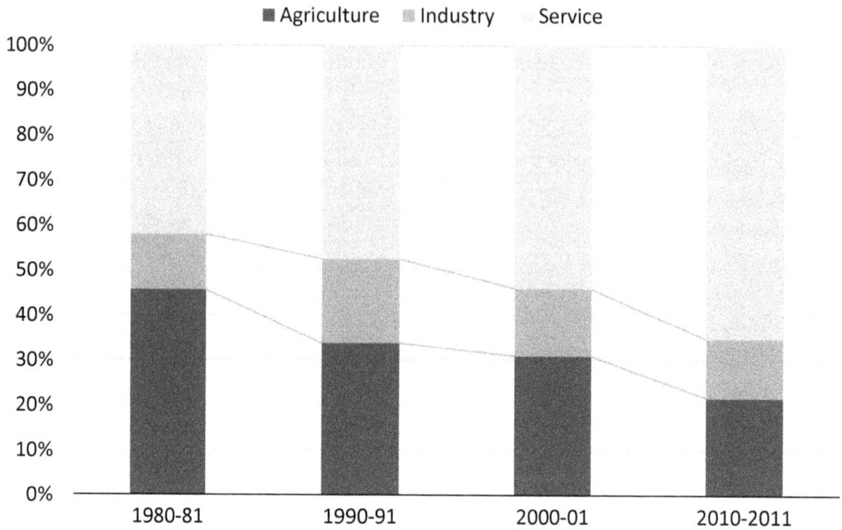

Figure 4.1 Percentage of components of AP's NSDP at factor cost by industry of origin (at constant prices).

Source: *Handbook of Statistics on Indian Economy 2005–06* (2006), and *Handbook of Statistics on Indian Economy 2014–15* (2015), drawn by the author.

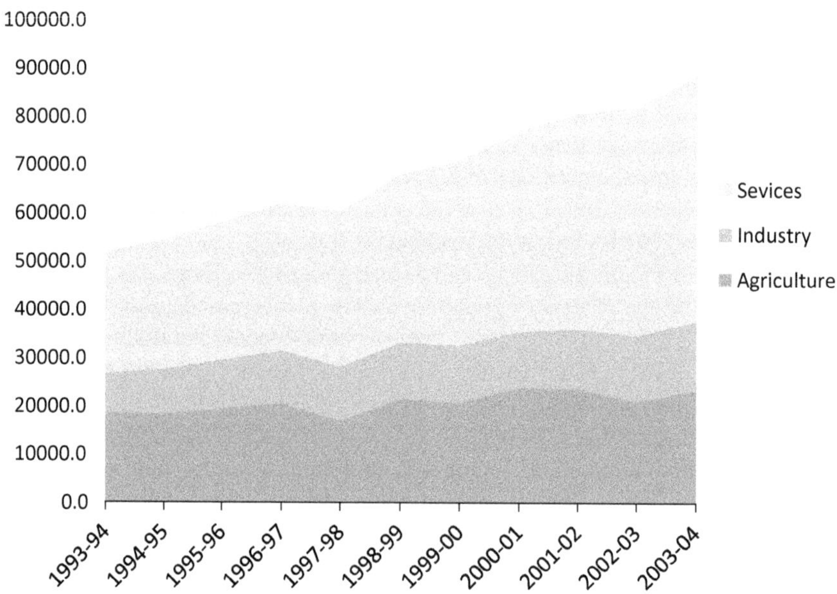

Figure 4.2 Components of AP's NSDP at factor cost by industry of origin (at constant prices, base year 1993–1994) in Andhra Pradesh.

Source: *Handbook of Statistics on Indian Economy 2005–06* (2006), drawn by the author.

significant State in terms of NSDP per capita. When Chandrababu Naidu started his tenure as the chief minister of Andhra Pradesh (1994–1995 financial year) per capita NSDP at a constant price[7] was Rs 7711 in Andhra Pradesh. It was below the average of Rs 8070. At the end of his tenure (2004–2005 financial year), this amount increased to Rs 19,963, which was more than the national average of Rs 19,330. This trend of growth continued until the bifurcation of the State.

The next important issue is the pattern of economic growth in the State. As Figure 4.2 depicts, the post-reform growth in the NDSP is mainly based on the growth in the service sector. Chandrababu Naidu's focus on IT and the telecommunication sector can be one the most significant explanatory variables for explaining this trend.

Table 4.1 presents detailed information about Andhra Pradesh's society and economy.

Table 4.1 Andhra Pradesh factsheet

Name	*Andhra Pradesh*
Capital city	Hyderabad
Established	1 November 1956 2014: Telangana region was recognized as a separate State
Population	1991: 66,508,008 2001: 76,210,007 2011: 84,580,777
Rank	Fifth (2011)
Total area	275,045 km^2
Rank	Fourth (2011)
Districts	23 total
Religions	Hinduism: 89.01%, Islam: 9.16%, Christianity: 1.7%, other: less than 1% (2011)
Official languages	Hindi and Urdu
Urbanization	1981: 23.32% 1991: 26.89% 2001: 27.30% 2011: 33.49%
Literacy rate	1981: 29.9% 1991: 44.1% 2001: 61.1% 2011: 67.7%
HDI rank	15th (2011)

Sources: Census of India (2011) and Paul and Sridhar (2015), drawn by the author.

Pre-1990s politics in Andhra Pradesh

Historical backgrounds: from state formation to the first Telangana movement

The State of Andhra Pradesh (prior its re-bifurcation in 2014) came into being on 1 November 1956. The formation of Andhra Pradesh was the outcome of combining two different Telugu-speaking regions with two distinct colonial backgrounds. Before the independence, the Telugu-speaking people lived under the Madras State (Coastal Andhra and Rayalaseema regions) and the Princely State of Hyderabad (Telangana region).

After independence, Telugu-speaking elites of Madras Presidency demanded that the Center create a separate linguistic state. As a result, the Telugu-speaking regions of the Madras Presidency were separated on 1 October 1953 and formed the 'Andhra state.' Andhra state was the first state, created based on linguistic basis after the independence. The capital city of the new state was Kurnool (see Suri 2002).

The Telangana region had a different story and was part of Nizam state of Hyderabad. The Princely State of Hyderabad became part of the Indian Union following an armed action, known as Police Action by the Government of India in September 1948. It remained under military governor until 1949. After the recommendations of the 'States Reorganization Commission,' Marathi-speaking districts of the Hyderabad state were included in the then Bombay state, and the Kannada-speaking districts were merged with the then Mysore state. Nevertheless, the Commission was careful about the situation in Telugu-speaking regions and their social and economic differences.

Therefore, the members of Commission recommended that "the unification of Telangana with Andhra, though desirable, should be based on a voluntary and willing association of the people and that it is primarily for the people of Telangana to take a decision about their future" (Forrester 1970, 12). While some of the Congress leaders in Telangana like K.V. Ranga Reddy or Dr. M. Channa Reddy opposed a unified state of Andhra Pradesh and demanded a separate State of Telangana (Seshadri 1970), there was a tendency among both region political leaders especially MPs of some Telangana districts to create a united State based on the linguistic border.

Finally, after a discussion among the Congress leaders of both regions in Delhi, they signed a comprehensive agreement on the 'Safeguards for Telangana' or 'Gentlemen's Agreement' in February 1956. This agreement paved the road to form a new state. The primary objective of these safeguards was to provide some privileges for Telangana as weaker and less developed region of the state in terms of jobs, education, the spending of revenues and power-sharing.

Finally, Telangana was merged with the Andhra state on 1 November 1956 under the State Reorganization Act to create the *Visalandhra* (greater Andhra), called Andhra Pradesh (see Suri 2002 and Rothermund 2008).

After the formation of the united Andhra Pradesh, this State became one of the strongholds of the Congress; therefore, other political parties could not challenge the supremacy of this party for nearly three decades. Even after Indira Gandhi's defeat in the 1977 Lok Sabha election, the people of Andhra Pradesh voted for a Congress government in 1978 (Rothermund 2013, 86). That is why Ram Reddy (1976) describes Andhra Pradesh as a 'loyal Congress state.'

However, the political climate did not remain calm in the newly formed state, and the separatist tendencies arose in the form of a demand for a separate Telangana state in 1969. Although in the later stages the Telangana movement has acquired more identity-oriented elements, it was initially an interest-oriented movement. After a combination of the bureaucratic system of two regions, the problem of jobs allocation between two regions arose. As Forrester (1970, 13) explains, bureaucrats in Andhra were more competent than their counterparts in the then Hyderabad state; therefore, the critical positions in Telangana were occupied by *none-Mulkis*[8] or outsiders from Andhra region. The State Government argued that because the education system in Telangana is relatively backward, filling posts with the well-qualified *none-Mulkis* is inevitable. Students of Osmania University (the key educational institute of Nizam State) perceived this decision as an example of a violation of a Gentlemen's Agreement and began an agitation for the continuation of the agreement. The primary objective of movement transformed gradually to a separate state. Whereas the bulk of literature highlighted the role of students and unsatisfied government officers in the movement, as Mitra (2012) specifies, dissident factions of Congress, directed the separatist Telangana agitations. For instance, M. Chenna Reddy, ex-member of the Congress founded the *Telangana Praja Samithi* political party in 1969.

A neo-institutional model of governance can explain the rise and decline of the first Telangana movement. As Huntington (1968) elucidates, in the post-colonial states, the structural changes not only did not lead to more political stability but also enhanced ethnic identity movements, relative deprivation, and social inequality; therefore, political mobilization and even collective violence can be the outcomes of these structural changes. In South India, the merger of Andhra state and Hyderabad state can be seen as a fundamental post-colonial change with several institutional transformations. These transformations, particularly in the state bureaucracy, created the sense of relative deprivation, and led to political mobilization in the form of student agitations to demand a separate state of Telangana. The deprivation sentiment and inequality has been even echoed in the contemporary works of pro-Telangana scholars such as M. Kodanda Ram (2007, 93), writing:

> Telangana has thus been converted into an internal colony as a result of the economic development process pursued by successive governments. Its resources have been diverted and utilized for the development of other regions. The movement for separate statehood seeks to articulate the demand for a fair share in the resources. It is an outcome of injustice meted out to the region by the successive governments in Andhra Pradesh. Separation is seen as the only answer to these grievances.

However, as Mitra (2006) clarifies, based on the neo-institutional model of governance, the elite agency at the Center can play a significant role in the durability of the orderly rule in the state. Strategic choices of elites at both the Central level and the state level are the key explanatory variables for an explanation of the decline of political instability in the state. Not only had the Center implemented law and order management by calling army and closing Osmania University, the affiliated colleges, and schools for an indefinite time, but it also created a framework for a political settlement through a Six-Point Formula, amended in India's constitution (the 32nd amendment). Additionally, the regional leader of a dissident faction of the Congress, M. Chenna Reddy, was appointed as the governor of Uttar Pradesh (1974–1978) and later as the chief minister of Andhra Pradesh (1978–1980). Because of these elite interventions, the sub-regionalism in Andhra Pradesh in the form of the agitation for a separate Telangana did not engender a high level of deinstitutionalization and collective violence and further political instability.

Following Mitra (2006), this study employs the aggregated indicator of incidents of murder and riots per million to measure orderly rule and the ability of the state to govern. As Figure 4.3 elaborates, Andhra Pradesh had a lower level of political violence than average in India in the post-colonial period. However, the first wave of increased violence took place in the late 1960s and early 1970s. This wave can be attributed to the results of Jai Telangana and Jai Andhra's political movements. Interestingly, the first increase in orderly rule in the mid-1970s synchronized with the implementation of the Six-Point Formula. Nevertheless, like other parts of India, Andhra Pradesh experienced a lower level of the orderly rule in the late 1970s because of the after-effects of the emergency and the consequent decline of the Congress system in AP. Remarkably, with the beginning of the rule of the TDP as the first regional party, the trend reversed and showed a slight fall. However, with the return of the weak Congress

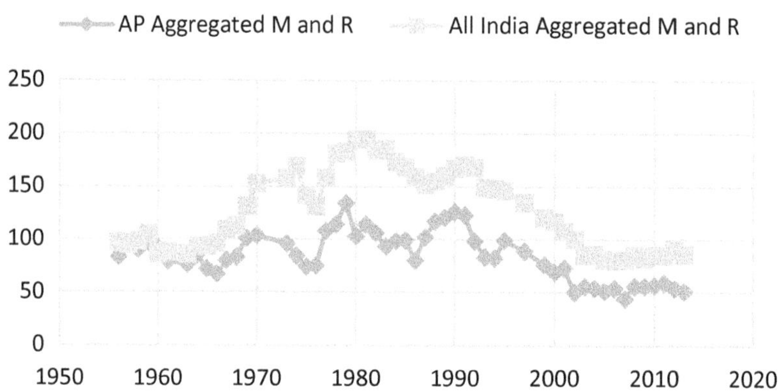

Figure 4.3 Combined index: murder and riots in Andhra Pradesh and India (number of riots and murders per million population).

Source: *Crime in India* (Government of India 1951–2013), drawn by the author.

governments between 1989 until 1994 the index increased meaningfully. Since the mid-1990s, and stable governments of the TDP, the level of the orderly rule has increased gradually.

Caste and politics in Andhra Pradesh

Most of the scholars maintain that post-colonial politics in Andhra Pradesh have been influenced mainly by the caste politics and the confrontations between traditionally dominant castes in the state (Forrester 1970; Srinivasulu 2002; Ram Reddy 1989; Keiko 2008). According to Kohli (1988), during the 1970s, around half of AP's population consisted of backward classes. In addition, Harijans was an additional 15%. On the other hand, the Reddy caste constituted 10–12% of AP's population, and they were spread in the whole state.[9] The Kamma with 5% of AP's population were concentrated in the coastal Andhra region. Brahmins also constituted about 2 to 3% of AP's population.

While backward classes and Harijans constituted the majority of AP's population, the political power remained in the hand of Reddy and Kamma castes after independence. One of the popular approaches for explaining AP's politics is concentration on the rivalry between these two traditional dominant peasant castes. Harriss (1999, 3369) compares the dominance of Reddies Kammas in Andhra politics with Maratha dominance in Maharashtra. Ram Reddy (1976, 4) introduces the Kamma and Reddy castes as the most significant castes in Andhra Pradesh, politically and economically and writes:

> Politically, the most important castes in the state are the Reddis and Kammas. These can be regarded as the dominant castes for they are numerically the strongest in the village or local area, and economically and politically exercise a preordering influence. The most significant source of their power is their control over land. As the major landholders and occupants of important positions in the villages, they control the village political life. More often than not, in many respects, political power is derived from positions of dominance in other areas of the village.

Although it was expected that Brahmins as the top of the pyramid of caste system have more opportunity to organize themselves in the form of new political institutions after the independence, Reddies as the dominant peasant caste have become dominant in the Congress. As Forrester (1970, 9) delineates, while Telangana people become politicized later and did not participate in setting up a Telugu state, Telugu Brahmins in Madras Presidency who were upset by the supremacy of Tamil Brahmins, led the first wave of demand for a separate state for Telugus. Also, the leadership of the Congress in Andhra region during the freedom movement was in the hand of Brahmins. These Brahmins kept their dominance in the Congress in the first years after independence; nevertheless, their position had been challenged gradually by the rise of Kammas and Reddies after formation of new Andhra Pradesh (Reddi 1994).

Remarkably, unlike Brahmins in Bihar and Uttar Pradesh, there was a clear cut between Brahmins' ritual status and economic position in Telangana region. While Brahmins in Bihar enjoyed both ritual and property privileges, Brahmins in Telangana had only ritual status and did not possess the significant landed properties (Satyanarayana 2007, 15–16). On the other hand, they should lease the lands from other agriculture upper castes such as Reddy/Kamma. Therefore, Reddy and Kamma castes, possessing land and dealing with lower castes, had a more potential objective source of power.

While Brahmin community lived in the cities in both regions, both Kamma and Reddy castes had rural origins. Sharma and Reddy (1979, 469) underline this significant shift in the Congress era and write

> The party's leadership gradually shifted in the late fifties and early sixties from the urban centers to the rural periphery, from the educated middle class in the cities to the rural elite, from the higher urban-based castes to middle peasant castes.

After the merger of Andhra state with Telugu-speaking regions of Hyderabad state, Reddies became more dominant than Brahmins and Kammas in the Congress. As Von Fürer-Haimendorf (1963, 62) outlines, "the inclusion of the Telangana districts of the dismembered Hyderabad state in the greater Andhra Pradesh has definitely tilted the scales in favor of the Reddies, who in those districts are far stronger Than the Kammas."

According to Satyanarayana (2007, 10–12), in the Telangana region, the political dominance of the Reddy caste manifested in terms of control of landed property and other economic resources in the villages. Moreover, they possessed the important positions such as the villager's officer post, which provided them with access to more economic resources and the support of lower castes. These socio-political backgrounds paved the path to power for Reddy proprietors as the more-organized rural elites after the collapse of Hyderabad state and the decline in the role of Muslim or Brahmin elites.

Consequently, the most prominent political elites came from the big landholding Reddies (Thirumali 2013, 94) and Brahmins, Kammas, and backward castes had been mostly excluded from the Congress politics.

The well-known example of transition in power from Brahmins to Reddies can be found in the first days of the formation of Andhra Pradesh. Ramakrishna Rao, the Brahmin chief minister of Hyderabad state before the formation of Andhra Pradesh, has a pro separate Telangana state attitude; nevertheless, he realized that the rising power of the Reddy caste in Telangana with the leadership of K.V. Ranga Reddy would end his tenure in the separate state. Hence, he changed his mind in favor of a unified state of Andhra Pradesh; however, a more powerful Reddy politician from the Andhra region, Sanjeeva Reddy,[10] who served as deputy chief minister in Andhra state, became chief minister of the new state (Seshadri 1970, 66).

As Table 4.2 illustrates, the absolute majority of Congress's chief ministers in AP had a Reddy caste background. While the majority of chief ministers in the

Table 4.2 List of the Congress's chief ministers in AP

Name	*Term of office*		*Caste background*	*Region of origin*	*Political party*
Neelam Sanjiva Reddy	1 November 1956	11 January 1960	Reddy	Rayalaseema	Congress
Damodaram Sanjivayya	11 January 1960	12 March 1962	Dalit	Rayalaseema	Congress
Neelam Sanjiva Reddy [2]	12 March 1962	20 February 1964	Reddy	Rayalaseema	Congress
Kasu Brahmananda Reddy	21 February 1964	30 September 1971	Reddy	Coastal Andhra	Congress
P.V. Narasimha Rao	30 September 1971	10 January 1973	Brahmin	Telangana	Congress
Jalagam Vengala Rao	10 December 1973	6 March 1978	Kamma	Telangana	Congress
Marri Chenna Reddy	6 March 1978	11 October 1980	Reddy	Telangana	Congress
Tanguturi Anjaiah	11 October 1980	24 February 1982	Velama	Telangana	Congress
Bhavanam Venkatarami Reddy	24 February 1982	20 September 1982	Reddy	Coastal Andhra	Congress
Kotla Vijaya Bhaskara Reddy	20 September 1982	9 January 1983	Reddy	Rayalaseema	Congress
Marri Chenna Reddy [2]	3 December 1989	17 December 1990	Reddy	Telangana	Congress
Nedurumalli Janardhana Reddy	17 December 1990	9 October 1992	Reddy	Coastal Andhra	Congress
Kotla Vijaya Bhaskara Reddy [2]	9 October 1992	12 December 1994	Reddy	Rayalaseema	Congress
Y.S. Rajasekhara Reddy	14 May 2004	2 September 2009	Reddy	Rayalaseema	Congress
K. Rosaiah	3 September 2009	24 November 2010	Vaishya	Coastal Andhra	Congress
N. Kiran Kumar Reddy	25 November 2010	1 March 2014	Reddy	Coastal Andhra	Congress

Source: Drawn by the author.

Congress era belonged to the Reddy caste group, only one Kamma, one Dalit, one Brahmin and one Velama secured this position in the framework of the Congress.

This domination of the Reddy caste in the Congress has been called 'Reddy Raj.' Reddi (1994, 201) in his work on politics in AP specifies that since 1956 until 1983 non-Reddy chief ministers like Sanjivayya or P.V. Narasimha Rao[11] found it tough to continue their tenure in AP. For instance, P.V. Narasimha Rao as the chief minister with the support of the Center introduced several progressive land reforms. The upper caste peasant caste in the state opposed this agrarian reform. Moreover, Brahmananda Reddy, the ex-chief minister of AP, and his faction in the Congress directed the Jai Andhra agitation, leading to political instability. Finally, Rao could not finish his tenure, and President's rule was imposed in 1973.

After independence, the Congress Party implemented a progressive reform agenda[12] including the abolition of the *Zamindari* and *Jagirdari* systems; nevertheless, the real beneficiaries of the reforms were dominant peasantry castes, like the Reddy caste. As Srinivasulu (2002, 6) observed, "while the lands of these *doras* were distributed among the Kapu-Reddy *ryots* and tenants, the common pastures and waste lands became a lot of the landless Dalits and other lower castes." That is why the land reforms in Andhra Pradesh not only did not weaken their political power and status but also improved it.

As Seshadri (1970, 67) points out, while the elites of Reddy caste organized themselves in the framework of the Congress Party in the State and secured high political positions, Kamas moved to other professions like business, farming, and the growing film industry. Remarkably, in the majority of political opposition movements against the Congress, Kammas played a significant role. Forrester (1970, 10) highlights the role of some Kamma groups, who supported the first Telangana movement to reduce the political dominance of the Reddy caste in Andhra politics. According to him, the pro-Telangana position of Swatantra Party, led in Andhra Pradesh by a Kamma, N.G. Range, can be interpreted in the same way.

Kohli (1987, 996) elaborates the transformation in the nature of Reddy–Kamma rivalries and of their relative power positions in the 1970s. Distancing themselves from politics, the Kammas become more enterprising than the Reddies, and they initiated several commercial activities such as "rice milling, sugar production, hotels, tobacco processing, newspapers and the film industry." Therefore, as Kohli clarifies (1987), their economic basis transformed from a rural dominant agriculture caste to a more modern commercial urban force. These growing local businesses also needed political support, especially from the State Government and bureaucracy. Consequently, Kammas became again more politicized to gain more political power. The support of the Kammas boosted NTR's political career. As Sarangi (2004, 109) points out, N.T. Rama Rao as a Kamma provided an opportunity for this caste to realize their political capabilities and ambitions. Nevertheless, NTR did not remain in a narrow frame of his caste; on the other hand; he made a mindful attempt to ally with several backward castes that were unhappy with the long-term Congress dominance.

From the one dominant party system to a two parties system

While the emergence of the alternative political parties had begun in several States in 1967, 1971 or 1977, Andhra Pradesh remained under the dominance of the Congress until 1983.[13] Andhra Pradesh had not followed the way of Tamil Nadu, which witnessed the rise of regional parties and anti-Center tendencies after 1976. Andhra Pradesh remained the stronghold of the Congress until the rise of the TDP in the 1980s.

Although there is a tendency in the literature to perceive the Congress era (1956–1983) as a whole, Ram Reddy (1989, 281–283) distinguishes three distinct political phases. In the first phase (1956–1964) or Nehru era, the party leadership at the State level enjoyed relative autonomy under a stable political system. In the second stage (1964–1971), while the central leadership was significantly weakened, the chief ministers and regional leaders became more autonomous and even played a role in the decision-making at the Center. In the second era, factionalism becomes common in the Congress, and the discontent Congress leaders had led both the Telangana and Andhra movements. Unlike the second phase, the third stage (1971–1982) witnessed the increase in the role of the Center in the State's affair. Therefore, the State lost its autonomy; thus, the Center became the primary determinant in the State's politics. Luther (2006, 366) delineates this unbalanced relations.

The office of chief minister became an object of mockery and held no sanctity. Chief ministers were being manufactured in Delhi and like defective pieces were cast away one after another. Nominated by the high command of the party in rapid succession, these appointments brazenly disregarded the local sentiment. They were not leaders of their legislature party. They were the followers of the powerful leaders in Delhi.

Indira Gandhi's policies in the State targeted the dominance of the wealthy peasantry castes over the vote banks. For instance, P.V. Narasimha Rao as the chief minister with the support of the Center introduced several progressive land reforms in favor of less advantaged peasants (see Sitapati 2016). S.R. Sankaran,[14] a Gandhian and pro-poor IAS officer, provided the first draft of the legislation. The Legislative Assembly passed the bill.[15] While the rival communist party and the Center supported the land reforms, several Congress leaders at state level opposed it. Reddi (1994, 201) in his work on politics in AP and Sitapati (2016, 38–41) elucidate how the upper caste landlords and their allies in the Congress opposed this agrarian reform.

Sankaran (1996, 22) who served as an IAS officer in AP, underlined the lack of political will, dysfunction of the State bureaucracy and the vested interest of landlords as the main causes for the failure of land reforms:

> The principal reasons are the total lack of political will, the halting and ambivalent formulation of policy, the painfully slow process of legislation, lukewarm and inefficient implementation, the absence of pressure from below inadequacies of the administrative machinery, indiscriminate judicial intervention,

> and lack of correct and up-to-date land records. Indeed, it cannot be denied that many of the senior officers of the government were sympathetic to the landlords or on friendly terms with them, while the lower echelons of the revenue administration, apart from lacking in integrity, were also under the sway of large landowners who wielded considerable political power.

While the landowners of coastal Andhra region with the support of their political allies in the Congress blocked the land reform in AP, Indira Gandhi was determined to deteriorate their influence by installing the weak chief ministers without political capital in the State. To ensure the political fortune in AP, she initiated several anti-poverty schemes and socio-economic programs. These agendas enabled her to create more direct contact with minor farmers, the scheduled castes, the scheduled tribes, backward classes, and women. While these policies created more support from weaker segments of society such as backward castes and Harijans, the traditional allies of the Congress withdrew their support for Indira Gandhi. That is why the majority of dominant agricultural castes in all regions supported the Janata Party in the 1977 election.

As Kohli (1988) specifies, not only did the Congress in the Center face the challenges that arose from the strategic choices of Indira Gandhi in the 1970s (centralization of power, state of emergency), but also her interventions in AP's politics led to public dissatisfaction especially among dominant castes. Between 1978 and 1983, Indira Gandhi appointed four different chief ministers in AP. These chief ministers did not possess a strong personal political support in the region; on the contrary, their appointment was mainly based on their loyalty to Indira Gandhi. Ironically, two of these chief ministers lost in the legislative assembly elections and were just installed because of their loyalty to the central leadership. After the appointment of these weak chief ministers without a firm political basis in the State, the way was paved for competing elites and rebels in the party who did not accept the authority of these leaders. Thus, the position of the Congress became weaker and a 'power/authority vacuum' was created in AP.

This political and institutional erosion of the Congress in the State, factionalism in the Congress and the regional leadership vacuum paved the path for the emergence of a second political force in AP. Ram Reddy (1989, 286) describes this situation as an 'opportune juncture' for the TDP to come into existence. The 1983 assembly election ends the one dominant party system in Andhra Pradesh. While several interventions by the Center and factionalism had weakened the Congress, the TDP as an anti-Center party emerged and became the second political actor in AP.

As Figure 4.4 depicts, the party system in Andhra Pradesh had transformed from the one dominant party system to a two-party system from the 1983 election until 2014 election. Two main political parties in the State, the Congress, and the TDP have competed for the Assembly election as well as general parliamentary elections. Neither the leftist parties such as CPI and CPM nor

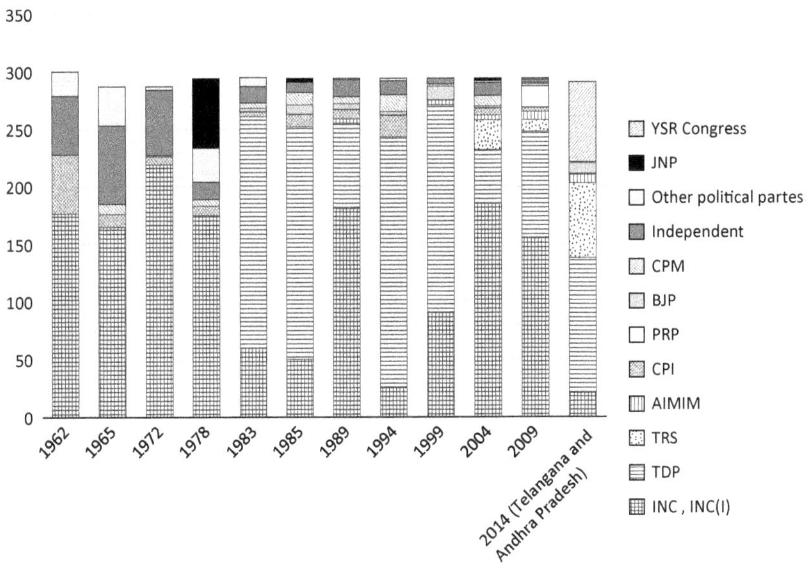

Figure 4.4 Andhra Pradesh Assembly election results (1962–2014).

Source: Statistical Report on General Legislative Assembly of Andhra Pradesh series (Election Commission of India 1951–2014), drawn by the author.

right-wing BJP played a significant role in the State's politics; however, the TDP participated in the NDA governments.

As Kennedy (2014, 48) points out, after the emergence of the TDP in the 1980s as the primary challenger of the Congress in Andhra Pradesh, two main parties competed in the framework of a two-party system at the state level. Therefore, this relative stability allowed TDP especially during the Naidu Government to "adopt an aggressive policy stance on economic reforms without taking too much of political risk."

The TDP was not the only regional party in the State in the post-Congress era. All India *Majlis-e-Ittehadul Muslimeen* (AIMIM) represents the Muslim minority especially in the Old City of Hyderabad in national as well as State politics. Kalvakuntla Chandrashekar Rao (KCR) established *Telangana Rashtra Samithi* (TRS) as a sub-regional party in 2001 to pursue the demand for a separate Telangana state.

Finally, the party system in the State has transformed from the two-party system to a multi-party system since the 2014 election. After the formation of Telangana, the TRS became the majority party in the new State's Assembly and formed the first government of Telangana state. On the other hand, the TDP in Andhra Pradesh formed a new government, and the YSR Congress Party[16] became the main opposition party. Remarkably, in both states, the Congress's share of votes and seats decreased drastically in the 2014 election.

The fall of the Congress, the rise of the TDP, and the Telugu subnational movement

Although the Janata Party won 60 seats in the 1978 Assembly election in Andhra Pradesh, implying the decline of the Congress's power, it was nevertheless not sufficient to challenge the supremacy of the Congress in the State. Indira Gandhi's several interventions in the State politics after 1978 accelerated the decline of the Congress in AP. Appointing weak chief ministers for a short time had polarized the political scene in AP. As Kohli (1988) notes, the decline of the Congress in AP not only attributed to the Center's intervention but also was the result of the crisis in the regional leadership in AP. During the 1970s, the majority of the Congress leaders, MPs or MLAs did not win the election based on their popularity; on the contrary, they secured the seats because of the wave of Indira's popularity.

Finally, the dominance of the Congress was ended by the Telugu Desam Party (or TDP, Party of Telugu country/land), formed by N.T. Rama Rao, the famous film star in Telugu cinema. According to Thirumali (2013, 104), NTR formed the TDP, when he became disappointed about the possibility of nomination for Raja Sabha. The Andhra's Congress was against his candidacy, and he realized that there was no room for him in the Congress politics. Only nine months after its formation, the new party defeated the Congress and won two-thirds of seats in the Legislative Assembly. The notable victory of the TDP was accompanied with the rise of the Telugu subnational movement. Mitra and Enskat (2004, 15) describe the TDP as "one of the finest examples of the trend towards regionalization of India's party system," which also plays a significant role in the coalition politics at the national level.

As Suri (2013, 168–169) explains, Telugu nationalism, propagated by the TDP, had substantial differences with other subnational movements in India. NTR expressed slogans such as "restoration of self-respect of Telugu peoples," and criticized the local Congress leaders who underestimated the self-esteem Telugu people. Unlike initial years of the DMK in Tamil Nadu or National Conference in Jammu and Kashmir, the TDP did not possess secessionist tendencies. As Rao (1994, 107) reports, NTR's key slogan in his speeches was '*Jai Telugu Nadu, Jai Hind.*' Also, the Telugu subnational movement had not any hostility toward the outsiders or particular group (religious community, specific caste or ethnic group) in the society. Moreover, a particular caste, religious community or class had not supported the TDP as the manifestation of Telugu subnational movement. Although the Kamma caste controlled the leadership of the TDP, they only constitute around 4 or 5% of AP's population. Therefore, the widespread support to the TDP cannot be seen as the support of only Kamma community.

Mukherji (2014, 151) recognizes the Telugu pride, anti-Congressism, and populism as the key basis for consolidation of the TDP. The focus of the TDP party was the dignity and respect to the Telugu people, which was missed by the Congress in the Center and their 'yes-men' in the State. NTR's message was clear: The Central Government neglected and humiliated Telugu people for 35 years; therefore, Telugu people should revive their glory and dignity (Bernstorff 1998a, 12). NTR and the TDP constructed the Telugu identity based on the unity of all Telugus, regardless of their caste, class, region or religion against external interventions (mostly the Center and their allies in the state) in order to revive the glory of Telugus:

> Telugu Desam wishes to improve the lot of the Telugu society which has remained unchanged over the years in spite of the fact that the so-called leadership changed so often and also to assert the unity of Telugu Speaking people and channelize their potentialities.
>
> (Telugu Desam Party 1983 – TDP's election manifesto 1983)

While, there are several social and political cleavages in Andhra Pradesh such as Hindu–Muslim, higher caste–lower caste, Andhra–Telangana and Kamma–Reddy cleavages, a tendency toward the unification of all Telugus was the key characteristic of the Telugu subnational movement. Consequently, N.T. Rama Rao preferred the term 'Telugu Nadu' (the land of Telugus) to Andhra Pradesh. To show his emphasis on Telugu identity, he affixed the word 'Telugu' before most government programs and schemes. For example, an irrigation project was called 'Telugu Ganga Project' (Nag 2011, 72). These tendencies have been reflected at the beginning of the first manifesto of Telugu Desam Party (1983):

The emergence of 'Telugu Desam' is the harbinger of the renaissance of the glory of Telugus. Telugu Desam transcending the loyalties of caste, religion, and region has shaped itself with the goal of seeing the Telugu brightness, freed from the eclipse of evil forces. It is the hope of the Telugu Desam that all the Telugus should be prosperous and that the Telugu Nadu (Andhra Pradesh) should forge ahead in all spheres. It is its aspiration and life force. 'Telugu Desam' is the march against the rulers, who work against the greatness of the nation.

One of the major outcomes of the rise of Telugu subnationalism was the decline of the Telangana movement as a sub-regional movement. NTR with his slogan of 'self-respect for Telugu people' could unify several castes and classes in which all inhabitants of each three regions consider themselves as a Telugu. As Haragopal (2010, 55) observes:

> The Telugu regional identity was so articulated that the Telangana identity got submerged in the larger Telugu identity. The self-respect of Telugus, which TDP raised as an important issue obviated the Telangana identity for the time being. It is not that what happened through the rhetoric of Telugu identity was the integration of the regions but subjugation.

Charismatic leadership of NTR

Mitra and Enskat (2004, 15) described the 'NTR Phenomenon' as a classic example of party building based on the 'charismatic power of an individual leader.' The emergence of N.T. Rama Rao (28 May 1923–18 January 1996), the superstar of Telugu cinema as a political leader, was a turning point in the history of Andhra Pradesh. Born in the Krishna district and studying in Vijayawada and Guntur (both in Andhra region), he was a film actor and worked on over 320 movies (Rothermund 2013, 86). As Kohli (1988, 998) notes, before NTR's political career, on account of the fact that he acted in several Telugu movies, he became very well-known in Andhra Pradesh. He played the role of gods of Hindu mythology or savior and liberator of the poor. Srinivas (2009, xvi) highlights the role of cinema as a public institution in South India and writes:

> The cinema is a public institution facilitates a range of transactions, which, in parts of India – Tamil Nadu, Andhra Pradesh, and, to a certain extent, Karnataka – have extended into electoral mobilization.

Srinivas (2009) in his study elaborates how Telugu cinema is capable of producing star-politicians. Analyzing the role of fan clubs[17] and the linkage between politics and Telugu cinema, he suggests Telugu cinema is 'fundamentally populist' and can create political superstars.

Srinivasulu and Prasad (1987, 151) stress the role of Indian cinema in the construction of hero and myths and its political implication:

> Cinema, more so commercial Telugu cinema creates powerful myths about individual and society… The cinematic myth of a hero as a savior operating outside the terrain of social barriers like caste, class, and religion is more powerful than the political charisma, which is limited to periodic electoral politics – nothing more… Telugu cinema (like Madras or Bombay cinema) projects a voluntaristic image of the hero. The hero is seen to be, autonomous of the situations, and determines its development and not vice-versa. In a volatile political situation, it has a serious implication. Using it as imagery, one can suggest – as NTR himself did in his election speeches – that all the Telugus were victims of 'Congress I· misrule' and NTR uncontaminated by it is there to rescue them.

Therefore, NTR acquired considerable popularity, especially among illiterate rural folks and women. He employed this popularity to found the Telugu Desam Party in on 29 March 1982 and emerged as a charismatic political leader in Andhra Pradesh.

In the era of factionalism in the Congress in which the first generation of influential chief ministers was replaced with the more dependent leaders to the Center, NTR emerged as a popular regional leader who can attract the masses. He was a mythological hero in the Telugu cinema, which transformed into a real-life hero of the masses. That is why Ram Reddy (1989, 286) describes his image as 'incarnation of God' for most of the rural poor in Andhra region. Because of this extraordinary level of popularity, he had popularly been called

Anna or elder brother (Neuss 1998). Suri (2004b, 1483) describes the charismatic appeal of NTR as the crucial factor in TDP's success and writes:

> People reposed great faith in him, as someone who could deliver the state from the Congress misrule. He also worked with great zeal and conviction. His idealism, determination, cine popularity, and hard work mesmerized many. He was looked upon with admiration and awe, as a leader with superhuman capacities. He was a great public speaker. He knew that people hardly care for what the speaker says, but are only interested to see how the leader speaks. He spoke in chaste Telugu. The histrionics were perfect. The delivery was excellent. His exhortations fell on receptive ears. NTR, the cine-idol for millions of people, known more for his excellent performances in mythological films, especially in the divine roles of Rama and Krishna, used his celluloid image most effectively to carry his political message.

NTR in his electoral campaign traveled to every city and most of the villages in the State by his van. For the first time, people of Andhra Pradesh saw personally their cine-super star who several times played the role of the Hindu gods and legendary heroes. In his electoral meeting, the videotapes including his electoral speeches as well as important scenes of his movies were displayed (Bernstorff 1998a, 12). Kohli (1988, 998) underlines the political symbols and the idiom that NTR used to transmit his message and writes:

> Clad in his saffron robe-the traditional garb of India's holy men and riding around in a convertible transformed to look like a chariot, NTR might have been a figure from the Mahabharata, reincarnated to protect the dispossessed from worldly evils.

This successful electoral campaign created massive support for NTR and his TDP. As Rajendra Prasad (2004, 43) reports, at one electoral meeting in Nandyal town in Kurnool district, when a candidate from the Reddy caste asked the crowd "whether they wanted a tried and trusted friend of the weaker sections like Indira Gandhi or a film personality that playing gimmicks to get publicity," the crowded responded "we want NTR!" In a similar case at Tirupati, while Indira Gandhi was addressing her last electoral public meeting, NTR arrived in the city, so people started leaving Indira Gandhi's speech to meet NTR. In the 1983 Legislative Assembly election, the TDP won a landslide victory and came to power in January 1983; hence, he ended the Congress's dominance in AP for the first time. He and his party enjoyed massive support in the early years of the 1980s. The TDP secured 202 seats out of 294, and the Congress could secure only 60 seats. Despite a sympathy wave at the national level in favor of the Congress following the assassination of Indira Gandhi in 1984 Lok Sabha elections, the TDP again secured a majority of Andhra Pradesh seats in Lok Sabha.

As a populist leader, he emphasized mainly the regional Telugu identity against the Center and its Hindi character; nonetheless, the TDP never was a separatist party and remained loyal to India's federalism. The main slogan of NTR was the need for self-respect for Telugu people *(Telugu Atma Gowrawam)* and highlighted the regional themes of Telugu identity (Yadagiri 1994, 301).

As Suri (2004b, 1481) indicates, whereas other regional political parties such as National Conference, Dravida Munnetra Kazhagam (DMK), or Shiv Sena emerged as an outcome of a long-term struggle or sustained social movement, the TDP mostly was the result of the personal decision of NTR. For that reason, at the beginning of the TDP, this party has neither the leaders trained in politics nor any ideology. According to Thirumali (2013, 104), the TDP was the first example of a political party that set up as a business concern with "one's own money, resources, and men." Although the TDP initially did not have any ideological orientation, NTR's political agenda was constructed based on conflict with the Congress. The focus of NTR in his speeches was the Congress's corrupt political culture. Moreover, he several times criticized the Congress leaders at the Center, because of their frequent interventions in the State politics that "destroyed the capacity for and pride in self-government" (Kohli 1988, 54). Not only did the TDP with its emphasis on regional pride win the 1983 election, but it also attracted some Congress politicians such as Chandrababu Naidu.

Economic populism and identity politics in the TDP (I) regime: seeking the horizontal rewards

Mitra and Enskat (2004, 15) attribute the successful emergence of the TDP to effective blending of the politics of personality, identity, and popular welfare policy. While the strategic choice of NTR as a charismatic leader was a confrontation with the Center based on identity politics in the vertical game, he chose populist welfare policies at the horizontal level.

The Congress in Andhra Pradesh sought to create a pro-poor and minorities image by the implementation of land reforms programs and anti-poverty schemes, particularly after the victory of Indira Gandhi with the slogan '*Gharibi Hatao*.' Traditionally, scheduled castes (SCs), scheduled tribes (STs) and Muslims supported the Congress in Andhra Pradesh. In the first years of Congress politics in AP the Congress's access to the lower section of society was provided by traditional dominant castes in the region; nevertheless, Indira Gandhi's policies marginalized the role of the dominant agricultural castes and created a direct contact with the potential vote banks in the State.

The most important strategic choice of NTR was to sustain and to enhance the populist economic measures in the State. If Indira Gandhi had defeated her rivals (both in the party and outside of the party) with the slogan '*Gharibi Hatao*,' the TDP could use the same weapon against the Congress in AP with the motto 'basic needs to the poor.' Particularly when the main strategic choice of NTR in the vertical game was the confrontation with the Center (which was symbolized in Andhra's collective memory as Amma (Indira Gandhi) versus

Anna (NTR)), he needed more support from the State. With the implementation of several welfare schemes and an increase in the subsidies, NTR tried to prove that his government could deliver services better than the Congress, especially to the poor and backward caste and classes. In NTR's rhetoric, the Congress in the State was equal with corrupt and greedy politicians, following Delhi's rule and forgetting the interest of poor Telugu people. Accordingly, NTR as a superstar wants to save Telugu people, revive their dignity and fight against the poverty. Therefore, he needed short-term policies with clear outcomes. Remarkably, there is no reference to or promise for the land reforms in the TDP election manifesto in 1983 Legislative Assembly elections. NTR realized that distribution of lands of major landlords could jeopardize his mass mobilization; therefore, he concentrated on inclusive welfare measures for the poor and rural population that the state government was the main sponsor for it. With an interventionist tone, TDP's election manifesto (Telugu Desam Party 1983) stated:

> Though there is an abundance of food production in the State, the shortage of the essential commodities in the market has become a regular phenomenon causing annoyance to the woman folk. It is the duty of the popular Government to see that the essential commodities are supplied to the public at reasonable prices. Telugu Desam shall create a proper distribution system for essential commodities and put a check on the indue profits that are being made so far by the middlemen.

Indira Gandhi had enunciated the 20-Point Program for implementation in the country; similarly, NTR began a 15 Point '*Pragati Patham*' (the path of progress). These ambitious popular welfare policies are as follows (Rao 1994, 85–86):

- i Water for every village
- ii Midday meals for schoolchildren and construction of school buildings for schools
- viii Rice at Rs 2 per kg
- iv Welfare of SCs
- v Welfare of STs
- vi Welfare of backward classes
- vii Women's welfare
- viii Houses for the weaker sections
- ix Helping the farmers
- x Improvement of roads
- xi Integrated rural development
- xii Encouraging the youth

The most significant NTR's populist policy, indicated in both the manifesto of TDP and '*Pragati Patham*' was to sell rice at Rs 2 per kilo; as a result, NTR has become synonymous with the Rs 2 per kilo rice scheme for the poor. As

Rajendra Prasad (2004, 39) reports, after announcing the scheme in March 1983, the government must pay the subsidy of approximately Rs 33 crores a year. Although with an extraordinarily ambitious tone, the manifesto promised such rice for all, the NTR Government limited it for those with an annual income of less than Rs 6000 per annum; as a result, the scheme covered 60 lakh families.

In a similar scheme, the Telugu Desam Government decided to offer the subsidized Handloom *Sarees* and *Dhotis* at half price to people with an annual income of less than Rs 6000. As Rao (1994, 86) remarks, 31 lakhs benefited from the *Janata cloth* scheme by the end of 1984–1985. However, TDP with the implementation of populist policies such as Rs 2 per kilo of rice scheme, Janata cloth scheme or subsidized housing for the poor, not only engendered new supporters from other backward classes (OBCs), women or youth but also attracted support from the Congress's traditional vote banks.

The vertical game: TDP in the State and Congress at the Center

After three decades of harmony between the State Government in Andhra Pradesh and the Union Government in New Delhi, Center–State relations became a critical issue after the emergence of the first non-Congress government in AP. Particularly, the TDP with its anti-Congress orientation that criticized the Congress in both the Center and State for being responsible for the backwardness of Telugu people sought to prove that this party would be more independent in its decision-making. Suri (2013, 173) describes NTR's rhetoric against the Congress as "aggressive and vituperative." Emphasizing Telugu dignity, he criticized the Center frequently and stated:

> Our Telugu self-respect is being daily butchered on the streets of Delhi. We will be nobody's branch office. They go to Delhi to seek permission to transfer a clerk in Tehsildar's office. The Congress (I) of today has nothing to do with the Congress of Mahatma Gandhi. It split into as many letters as there are in the alphabet. Indira Congress! Quit Andhra Pradesh.
>
> (Quoted in Rajendra Prasad 2004, 34)

NTR's anti-Congress and anti-Center slogans had been supported and rewarded by public disenchantment with Congress politics. The Center did not remain silent toward the TDP's rhetoric against the Congress. Indira Gandhi perceived NTR as an emerging threat to the Congress both at the State and the national level; as a result, she used the old instrument of President's rule for removing N.T. Rama Rao. While Indira Gandhi appointed Bhaskara Rao, a dissident TDP leader, as the chief minister, NTR moved the court and won this case. Furthermore, NTR launched a 'Save Democracy Movement' with the support of other non-Congress parties and called it '*dharma yuddham*.' With the rise of anti-Center and anti-Congress sentiments in the State, the Congress gave up its effort to dismiss NTR; therefore, he came back to power and completed his term (Rothermund 2013, 87; Suri 2013, 103).

The TDP tried to introduce the Center's reactions toward NTR to public opinion as an insult to six crores of Telugus. Consequently, NTR attained more support for his anti-Center and anti-Congress attitude. Not only did NTR several times blame Indira Gandhi for her policies at both the national level and state level, but also he continued the confrontation with the Center throughout the tenure of Rajiv Gandhi as prime minister of India.

The Center also did not have a positive attitude toward the Telugu Desam government. When Indira and Rajiv Gandhi visited Hyderabad, both prime ministers criticized the State Government for its insufficiency or delay in submitting proposals or accounts. The confrontation between the State Government and the Central Governments not only had political outcomes but also influenced the State's economy. According to Prasad (1994, 146), during the tenure of NTR, Andhra Pradesh was faced with both drought and cyclones; as a result, the State Government needed massive aid from the Center. Although the chief minister asked for a considerable amount of aid, the Center – after a delayed visit by the central mission – sanctioned measly sums for relief work.

In addition, the demand for allocation of more revenues to AP was another root for a confrontation between State and the Center. The Telugu Desam government argued that distribution of revenue to states should not be based on the criteria of the population; on the contrary, it should be based on the contribution to the central revenue pool. The Center rejected the TDP government's requests for allocation of financial resources for the NTR's popular welfare policies. As Gopal (1994, 156–157) elaborates, NTR asked the Planning Commission for more allocation of resources to meet developmental goals of the State. He declared furiously "We are not beggars to ask for charity or alms. We are entitled for a legitimate and due share from the Center." NTR asserted these views several times in various fora such as the planning commission; however, the Center did not accept his demands.

The State's plan outlay was another example of the confrontation between the State and the Center. According to Gopal (1994, 157–158), NTR was discontented with the annual plan outlays; in other words, he felt that the approval of plan outlays by the Planning Commission was unfair and based mostly on political considerations. Figure 4.5 depicts a wide gap between the State's proposals and the amounts approved by the Planning Commission:

In the same way, while the AP Government demanded Rs 7500 crores for the Seventh Plan outlays (1985–1990), the Planning Commission approved 5200 crores. Therefore, NTR almost criticized the Center and charged it with a 'stepmotherly attitude.' Therefore, NTR felt that there was no possibility to work with the Congress at the Center; hence, he tried to find an alternative to the Congress in the Center. NTR considered the TDP a strong anti-Congress platform. He was eager to cooperate with other regional parties against the domination of the Congress. NTR advocated the idea of strong states and called the Centre a 'conceptual myth.' He asserted:

> It is as though the people of the country who elect the State Governments had persuaded to delegate their authority in subjects such as defense and

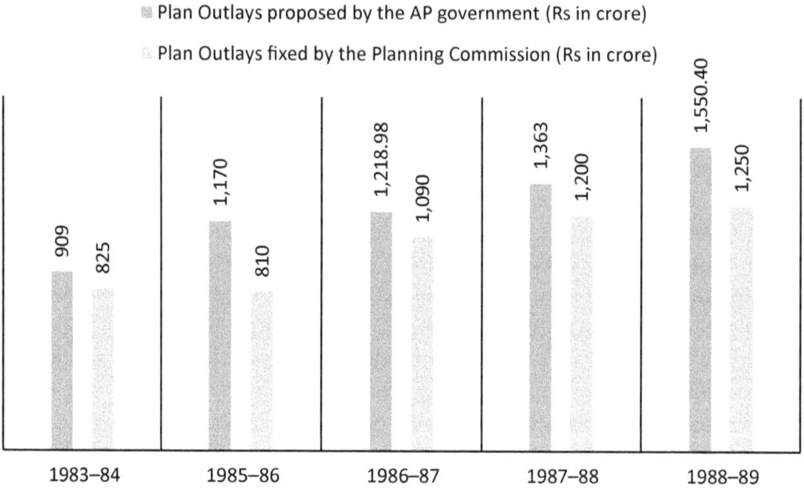

Figure 4.5 AP's annual plan outlays between 1983 and 1989.
Source: Gopal (1994, 157), drawn by the author.

> foreign policy to the Centre so that there is no overlapping in the discharge of powers by the Centre and State Governments.
>
> (Quoted in Prasad 1994, 146)

NTR assembled the non-Congress leaders from 13 parties[18] to Hyderabad to form a political platform against Rajiv Gandhi in 1986. Non-Congress politicians not only complained about the unbalanced economic policies of the Centre and what they called "the Centre's discriminatory attitude towards non-Congress Governments," but also they criticized the elitist approach of the seventh five-year plan (Rajendra Prasad 2004, 69–70).

Finally, the TDP and other political parties such as DMK, JP, LD and Congress(S) formed the 'National Front' in 1988. NTR was the elected Chairman, and V.P. Singh became the governor. NTR played a significant role in the formation of the 'National Front Government' (2 December 1989–10 November 1990) at the Center, unified all non-Congress opposition parties in India. For the first time, a regional party such as the TDP was actively involved in the formation of government at the national level. However, the TDP could not benefit from the 'National Front' government in Delhi, because the TDP had already been defeated in the 1989 Assembly election. To sum up, Yadagiri (1994, 305) notes the confrontation strategy with the Center did not benefit NTR in the longer term and indicated:

> Deliberate confrontation with the Centre and the antagonistic posture snapped all ties and rapport between the Centre and the State. The State suffered isolation from the mainstream of national life.

Moreover, the policy of confrontation with the Center, adopted by NTR, led to the limited amount of the transfers such the approved annual plan layout. Consequently, the available funds for development and investment in infrastructures were not sufficient to engender a sustainable growth. NTR needed more financial resources for implementation of his welfare policies, and the Center did not provide adequate central transfers; thus, he increased the rate of taxes, particularly in the cities. For instance, he increased house and professional taxes, house taxes, entry tax on textiles, and sale tax.

The coup in TDP and the rise of Chandrababu Naidu

The Congress in the1989 assembly election defeated the TDP. Yadagiri (1994) sums up factors such as improper selection of candidates, family rule, and the unhappiness of bureaucracy, alienation of dominant sections, populist measures, and confrontation with the Center, hollow election promises, and ineffective campaign as the primary causes of the decline of the TDP.

While there is a widespread idea that Chandrababu Naidu has introduced the reforms in Andhra Pradesh since 1995, as Suri (2005, 136) indicates, the new Congress government of Andhra Pradesh took the initial steps for economic reforms. In line with the new industrial policy, announced by the Center, the Congress government in AP declared "its commitment to creating a condition conducive to industrial development" (Suri 2005, 136).Under the guidance of P.V. Narasimha Rao, the AP's Congress government introduced a scheme to attract foreign direct investments (FDI) from non-residence Indians (NRIs). The Congress government not only paved the way for the establishment of one software park in Hyderabad but also took loans from the World Bank for the road and agrarian projects.

In the framework of the liberalization, the Congress government increased the price of subsidized rice from Rs 2 to Rs 3.5. Moreover, the foreign fund component in the annual budget increased from Rs 480,000,000 in 1990–1991 to Rs 8,500,000,000 in 1994–1995 (Suri 2005, 136).

The TDP as the main opposition party in Andhra Pradesh along with its allies (CPI and CPM) launched attacks against the liberalization policies, introduced by P.V. Narasimha Rao and the Congress. In the Assembly, the TDP along with CPI and CPM criticized the liberalization as anti-people and anti-poor policy.

Whereas it was supposed that NTR as the leader of the opposition party plays a significant role in the assembly sessions, his son-in-law Chandrababu Naidu emerged as the key actor of the opposition party. NTR was not a professional politician and could not lead the opposition in the Assembly successfully. Instead of reading the Assembly procedures, NTR played several roles in the movies such as *Samrat Ashok* and *Major Chandrakant.* Consequently, professional politicians like Chandrababu Naidu supported him in the leadership; as a result, the influence and power of Naidu increased among the TDP's MLAs (Narisetti 2002, 201).

As Sarangi (2004, 111) elucidates, despite the hopes of the voters and the Congress's efforts for economic reforms, this party continued its political mistakes in AP. The Congress entangled with internal bickering and factional conflicts; as a result, AP was witness to the frequent change of chief ministers. Marri Chenna Reddy, the Congress leader from Telangana for the second time, was appointed as the chief minister of AP in 1989; however, because of factionalism in the Congress, Nedurumalli Janardhana Reddy became the chief minister after only one year. He also remained in power only until 1992, when P.V. Narasimha Rao, the prime minister of India, appointed K. Vijaya Bhaskara Reddy for the second time as the chief minister of AP. While Narasimha Rao took the first steps of the economic reforms in the Center, the Congress government in AP persisted in the old pattern caste politics, regionalism, factionalism and internal conflicts.

The 1994 election was a decisive moment for both parties. The Prime Minister P.V. Narasimha Rao campaigned personally in his home State in favor of liberalization. As Suri (2013, 171) points out, the Prime Minister "counterposed development and welfare," arguing that the development would suffer by NTR's populist schemes. While the Prime Minister sought to explain the significance of liberalization and pro-business approaches, NTR stressed the role of the government in providing the basic needs of all people: food, clothes, and shelter.

The TDP entered again in the election stage with the motto of 'basic needs to the poor' and promised subsidized rice, cloth, and providing a house for the poor. Finally, although Narasimha Rao campaigned in his home state for the reelection of the Congress, the causes above significantly contributed to the return of the TDP to power in the 1994 Assembly, capturing a massive 217 seats out of 292 seats.

However, the new TDP government did not oppose the reforms practically after the election. While the TDP government restored the populist welfare schemes officially, it initiated measures to reform the power sector. Chandrababu Naidu, the new finance and revenue minister and the new key player in the party, tried to convince his father-in-law to initiate new measures to reforms and ban new recruitments in the public services (Suri 2005, 139). Although Naidu attained considerable power and influence in the TDP, he was not the only emerging star in the party.

As Rothermund (2013, 87) notes, when NTR was out of power, he married Lakshmi Parvathi. NTR's young wife, who was the author of his biography, gained more political influence on NTR than other TDP leaders. NTR trusted his young wife enthusiastically; hence, she became the key figure in the Telugu Desam Party. The high-ranking members of the party and some members of NTR's family worried about increasing the role of Lakshmi Parvathi; therefore, they decided to remove NTR from his position. His son-in-law, Chandrababu Naidu, led the rebellion against NTR and overthrew the old charismatic leader in "a kind of palace revolution." He could unify NTR's family members, the TDP's MLAs against the NTR and his beloved Lakshmi Parvathi. In fact, the family members and the high-ranking members of the TDP knew that NTR had several health problems; as a result, the second wife of NTR could emerge as the successor of NTR.

After Naidu's claim that he had the support of the majority of TDP's MLAs, the Governor asked NTR to prove his majority in the Assembly. As Rajendra Prasad (2004, 117–118) reports, because of pain in his chest, NTR could not meet the governor and was admitted to a hospital. After a meeting between the chief minister and the Governor of the hospital, NTR wrote his letter of resignation.

On 1 September 1995, Chandrababu Naidu was sworn in as the new chief minister of Andhra Pradesh. In the first move, he promised to sustain NTR's populist schemes such as rice at Rs 2 per kilo, total liquor prohibition and the subsidized power to houses; however, he abandoned all these schemes in the next two years.

Conclusion

This chapter has elaborated the socio-political context of the adoption of the confrontationist approaches in the vertical game and populism (based on the lingo-ethnic identity and direct redistribution) in the horizontal by NTR as a rational leader to maximize his political gains. Nevertheless, because of these populist welfare measures and confrontation with the Center, the TDP government experienced a critical fiscal imbalance in the 1980s. Lalitha (1997, 108) identifies two main roots for this imbalance: First, government expenditure had been oriented toward consumption rather than a capital formation that has shrunk the base for raising revenue. Moreover, the TDP government welfare program had led to decreasing the availability of resources for economic development. The TDP Government distributed rice at Rs 2 per kilo with an estimated subsidy of Rs 5.20 per kilo. With vast beneficiaries of the scheme (households with less than Rs 6000 per month), the rice subsidies had become the primary burden on the shoulder of the annual state budget. For instance, in the 1987–1988 financial year, whereas the state government allocated Rs 300 crores for the rice subsidy, it spent Rs 100 crore on urban health, Rs 26 crore on rural health, Rs 16 crore on medical research, Rs 48 crore on public health, and Rs 39 crore on family welfare. The entire expenditure for elementary education in the state was Rs 343 crore, a little bit more than rice subsidies. More noticeably, the state spending on secondary education and university and higher education was Rs 210 crore, and Rs 138 crore respectively. Therefore, after the 1995 Palace coup, Chandrababu Naidu as the new leader of the TDP along with the State bureaucracy realized that while populist and inclusive welfare measures are significant to get votes in the horizontal game, the donative distribution of essential commodities not only fiscally is not sustainable. The Telugu Desam government could not sustain the fiscal weight of NTR's populist schemes, and it was on the edge of bankruptcy.

Notes

1 Tollywood refers to the Telugu cinema. Tollywood is part of Indian cinema, producing films in the Telugu language. The main film production companies of Tollywood are centered in the Indian states of Andhra Pradesh and Telangana. The Telugu film industry is the second largest in India; nevertheless, there is not a lot of information about it outside of Andhra Pradesh (Srinivas 2009, xviii).

2 Party of Telugu People.
3 The current bifurcation of Andhra Pradesh and formation of Telangana state is based on historical borders between these two regions before the formation of a united Andhra Pradesh in 1956. Since July 2014, the Telugu-speaking region of the previous Princely State of Hyderabad has been named Telangana state and the Telugu regions of Madras Presidency have been called Andhra Pradesh state.
4 Telangana includes ten districts with 40.5% of the population (Census of India 2011).
5 The coastal Andhra region includes nine districts and compromises 41.7% of the State population.
6 Rayalaseema consists of four districts with 18% of the population.
7 Base year 1993–1994.
8 Since the early 1930s, the Princely State of Hyderabad had implemented a new employment policy, called Mulki rule. According to Mulki rule, all applicants for government jobs required Mulki certificates. It was an answer to the negative sense among the native residences of Hyderabad state who felt the majority of top governmental jobs had been allocated to non-native Muslims.
9 Bernstorff (1998b, 82) describes Reddys as peasant proprietors who often hold hereditary village offices. While Reddys speaking *sat-shudras*, they claim *Kshatriya* status, because they have been warriors in the *Kakatiya* court.
10 Sanjeeva Reddy was the chief minister between 1956 and 1960 and 1962 and 1964. He was later elected as the president of India.
11 He served as the tenth prime minister of India (1991–1996).
12 For example, legislations like The AP (Telangana Area) Tenancy and Agriculture Act, 1950, AP Tenancy Act 1956, and AP Ceiling and Agricultural Holdings Act 1961.
13 The first opposition party that won in an assembly election at the State level was the Communist Party of India. The party won the election in Kerala in 1957; however, the Communist party was a national party, which was successful at subnational level. Dravida Munnetra Kazhagam (DMK) was the first example of a successful regional party at State level. The DMK won the assembly election in then Madras State in 1967 (Rothermund 2008, 17–18).
14 S.R. Sankaran graduated from Madras University in 1954. He worked as a lecturer for three years in Madurai. He joined the IAS in 1957 and was allotted the Andhra Pradesh Cadre. Among his important positions are Collector and District Magistrate, Nellore (1968–1969), Special Assistant to Union Ministry for Steel and Mines (1971–1973), Secretary, Social Welfare Dept. Andhra Pradesh Government (1976–1978), Chief Secretary, Government of Tripura (1978–1984) and Secretary, Ministry of Rural Development, Government of India (1999–1992). He was President of the Bharat Gyan Vigyan Samithi.
15 The Land Reform Bill, 1972.
16 YSR Congress Party is a new regional political party in Andhra Pradesh and Telangana. The leader of this political party is Y.S. Jagan, the son of former Andhra Pradesh chief minister Y.S. Rajasekhara Reddy (known as YSR). After the death of his father and political developments in AP Congress, he decided to run his political party.
17 NTR had 600 fan clubs all over Andhra Pradesh, mainly in Coastal Andhra region (Bernstorff 1998a, 12).
18 For example, two other chief ministers, Ramakrishna Hegde of Karnataka and Surjit Singh Barnala of Punjab, and K.P. Unnikrishnan of Congress (S), Dinesh Goswami of Asom Gana Parishad, Abdul Rashid Kabuli of National Conference, C.T. Dandapani of DMK, and Ram Naresh Yadav of Samata Party.

5 Elite agency and development in Andhra Pradesh (II)

Pragmatism, cooperation, and pro-growth policies in the era of the CEO of Andhra Pradesh

Introduction

Chandrababu Naidu, as the finance minister of NTR's second government, in his budget speech of 1995–1996 (Naidu 1995) supported the massive subsidies such as rice subsidy program as a useful tool to fight against poverty:

> If there is one distilled lesson out of our "development experience" spanning nearly a half-century, it is that "trickle down" theories of growth do not work. Our anti-poverty programs, arguably designed and implemented with the best of intentions, have failed to reach the most deprived and the most indigent. And as we all know well by now, poverty anywhere is inimical to growth and welfare everywhere. The lesson is, therefore, clear. The most effective and possibly the only way, to alleviate poverty is by direct income transfer methods such as the rice subsidy program.

Nevertheless, five years later, Chandrababu Naidu, as the new chief minister of Andhra Pradesh (2000b, 115) criticized the previous schemes in term of effectiveness and fiscal burden:

> In the 1980s, in its first term in power in Andhra Pradesh, the Telugu Desam Party was voted in on the platform of Telugu pride and the promise of rice at Rs 2 a kg for those below the poverty line. However, it is difficult to implement the targeting of a subsidy like this. With even the relatively well-off sections of the population accessing the subsidized rice, it proved to be a very costly promise in the long run.

Two above statements, made by the same regional leader, draw attention to a critical question, addressed by this chapter. Why had Chandrababu Naidu supported the rice subsidy program despite massive fiscal constraints as the Finance Minister of Andhra Pradesh under NTR rule? Moreover, why did he later opt for more fiscal friendly and pro-growth policies as the chief minister of Andhra Pradesh by eradicating the subsidized rice scheme or total prohibition of liquor?

This chapter concentrates on the historical process and institutional transformations that shaped the strategic choice of the new chief minister of Andhra Pradesh in favor of cooperation with Center in the vertical interactions and pro-liberalization polices in the horizontal interaction. Naidu was sworn in as chief minister of Andhra Pradesh as the new leader of the TDP in September 1995. Immediately, he faced two main obstacles in the horizontal level to consolidate his power in the State. Not only was he not as popular and charismatic as NTR, but also the State's fiscal stance was unsustainable. These two difficulties played a crucial role in Naidu's strategic choices to revise his economic views on the subsidies and economic reforms in the State.

From charismatic populism to pragmatist technocracy: the rational actor and the horizontal determinants

Nara Chandrababu Naidu (born 20 April 1950) personifies the new generation of regional politicians who emerged in the context of post-independence India. Naidu was born to a farming family in a small village near Tirupati (Chittoor district, Rayalaseema region). He was a member of one medium-size farm family (Naidu 2000b, xiv). Like NTR, Naidu belongs to the Kamma caste (Balasubrahmanyam 2004; Rajendra Prasad 2004, 127). While studying at Sri Venkateswara University, he became interested in politics. Later, he joined the Youth Congress as a student leader (Naidu 2000b, xiv). He obtained a Master's degree in economics, but he could not find a job as a lecturer at the university. Therefore, his academic mentor, Professor D.L. Naraina, suggested that he enroll in a Ph.D. program in economics under his guidance; however, because of his political activities, he could not finish his doctoral studies.

As a young Congress leader, he ran for the Assembly election from the Chandragiri constituency in the 1978 election (Bernstorff 1998a, 14).Two years later, he became a Minister of State in Tanguturi Anjaiah's government. While he had been appointed as Minister of State in libraries, his future rival, Y.S. Rajashekara Reddy (YSR), served as Minister of State for rural development (Narisetti 2002, 239). The young and successful leader attracted the attention of Congress Party leaders as well as of N.T. Rama Rao. Young Chandrababu Naidu married NTR's daughter in 1980, before NTR chose to enter politics. In Bhavanam Venkatarami Reddy's government, he also served as Minister of State. As a young Congress leader, Naidu was also appointed as Minister of State for technical education in Kotla Vijaya Bhaskara Reddy's government (Narisetti 2002, 240–242). When NTR, his father-in-law, founded the TDP, he was still a member of the Congress. Even in a press conference, he declared that he would contest against his father-in-law if the Congress asked him to do so (Rajendra Prasad 2004, 128).

In the 1983 Assembly election, the TDP candidate defeated Naidu in the Chandragiri constituency; hence, he decided to give up politics and initiate a business. Later, he joined his father-in-law in the TDP. He had no official position in the first NTR's cabinet; he did not run for both the 1984 and 1985 Vidhan Sabha and Lok Sabha elections. Ninan in the introduction to his interview with

Naidu (2000b, xvi) asserts that Naidu at this stage was the 'backdoor organizer' of the TDP. Naidu not only used a computer to set up a database of the TDP's MLAs but also tried to train the TDP's party workers through a new educational institute that offer nine-month courses.

Finally, Naidu was elected in 1989 from the Kuppam constituency as TDP's MLA; nevertheless, the TDP was in opposition, so there was no possibility of him entering the cabinet. While NTR did not participate actively in the Assembly as the opposition leader, Naidu served as coordinator and secretary general of the TDP and became more influential on the TDP's MLAs. Naidu finally became the virtual leader of the opposition, when NTR decided to boycott all Assembly sessions in 1993 and 1994, asserting he would not attend the Assembly unless he became the chief minister (Rajendra Prasad 2004, 128). After reelection of Naidu as an MLA in the 1994 Assembly election, NTR, who became chief minister again, appointed Naidu as minister of finance and revenues. Although Naidu tried to encourage NTR to approve some economic reforms, as a minister of finance, he still advocated the TDP's populist views. Following the 'palace revolution' in the TDP, Chandrababu Naidu became chief minister of Andhra Pradesh at the age of 45 (Bernstorff 1998a, 14).

Legitimacy challenge

Since its formation, the TDP had mostly relied on the charisma of NTR, rooted in his cinematic career and personal characteristics. This personal charisma influenced the masses as well as party workers. The TDP had no apparent political ideology since its inception and could attract votes just based on the public interest in NTR. That is why the TDP was fundamentally dependent on its charismatic leader. Suri (2004b, 1483) describes the role of NTR in the party and writes:

> He thought himself to be infallible. His opinion was the opinion of the party since he was the party; his commands were law since he was the embodiment of the will of the people. He was the party patriarch. All party leaders and activists were his brothers ('tammullu') and sisters ('ada paduchulu').

NTR dominated government as well as the party. Kohli (1988, 999) describes NTR's decisions as 'impulsive and arbitrary' and writes:

> Decision making within the TDP is highly centralized, and the legislators play hardly any significant political role. Attempts to build the TDP into an organized party also have not amounted to much. The TDP remains a one-man show. The 'central theme' at the TDP's organizational forums is 'hero worship,' the hero, of course, being NTR.

Therefore, NTR knew the TDP as a synonym of himself and believed that "TDP came with me and will go away with me" (quoted in Suri 2004b, 1481). After the 'Palace Coup' NTR never accepted the legitimacy of Naidu. As Rajendra Prasad (2004, 118) reports after the swearing ceremony of Naidu, he along with NTR's son and daughter went from *Raj Bhavan* to NTR's house for his blessing. NTR not only did not receive them, but also a huge group of NTR's supporters shouted slogans against them. NTR submitted a case against the governor of AP to the court. He argued that the governor must dissolve the Assembly and announce a new election. He, however, lost his cases in the Courts; therefore, he prepared himself for the next Lok Sabha election in 1996 to fight against the 'traitors' and prove that "there is only one Telugu Desam, and only one leader" (quoted in Rajendra Prasad 2004, 122). Unhappy, NTR organized an electoral campaign against Naidu and asked his allies in the National Front such as V.P. Singh, Deve Gowda, and then Karnataka chief minister, Lalu Prasad Yadav, then Bihar chief minister, Surjit Singh Barnala and Prafulla Kumar Mohanta to come and address in his rallies. However, 73-year-old NTR did not see the 1996 election and died on 18 January 1996.

Even though Naidu became the chief minister of Andhra Pradesh, he remained under NTR's shadow. He knew that while the majority of MLAs opposed Lakshmi Parvathi and NTR, they could again become rebellious in favor of other NTR's family members. Moreover, the TDP was synonymous with the charismatic leadership of NTR. Chandrababu Naidu was not a cinema actor and never played a role of Hindu gods or heroes in Telugu cinema. He was neither a charismatic leader such as NTR, which could enchant the rural masses nor a member of Reddy caste or the Congress Party, which would guarantee for him the specific vote banks. Lakshmi Parvathi portrayed Naidu as a traitor who was responsible for NTR's death (Rajendra Prasad 2004). After the death of NTR, the TDP divided into two factions: the TDP Naidu or TDPND, and TDP Lakshmi Parvathi or TDPLP. Other children and family members of NTR could be a potential threat for Naidu. Lakshmi Parvathi traveled across AP with a campaign vehicle to remind the masses that she was the rightful successor for NTR.

Consequently, Naidu had a vulnerable position at the beginning of his tenure. Although he convinced a majority of the MLAs to support him in the short term, there was no guarantee that they would remain loyal to him. Moreover, Naidu needed to demonstrate his leadership skills to public opinion to escape from the vast shadow of his father-in-law.

Fiscal deficit crisis

The simplest way to convince the public opinion to support a leader such Naidu who would fight with the Congress as an opposition party, as well as unhappy supporters of NTR, was the implementation of a new wave of populist welfare measures. These policies could satisfy the OBCs, women or minorities and provide political rewards for a new leader with a disputed legitimacy. Despite all predictions in favor of sustaining populism, Naidu realized that he could not maintain the ambitious welfare policies and populist schemes. Although the pro-poor and populist policies of NTR led to a decrease in the level of mass poverty in the State (Balasubramanyam and Balasubramanyam 2012, 49–50), it also created a severe fiscal deficit at the State level. As Yadagiri (1994, 305) indicates, NTR's populist measures such as rice supply scheme (Rs 2 per kilo), the Sari dhoti, and permanent housing scheme became a massive strain on the financial resources of AP. For example, the subsidized rice supply scheme covered approximately two-thirds of AP's population; as a result, subsidies and non-developmental expenditures constituted a significant share in AP's budget and the proportion of developmental projects decreased. NTR's populism was the primary cause of the increase in public spending. Andhra Pradesh did not have a budget deficit before 1982; on the other hand, budget deficit emerged as the main challenge for all AP's government after 1990. Naidu encountered the shocking fact about subsidies. The cost of subsidies and populist schemes that began with NTR in 1983 multiplied 14 times in 1999 (Naidu 2000b, 116). Chandrababu Naidu (2000b, 116) compares providing a subsidy with 'clambering atop the proverbial tiger.'

Similarly, as Mukherji (2014, 151) illustrates, while the cost of generating electricity per unit was Rs 1.83, the State offered it to consumers for only Rs 0.03; therefore, AP's government should have paid Rs 15.3 billion (US$478.1 million) subsidy to the power sector in 1995. Similarly, housing subsidies and food protection schemes imposed heavy strains on the AP's budget. Chandrababu Naidu (2000b, 105) described the financial situation in the State when he started his tenure:

> When a State Government discovers that there is no money in the treasury to pay even salaries it is a moment of reckoning. Uttar Pradesh found in 1998 that its entire revenues were not enough to pay the salaries of its employees. In 1995, we in Andhra Pradesh were in the same situation. And in 1996–97 our expenditure on salaries and pensions as a percentage of the state's own tax and non-tax receipts was 94.5 percent.

Naidu (2000b, 105) compared the financial situation and fiscal crisis in the Center in 1991 that paved path to 'the reform' with the critical financial condition at the State level:

> If the beginning of the 1990s saw the Central Government recognize that the country's economy was in crisis, and drastic changes would have to be made in its functioning, most State Governments are facing that realization by the end of the same decade.

Therefore, he acknowledged the importance of the economic reforms, which had been introduced by the Congress government of P.V. Narasimha Rao and were criticized by the TDP. Although all of NTR's popular welfare expenditures created an atmosphere, which allowed the TDP to survive in Andhra Pradesh as the principal competitor for the Congress, Naidu realized that political gains through populism are not possible anymore. He (Naidu 2000b, 114) recognized the role of the political determinant in the TDP's economic policies and indicated:

> When the state provides a service for the people – be it irrigation, electricity, road transport, primary school education or municipal water supply – it is usually constrained to give it away free or at heavily subsidized rates. The reason for this economically aberrant behavior is quite simply called politics.

These financial realities, as well as the urgent need of Naidu to escape from the political shadow of NTR, accelerated the fundamental shift in the TDP's economic viewpoints. The TDP along with the leftist parties such as CPI and CPM had formed an opposition coalition against the Congress between 1989 and 1994, and opposed the reforms and economic liberalization.

One year later, as the chief minister of AP, Naidu decided for the opposite way. After the dismissal of NTR, while Chandrababu Naidu needed to demonstrate that he was a capable leader, he could not use the old instrument of welfare policies. Therefore, in a radical shift, he adopted neo-liberal economic policies and tried to portray himself as the vanguard of development in Andhra Pradesh. Although some of the other leaders of the TDP, CPI, and CPM criticized this shift, Naidu, however, abandoned most of the welfare schemes and tried to find new sources for investments.

The TDP did not have a coherent ideology, so the charismatic leadership of NTR shaped its approaches. Although social democracy, as well as neo-liberalism, influenced the initial manifesto of the TDP (Suri 2013, 170), the political realities in AP and the characteristics of the Telugu subnationalism highlighted both confrontation with the Center and populism. Nevertheless, unlike the leftist parties such as CPI or CPM, founded based on a solid economic perspective, the TDP as a non-ideological regional party could revise its economic approach fundamentally. Therefore, the first government of Naidu (1995–1999) made a departure from NTR's populist policies to pro-liberalization economic policies.

As Mukherji (2014, 151) notes, Naidu's background in economics (his Master's degree and uncompleted Ph.D. in economics) and his experience as the Finance Minister in NTR's second government (1994) convinced him to reconsider economic policies. The academic background of Naidu is also is reflected in his explanation (Naidu 2000b, 114–115) about the reasons for the entire shift in the TDP's economic approaches:

> I studied economics in college and was doing my Ph.D. on the economic policies of the eminent parliamentarian N.G. Ranga. Being an economist by training and a politician by experience, I can see quite clearly that political populism in recent years has in many ways been bad for the economy of State Governments. We got away with practicing this kind of aberrant management for some years, but as our population grows and our costs and

> inefficiencies mount, the specter of bankruptcy looms ahead for many State Governments. The more fragmented the electorate becomes as caste, and communal divisions come to the fore, the more political parties have to resort to populism to win their vote. Frequent elections have made matters worse: they have made responsible public finance extremely difficult. Political parties are constrained to promise that they will write off bank loans to farmers, or give them free electricity.

Only one year after the beginning of Naidu's tenure, the AP Finance Department released a White Paper stressing the necessity of fiscal prudence. In this paper, the TDP government analyzed several financial challenges and economic problems such as resource crunch, low developmental expenditures, and considerable debt. Therefore, the document recommended limiting subsidies, privatization in some public sectors and other similar measures. Consequently, The TDP government initiated several reform plans and schemes to cope with the financial crisis in the State and provide a more business-friendly environment in the State to attract domestic as well foreign investments. Naidu's decision to raise the price of subsidized rice and partial lifting of the ban on liquor was a visible sign of his intention in the implementation of the reforms:

> In the 1980s, in its first term in power in Andhra Pradesh, the Telugu Desam Party was voted in on the platform of Telugu pride and the promise of rice at Rs 2 a kg for those below the poverty line. However, it is difficult to implement the targeting of a subsidy like this. With even the relatively well-off sections of the population accessing the subsidized rice, it proved to be a very costly promise in the long run.
>
> (Naidu 2000b, 115)

The death of NTR in 1996 decreased the succession dispute within the party substantially. Not only NTR died in 1996, but also his populism was sacrificed in favor of the economic reforms. The 'Palace coup' in the TDP and death of NTR can be considered as a critical juncture in the development trajectory. As Sarangi (2004, 109–110) observes about the new TDP government, whereas anti-Congress tendencies and Telugu nationalism have continued in the TDP rhetoric, the populist economic policies and its pre-modem mode of communication with people are substituted with a modem *realpolitik* strategy of governance.

Similarly, Suri (2002) differentiates between the NTR era as 'politics of populism and confrontation' and the Chandrababu Naidu era as 'politics of pragmatism.' Naidu confirmed this shift explicitly:

> The politics of populism can be replaced with politics of development. The latter too can be made to pay electoral dividends. People have begun to recognize that it is not viable for governments to continue providing goods and services for free.
>
> (Naidu 2000b, 17–18)

The current book argues Chandrababu Naidu tried to create a dynamic, progressive and trustworthy image for the TDP leadership as an alternative to the charismatic image of NTR. Manor (2002, 54) compares the leadership of NTR and Naidu, and writes:

> NTR was a genuinely charismatic figure (a much-overused term in the analysis of Indian politics, but appropriate in his case). He could make a crowd laugh and weep by turns, and he often left them breathless with excitement. Naidu is a wooden speaker who is famous in AP for having no sense of humor. So he stresses expensive publicity campaigns in which much is said in his name, without his having to say things directly to large audiences.

Therefore, Chandrababu Naidu neither had NTR's charisma, which attracted the attention of constituents to him, nor enough financial resources to pursue populist welfare policies to convince masses to support him. The TDP under the leadership of N.T. Rama Rao was supported mainly by the coalition between the Kamma caste (Rao belonged to this caste), the OBCs, Muslims especially after Babri Masjid dispute, women and all masses who were inspired by NTR's charismatic character or his populist schemes (Suri 2004b, Kohli 1988). After the end of the political career of NTR, Chandrababu Naidu had several challenges to get support from his traditional supporters. To create a new political base in the State, the strategic choice of Naidu was to shift from the economic populism toward liberalization. This reshuffling not only displayed a progressive image from the TDP government and the new leadership, but also could attract votes and support from the emerging urban middle class, the youth, and Kamma entrepreneurs.

As Reddy (2007, 163–164) specifies, Naidu's pro-development image was constructed based on three pillars: "(1) Media management; (2) Depending on a few select bureaucrats combined with a corporate style of functioning; and (3) Making use of internationally aided projects for his image and party cadre building."

Although as Jenkins (1999, 172) indicates, skilled politicians introduced the economic reforms by stealth in their States, Andhra Pradesh is an exemption for this pattern. Kennedy (2004, 30) in his comparative study of Andhra Pradesh and Tamil Nadu realizes that while both states have pursued similar pro-market policies with the 'similar content' and liberalized their economy since the 1990s, they pursued a 'distinct approach' in terms of discursive framing and depth of policy change. As Kennedy (2004) elaborates, the successive governments in Tamil Nadu are cautious about openly endorsing liberalization; on the other hand, political leadership in Andhra Pradesh openly embraced a pro-liberalization stance. Although the Congress government (1989–1994) in the State already introduced the reforms (Suri 2013), Chandrababu Naidu publicly identifies himself with the economic reforms and advocates the reform process. As Mooij (2013) points out, unlike the other Indian States, Naidu did not introduce the reforms in Andhra Pradesh by stealth, but "by hype, by a skillful and cleverly managing leadership." Similarly, Balasubramanyam and Balasubramanyam (2012, 49) highlight Naidu's penchant for 'self-publicity' and discuss 'populist model of development.'

While scholars such as Suri (2004a, 5493) proposed the TDP's clear pro-liberalization stance was a reaction to the strong left tradition in the State, the current book suggests that Naidu opted for a pro-liberalization attitude to consolidate his power and create a new political and social support for his party position in the State, domestically and internationally.

The vertical game: the TDP as a member of the NDA – the Congress as the enemy, both at the State and the Center

When Chandrababu Naidu became the chief minister in 1995, P.V. Narasimha Rao was serving as the Prime Minister of India. The pattern of relationship between the Congress in the Center and the TDP in the State became very similar to NTR's era. As Suri (2013, 173) maintains, "The reason is that the very genesis of TDP lies in its opposition to the Congress, and its constitution depends on its ability to keep itself as the only opposition of the Congress Party in the State."

Naidu confronted the Congress at the State and Center level; nonetheless, it was not the only source of the threat. NTR and his loyal MLAs also challenged his legitimacy. Although NTR had challenged Naidu and other rebellious leaders of the TDP in the 1996 general election, his death weakened the position of Lakshmi Parvathi and her supporters in the party. Naidu could consolidate his position quickly, and the MLAs and other TDP workers stood behind him; as a result, the Election Commission recognized his party. Factionalism and the succession dispute, however, debilitated the TDP, and they won only 16 seats in the Lok Sabha election while the Congress secured 22 seats.

Despite the weak performance of the TDP in the election, Naidu played a significant role in Vajpayee's unsuccessful government formation at the Center.[1] Naidu as a member of National Front coalition did not support Vajpayee and preferred to support H.D. Deve Gowda as the prime minister of India. Later, Naidu realized that the political game with the Center could not be continued through the National Front. He looked for a stronger ally at the Center who could support the TDP in the regional competition with Congress. After the 1998 general election, Naidu joined the National Democratic Alliance (NDA) led by the BJP. The BJP required outside support for a stable government and elected MPs of the TDP played a crucial role in the formation of NDA. The TDP continued the coalition with the BJP until the 2004 election; however, both were defeated by the Congress at the Center and the State.

While NTR considered the Center as a 'conceptual myth' and confronted it, Naidu joined the ruling coalition and became a partner of the Central power. NTR's confrontation with the Center could be due to the fact that the Congress, the chief opponent of the TDP in AP, also was in power at the Center. Looking at the new political arrangements at the Center and States, Chandrababu Naidu realized that the TDP government could get maximum benefit from the Center by sustaining constructive and friendly relations with it.

As a pragmatist politician, Naidu emphasized the significance of positive relations between the State and the Center to attract more financial resources from the Center:

> A politician who wants to deliver cannot have an ego. He has to lobby with the Central Governments for funds, using every persuasion he can think of.
>
> (Naidu 2000b, 7)

Consequently, the TDP that emerged with the slogan of pride of Telugu culture and identity got closer to the BJP, just because of these political realities. After 1998, when the TDP became a prominent member of NDA, Naidu could convince the Union Government and the Planning Commission to allocate more financial resources to Andhra Pradesh. For instance, as Figure 5.1 illustrates the TDP government between 1998 and 2004 witnessed increases in the annual outlay for five-year plans by the Planning Commission. After 2004, the YSR's government as a member of the UPA government had close cooperation with the Center and benefited from the Center's financial allocation.

Although AP's government tried to improve the relationship with the Center to attract more financial resources, Naidu recognized that the Center had ended the centrally planned economic era. Moreover, the role of the Centre has transformed from an interventionist to a regulatory state since 1991. Instead of Nehruvian interventionist state, the post-reform state seeks to ensure accountability and transparency in the market, facilitate the growth, and discipline the States fiscally (Rudolph and Rudolph 2013). The new role of Union Government provides more autonomy for the State, enabling them to be more independent in economic policymaking, and negotiate directly with international financial and aid agencies such as the World Bank.

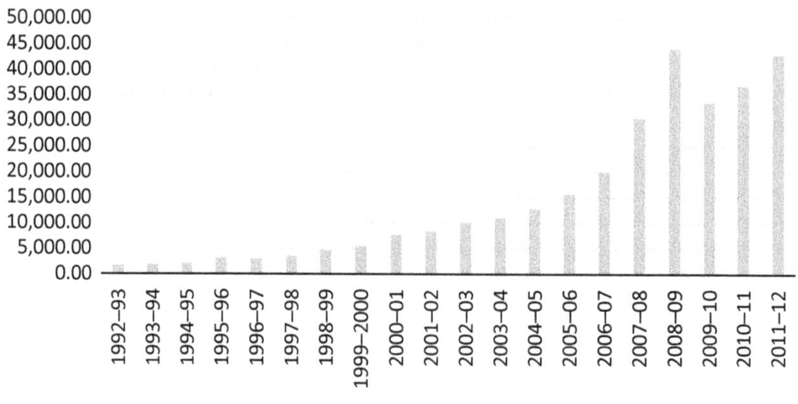

Figure 5.1 Approved annual outlay for 8th, 9th, 10th, 11th plans for Andhra Pradesh.

Source: *State Finances: A Study of Budgets* (Reserve Bank of India 2015), drawn by the author.

Andhra Pradesh as a developmental (subnational) state in the TDP regime

Although Andhra Pradesh is not an independent nation-state and operates within the framework of India's federal system, it has acquired some characteristics of a developmental state since the mid-1990s. As Jenkins (1999, 2003), Mitra (2011), and Kennedy (2004, 2014) indicate, the liberalization in India led to significant transformations in federal relations, especially in terms of economic policymaking. As a result, Andhra Pradesh attained more autonomy in terms of economic planning. Mitra (2011, 102) discusses the impact of 'big bang liberalization' of the Indian economy on the federal system in India:

> It has seen a radical transformation from the earlier 'ganging up of the States against the center' to a free-for-all competition between all stakeholders – Union, States, and mega-cities – to create conditions that attract investments from home and abroad. This has led to the decline of the center-dominated developmental model that was implemented after Independence. By scaling back the State's involvement in the developmental process and as such reducing the functions of the Central Government, liberalization removed the safety net on which regional governments had depended.

Before the 1990s, the departments of the Union Government and the Planning and Finance Commission had been responsible for making decisions associated with the allocation of resources; as a result, the States had little direct influence on economic planning and investment decisions. If the State Government had positive relations with the Center and could lobby with the responsible institutes (department, ministers or the Planning Commission,), the State Governments could get more resources for industrial and infrastructural projects in their territory (Sinha 2005). However, the regional parties such as the TDP, whose political agenda was challenging the Congress and confrontation with the Center, were mostly marginalized in the allocation of resources.

Since the economic liberalization in 1991, the deregulation and decentralization have created an environment for States to assert their greater autonomy in terms of formulation and implementation of their economic policy (Kennedy 2004, 31).

The policies of liberalization launched in 1991 dismantled the central planning model gradually; as a result, the significance of State–Center conflict declined. As Jenkins (1999, 135) delineates, "*the State-Center* conflicts has been at least partially displaced with *inter-State* competition for inward investment."

Thus, Andhra Pradesh transformed from the 'Congress citadel,' which followed the orders of Delhi to a more autonomous State in terms of economic policymaking. Unlike the NTR era, subjugated by the economic and financial consequences of confrontation with the Center, Naidu realized the necessities of inter-State competition; therefore, he tried to create a more business-friendly environment in Andhra Pradesh to attract private domestic and foreign investments.

> I want to make Hyderabad an economic and business powerhouse. I want to make Hyderabad a knowledge hub and Andhra Pradesh a knowledge state. When all my projects in tourism, healthcare, finance, and employment are successfully executed, Bombay or any other city or the state will be nowhere near Hyderabad and Andhra Pradesh.
>
> (Naidu 2000a)

As a rational actor, Naidu was faced with a leadership dispute and legitimacy vacuum at the State level, the change in power relations at the Center, creating more autonomy for the State, and the development of a paradigm shift both at national and international level; as a result, he had new potential choices. He realized that possessing political power in Andhra Pradesh is not possible anymore through mere populism and confrontation with the Center. In the new institutional setting, Naidu should compete with other States to attract both Central financial allocation and private investments. He perceived success in the competition as a way to attract voters in the State. In the next assembly election, the TDP not only would be challenged by the Congress with the long history of domination in the State, but also the TDP lost its charismatic leader who could mobilize the masses. Naidu believed that the new source of legitimacy of the TDP government was its socio-economic performance, which would be possible by the implementation of reform packages.

A developmental elite at the state level: Naidu as the CEO of Andhra Pradesh

The new institutional setup at the Center and State, as well as the strategic choices of the rational actor, paved the path for the birth of a 'determined developmental leader' in the TDP, which had been founded based on populism and charismatic leadership. Leftwich (1995, 405–407, 2000, 152–196) recognizes 'determined developmental elite' as one of the most significant and necessary factors for the emergence of developmental states. These visionary elites are driven by a sense of urgency to grow economically and industrialize to catch up with the developed countries (here, inter-state competition).

These leaders are relatively uncorrupted, patriotic, visionary, and nationalistic with a genuine intention to develop their states rapidly. Leftwich (2000, 167) describes the developmental state as a "transitional form of modern state where political and bureaucratic elites have generally achieved relative independence from socio-political forces in the society"; thus, they have used this autonomy to support policies which boost economic growth.

As Rudolph and Rudolph (2013, 316–317) in *The Iconization of Chandrababu* elaborate, while Prime Minister Jawaharlal Nehru played a crucial role in the centralized economic planning during the 1950s and 1960s, chief ministers of States are the principal actors in India's emergent federal market economy after the 1990s liberalization.

Andhra Pradesh has emerged as a subnational developmental state with the leadership of Chandrababu Naidu, who provided a developmental vision for Andhra Pradesh, improved the current bureaucratic structure in State, and implemented new policies to enhance economic growth. While India's political economy in the 1950s and 1960s cannot be analyzed without studying the central role of Jawaharlal Nehru, his ideas and management style, in the post-1991 economic reforms of the role of chief ministers such as Chandrababu Naidu or Narendra Modi in the States and their ideas and policies should be underlined. That is why Kapoor and Ahluwalia (2015) attribute the economic successes in Andhra Pradesh to the visionary leadership of Chandrababu Naidu as the chief minister of Andhra Pradesh between 1995 and 2004.

Naidu's leadership in various ways influenced the development trajectory in Andhra Pradesh. His personal and political background along with his strategic choices in the vertical and horizontal games played a significant role in the development of Andhra Pradesh in the post-reform era. Like NTR, Naidu's leadership style was autocratic in both the party and the State (Balasubramanyam and Balasubramanyam 2012, 49); however, he had more management merits than NTR. As Manor (2002, 54) explicates, whereas NTR was reluctant in monitoring the performance of the TDP and State Government, Naidu dedicates an enormous amount of his time to control party and State. Manor (2002) reports that one district-level civil servant stated, "He personally hounds us constantly."

As Reddy (2007, 164) particularizes, on account of the fact that coalition politics were perceived as the cause of the relative political instability, Chandrababu Naidu's centralized and autocratic style of management was taken to be more appropriate for development. Naidu's leadership style emphasized effective management and swift implementation of projects more than democratic and bureaucratic procedures; therefore, it also suited the international aid agencies' governance agenda well.

Also, Naidu's educational and career background influenced his economic choices. As an economics graduate, he was aware of different economic theories and perspectives. Since the end of the 1970s, he had also served as an MLA for the Congress Party, minister, later as an MLA for the TDP and leader of the opposition, and as a minister of finance and revenues; as a result, he had first-hand knowledge and experience, enabling him to make more accurate decisions. During his studying and political career, Naidu was acquainted with developmental states in East Asia and their path to development. For him, the central question was why despite relatively similar initial conditions at the beginning of the twentieth century, East Asian countries such as South Korea, Singapore, Malaysia or China grew faster than India. Naidu (2000b, 19–20) insisted that his cabinet members and high-ranking members of the TDP should be acquainted with the East Asia countries' development experience:

> The orientation I gave my cabinet spelled out the lessons we have to learn from East Asia. First, you have to see India in relation to these countries to

> understand our mistakes in the way we have run our economy: in thirty years, from 1965 to 1995, the gross domestic product per capita in relation to the U.S. grew by 69.3 percent in Singapore, 39.8 percent in South Korea, 22.5 percent in Malaysia, 7.6 percent in China, and 1.3 percent in India. What were the factors behind East Asian growth? Several important ones: the transformation of agriculture through irrigation and power, private sector-led development, exports led growth and high savings and investment. These countries invested a great deal in infrastructure, and today their roads and ports would put ours to shame.

Naidu (2000b, 35) considered the East Asian states as a role model for Andhra Pradesh's development:

> There is the forceful lesson of the East Asian miracle emphasizing a strong commitment to human resource development. Towards this end, states need to invest in primary education, public health, female literacy and family planning to create a workforce equipped to take advantage of economic opportunity. The costs of these development initiatives have to be born by the states.

Naidu was not only interested in the development model of East Asian countries such as Singapore or Malaysia but he also copied particular infrastructural features of these countries. For instance, the so-called Singapore Township was constructed on the outskirts of Hyderabad. Also, the Multi-Modal Transport System in Hyderabad (MMTS) is modeled on the Mass Rapid Transport System in Singapore (Mooij 2013, 404).

Remarkably, Naidu was also intellectually aware of the theoretical debates about the transformation of the role of government in the post-cold war era. In the book titled 'plain speaking' (Naidu 2000b), there is a chapter on 'Simplifying Government.' At the beginning of the chapter, Naidu raises this question: "How much government do we need and what areas?" Immediately, he continues his discussion with reference to the well-known work of Osborne and Gaebler (1992) titled *Reinventing Government.* This book is one of the most influential neo-liberal works that tried to differentiate between the function of government. The first function is policymaking, called 'steering,' and the second function is service delivery, described as 'rowing.' Osborne and Gaebler (1992) consider bureaucracy as bankrupt for the rowing function, and it should be replaced by 'entrepreneurial government' that is dependent on markets and customers. Osborne and Gaebler (1992) conclude that governments would be more efficient "if they acted as steersmen rather than as oarsmen." These ideas were not only used during the neo-liberal attacks on 'big government' in the U.S. but also was represented in the growing governance literature. Bad governance became a synonym for extreme rowing function, and one of the aspects of good governance was seen as more capacity and effectiveness in policymaking by the government. Consequently, the neo-liberals emphasized the role of private sectors in public service delivery. Eight years after the publication of Reinventing *Government* Chandrababu Naidu considered it a theoretical foundation for reinventing Andhra Pradesh's government (Naidu 2000b, 46):

> David Osborne and Ted Gaebler, authors of Reinventing Government, write that 'the central problem of governments today is not what they do but how they operate.' Changing technologies make the old approach of people-intensive government redundant. Information technology can make a huge difference to citizen–government interfaces. It can also usher in transparency and flatter organizations. A simple three-point diagnosis of the systemic malady in Indian governance points to too many employees, too many levels and far too many files leading to excruciating delays. From these follow the manifestations of the malady: poor or no delivery of services, tremendous delays in decision making, absence of accountability, and corruption.

Therefore, Naidu admired the public-sector reforms[2] in the United Kingdom, initiated by Margaret Thatcher and followed by other Western countries. He was aware of the impact of these reforms on the nature and functions of governments:

> I emphasize the transformation of the public sector that has taken place in countries such as Australia, Britain, and New Zealand. New Zealand's Ministry of Public Works had 12,000 employees at one time and built most of the airports, bridges, power stations, roads, canals, dams and railways in that country. Today it no longer exists. First, it was split up, and all policy advice functions transferred to other departments. Commercially oriented services were converted into state-owned enterprises. These were reorganized along business lines and required to raise capital on the market. At the same time, they were freed from government regulations. Over time, each of these was sold to the private sector. New Zealand no longer has any government in-house capability to design, build or repair infrastructure. When these services are needed, they are purchased on the open market.

This neo-liberal background manifested in Naidu's developmental rhetoric in different ways. Despite the fact his management style was so centralized, Naidu portrayed a progressive, dynamic, and pro-development image in media at both international and national levels. In Naidu's developmental rhetoric, he several times asserted that politics and development could not go together, and politics impedes development:

> I have left politics behind in the last millennium, on the campaign trail. Now as Chief Minister of Andhra Pradesh, I do not want to talk politics. It is time for me to act and work for the development of the state, which I sincerely believe I am doing these days. My political agenda now is the economic empowerment of the poor and women. My political agenda now is to make Andhra Pradesh an economic powerhouse.
>
> (Naidu 2000a)

The regional, national and international media portrayed Naidu as the true champion of reforms (Suri 2005). The TDP party in its media campaign focused on the central role of Naidu in the reform. The reform not only could create political support among growing urban middle class but also it could increase his prestige in international level. Portraying himself as a developmental leader, Chandrababu Naidu (2000a) declared himself as the chief executive officer (CEO) of Andhra Pradesh:

> There is absolutely nothing wrong in a Chief Minister being called the CEO of a state. Like a CEO – who have short and long-term visions for their companies – I too have similar plans for my state. I am creating wealth for the people of the state. The 7.5 crore people of Andhra Pradesh are my shareholders. My immediate task is to generate 20 million jobs and reduce population growth from 1.4 percent to 0.83 percent. I want to achieve a seven to eight-fold increase in per capita income.

Although Naidu tried to depoliticize development in the State, the reform in the State, however, was introduced as Naidu's personal project. This 'one-man show,' reinforced by media, politicized the reforms and development; hence, it provoked other political parties especially the Congress (Balasubramanyam and Balasubramanyam 2012, 49–50; Suri 2005, 120).

Naidu introduced his government as a devotee to the development and economic reforms. That why the TDP's campaign for 1999 assembly election concentrated on reforms and asked voters to vote based on 'the performance of government.' This strategy along with the implementation of some welfare schemes for target groups such as women attracted voters in the 1999 assembly election. Suri (2013, 176) differentiates between NTR's populism and Naidu's 'welfarism.' While NTR considered himself as the savior of ordinary people and introduced undifferentiated and open-ended welfare schemes, Naidu's welfare schemes considered 'political expediency' and targeted specific social groups. That is why Reddy (2002, 881) describes it as 'targeted populism.'

Combining the reforms initiatives and targeted welfare schemes, Naidu not only could attract sufficient votes to win the 1999 election but also, he could convince international financial institutions such as the World Bank to support his reforms plans.

Edwin Lim (2005, 112), the World Bank Country Director for India, perceived Naidu as a new generation of Indian technocratic politicians who run his election campaign on the platform of reform and economic performance:

> Since the early 1990s, we saw the emergence of young, technocratic politicians at the state level, the most conspicuous of whom was Chandrababu Naidu in Andhra Pradesh. Naidu's technocratic credentials and records once won him the 'Businessman of the Year' award in India. Not only he was attempting to pursue a comprehensive reform strategy in his state, but also he had run his election on the platform of reform and economic performance.

Throughout India (in Madhya Pradesh, Karnataka, and Tamil Nadu), signs began to appear of performance becoming one of the criteria for the election contests. Recent state and national elections have, however, demonstrated the difficulty of maintaining such a course in the face of resistance from deeply rooted vested interests able to counter-reformist programs with hard-core populism.

A subnational state and international aid agencies: AP and the World Bank

The leftist parties such as CPI and CPM had considered the TDP as a strong secular anti-Congress force in the1980s and beginning of the 1990s. Frightened by the reforms and the economic liberalization, the TDP along with the leftists condemned P.V. Narasimha Rao's economic policies. Later, the leftist parties realized that their old partner in Andhra Pradesh works in close collaboration with the World Bank and other international donor agencies to implement neo-liberal economic policies.

Since the 1990s and after the decline of the centralized economic planning and the emergence of 'federal market economy,' the role of State Governments in the economic planning has increased (Rudolph and Rudolph 2013); as a result, the World Bank shifted its concentration from the Central Governments to State Governments.

As Kirk (2011, xviii) specifies, after the liberalization, the Center also decided to use selective state-level engagement by the World Bank. The World Bank officials wanted to demonstrate the effectiveness of their policy packages and the aids in India and wanted to create reform champions in the States. Thus, as Edwin Lim (2002, 57), the World Bank Country Director for India, indicates, the World Bank tried to create the role models for all Indian States:

> We shifted a lot of our work, the bulk of our work, in fact, to the State level, but it wasn't just any State. We began to differentiate. We wanted to concentrate on a few states only because we felt that India could be successful only if a few states were to break out of the pack and create a demonstration effect… And we felt that politically, it was possible to do that with the states and that some states would really engage in a partnership with the Bank.

The close relations between the World Bank and Andhra Pradesh started in 1996, and Andhra Pradesh under the rule of Naidu became the first focus of the World Bank in India in 1998. As Kirk (2011, 65) mentioned, the partnership between Andhra Pradesh and the World Bank began with a meeting between Naidu, Jim Wolfensohn, the ninth president of the World Bank, and Ed Lim. This meeting was not scheduled, and it was supposed that Wolfensohn visited the capitals of Karnataka and Odisha; then, he stayed three days in New Delhi. According to Kirk (2011), although Andhra Pradesh was not a priority for the World Bank's plan in India, Naidu used a connection in the central finance ministry to arrange a meeting with the President of the World Bank. As it was discussed, the TDP supported H.D. Deve Gowda as prime minister of India in 1996; therefore, for the first time, the TDP government had positive relations with the Center.

The role of the TDP in the formation of Gowda's government created the advantage to influence the Center. Therefore, Naidu used his influence to lobby the finance ministry and met the World Bank team in New Delhi.

Naidu inspired Wolfensohn and Lim with a PowerPoint presentation on his vision of the transformation of Andhra Pradesh; therefore, some weeks later, Lim took the World Bank team to Hyderabad for more discussion. After the negotiation in December 2006, they agreed in principle on an assistance program, which could run up to US$3 billion (Kirk 2011, 66).

The World Bank leadership perceived Naidu as a regional leader who has developmental potential. This potential and his commitment to implement the reforms attracted the attention of the World Bank. Lim (2002, 65), who already worked as the World Bank representative in China, realized the Naidu's interest in the East Asian Countries' development experience and wrote:

> In Andhra Pradesh, for instance, the Chief Minister was always telling me he wanted to transform his state into an East Asian tiger, so we found that political leadership in some of the states was very committed and very interested in getting assistance from the Bank; assistance in more than financial ways, and were also willing to accept it. They did not have any political problem with it. You did not find that in the Center.

The World Bank published a report titled Andhra *Pradesh: Agenda for Economic Reforms* in 1997, including the policy recommendations for strengthening Andhra Pradesh's public finances and achieving its developmental potential. The document (World Bank 1997a) recommended policies such as increasing the developmental impact of public expenditure via reorientation and a reduction of the welfare program and a decrease of consumption subsidies for rice, electricity and other similar items, reducing the salary bill, reforms in public enterprises, increasing in development expenditure, attracting private investment, and investment in physical infrastructures, primary education and health.

One of the most significant sectors that should be immediately considered by the State Government was electricity sector. As Mukherji (2014, 153) notes, Andhra Pradesh was witness to rapid growth in agricultural power consumption. Moreover, the enormous amount of subsidies had become a burden to AP government. One of the critical parts of the World Bank report was a recommendation for swift reforms in the power sector:

> The power sector has become a major obstacle for better utilization of the state's rich resources. A power shortage of about 16 percent of demand has deterred private investment and depressed capacity utilization, contributing to the recent slowdown of growth. Large financial losses by

> APSEB have put a heavy strain on state's finances. Power shortages result from inadequate past investment in the sector ... The immediate priorities in the power sector are to reduce the heavy and unsustainable financial losses of APSEB and to reduce power shortages. To address the state's power crisis, annual investments of at least $2.5 billion, ten times the level in recent years, are now needed in the next six years. Large private funds will undoubtedly be necessary to achieve such a high volume of investment. Depoliticization of tariffs and the management of the utilities in the sector and restoration of their creditworthiness are preconditions for this to happen.
>
> (World Bank 1997a, vi)

As Kirk (2011) elaborates, Naidu was influenced by the World Bank policy recommendations. Therefore, he pursued power sector reforms and proposed The AP Electricity Reform bill in 1998. The bill proposed to divide the State electricity board into two distinct corporations: first for generation and second for transmission. Moreover, the bill proposed to establish an independent regulatory authority. The Congress and the Left parties opposed the bill; nevertheless, the TDP with two-third majority in the Legislative Assembly passed the AP Electricity Reform Act in 1998. According to the Act, the AP State Electricity Board was divided into Andhra Pradesh Power Generation Corporation (APGENCO) and Andhra Pradesh Transmission Corporation (APTRANSCO) in 1999 (Mukherji 2014, 155). In June 1998, the World Bank expressed its support to the reforms and pledged US$543 million to the Andhra Pradesh Economic Restructuring Project, followed by another US$210 million for the Andhra Pradesh Power Sector Restructuring Project in February 1999. The World Bank's aids and loans not only had continued during the TDP government but also sustained during the Congress government despite all YSR's rhetoric against the loans in the 2004 assembly election (Kirk 2011, 63).

Although Naidu implemented several policy reforms in the State based on the World Bank recommendations, he also introduced some targeted populist measures pragmatically to attract specific groups of voters in the 1999 election. As Mukherji (2014, 155) maintains, the World Bank was patient about Naidu's populist initiatives in 1999 on the eve of his election campaign. The political support of the World Bank and its tolerance toward the Naidu's targeted populism is rooted in the pragmatist approach of the World Bank.

The 2020 vision

As noted, the TDP government published its first policy document in the form of a 'White Paper' in 1996. Subsequently, Naidu took a step further to display the State's growing autonomy in the economic planning. In January 1999, Chandrababu Naidu's government brought out the *Swarna Andhra Pradesh: Vision 2020* (Government of Andhra Pradesh 1999), an ambitious text, exposing what the AP Government should pursue in the next two decades.

As the previous section specified, Naidu had a keen interest in the East and South East Asian model of development and considered it as a role model for his government. Mahathir Mohammad, the prime minister of Malaysia, had published a document, titled 'Malaysia's Vision 2020' in 1991. The goal of this vision was full development of Malaysia by the end of 2020. Mahathir Mohammad's government also worked with the consultancy of 'McKinsey & Company,' the famous multinational management consulting firm, on a plan to transform Kuala Lumpur into a 'Knowledge Economy' hub (Kirk 2011, 65). This experience inspired Naidu to find a way to transform Andhra from traditional agricultural society to a developed high-tech market-led society. Therefore, Naidu started cooperation with McKinsey & Company to draft AP's own vision.

Andhra's 2020 Vision clarifies the State's developmental goals and the strategies to achieve it. The primary objectives of the vision included eradication of poverty, the empowerment of women and vulnerable groups such as SCs and STs, stabilization of its population, and the enablement of this population, through improved health and education, to participate in and fulfill the opportunities presented to it. Sen's 'capability approach' (1993) influenced this policy document; therefore, AP Vision 2020 aimed to eradicate poverty and provide access for all people to education and health, and declared:

> Our vision of Andhra Pradesh is a state where poverty is totally eradicated. Where every man, woman, and child has access to not just the basic minimum needs, but to all the opportunities to lead a happy and fulfilling life. A knowledge and learning society built on the values of hard work, honesty, discipline and a collective sense of purpose.
>
> (Quoted in Naidu 2000b, 234)

However, the capability approach is not the only inspirational view for the writers of the vision. The neo-liberalism and confidence in the emerging opportunities inspired by globalization also influenced the vision. As Naidu asserted, the document made an appeal for "a paradigm shift in our thinking on growth and development" (quoted in Suri 2005, 141).

The explicit paradigm shift is reflected at the beginning of the document where it advocated the neo-liberal nature of the state, transforming itself from controller of the economy to the facilitator and catalyst of its growth:

> to promote rapid development, the State Government will need to transform itself and quickly adopt a new role: from being controller of economy; it must become and facilitator and catalyst of its growth.
>
> (Government of Andhra Pradesh 1999, 7)

The Vision 2020 targeted Andhra Pradesh as the first State in India in terms of growth, development, and quality of life. The critical tool for achieving the goals is rapid economic development.

> Economic growth will stimulate development in two ways. First, it will increase incomes for the people by creating employment opportunities. Second, it will generate additional resources for the Government. The Government will invest these resources mainly in social development, that is, eradicating poverty, improving education and health, promoting rural and urban development, and providing services such as housing, water, power, transportation, and so on.
>
> (Government of Andhra Pradesh 1999, 6–7)

According to the Vision, Andhra Pradesh's economy should grow by 9–10% annually for 25 years. The Vision aimed at high economic growth and low population growth to eradicate poverty:

> The average per capita income should increase nine times, with incomes for the poor growing much more rapidly. Population growth should be limited to less than 1% (0.8%) a year. Finally, at least 18–20 million new jobs will have to be created.
>
> (Government of Andhra Pradesh 1999, 4)

The Vision 2020 identified its engines clearly for achieving economic growth.[3]

The Vision 2020 proclaims that 'knowledge-led growth' in fields such as information technology (IT), biotechnology, and pharmaceuticals along with other growth engines such as tourism, mining, and agro-industry pave the path for the State to achieve a "level of development that would provide its people tremendous opportunities to achieve prosperity and wellbeing and enjoy a high quality of life" (Government of Andhra Pradesh 1999, 1).

The Vision 2020 had specific attention to the role of IT sector in development:

> Andhra Pradesh will leverage Information Technology to attain a position of leadership and excellence in the information age and to transform itself into a knowledge society.
>
> (Government of Andhra Pradesh 1999, 276)

Chandrababu Naidu not only perceived information technology as a tool for more efficient governance but also believed that it could be seen as a powerful engine for development:

> I am confident that information technology can bring accountability, transparency and quick disposal of cases and redressal of grievances in all the villages. I believe it can alleviate poverty. I see three areas where information technology can be an effective tool: job generation, poverty eradication and wealth generation.
>
> (Naidu 2000a)

The focal point of the Vision 2020 were IT and other high-tech industries and services; however, Andhra Pradesh is one of the most important agricultural States in India; as a result, it should also consider this sector. The Vision 2020 instead of the old notion of 'self-sufficiency' and 'independence,' aimed to use export-led growth strategies for development of agriculture sector. By concentrating on the export-oriented agriculture, the Vision intended to make the sector globally competitive. Therefore, the document selected sectors such as horticulture, and fisheries, which possess the export potentials to act as growth engines (Raju and Rao 2001, 3–4).

The Vision 2020 defined a new role for the Government of Andhra Pradesh. The document tried to highlight the difference between the new TDP government and NTR's government as well as previous Congress governments. While the populist governments of Andhra Pradesh in the 1970s and 1980s had concentrated on the subsidies and welfare schemes to attract the support of voters, Naidu defined new roles for the government, which should enhance economic development in the State. According to Mohanty (2003, 2), these roles include:

1 refocusing government priorities and shifting spending from unproductive areas toward achieving high priority developmental goals;
2 decentralizing governance and making it participatory with the involvement of the people;
3 introducing 'electronic government,' using IT-based services to make government processes and procedures more transparent and improving citizen-government interface;
4 becoming a SMART (Simple, Moral, Accountable, Responsive and Transparent) Government by improving transparency and accountability at all levels and ensuring effective and responsive services to the people;
5 building the administration's capabilities, strengthening policymaking and improving performance;
6 taking a lead role in persuading the Central Government and initiating regulatory and other reforms.

The TDP government prepared the document in association with McKinsey & Company, a multinational management-consulting firm. Not surprisingly, several writers with leftist perspective criticized the Vision (Suri 2005, 141). For example, *Economic and Political Weekly* published an article, titled "Sweet Dreams: Andhra's Vision 2020" by an anonymous writer (V 1999, 392), criticizing the Vision 2020:

> Evidently, McKinsey is not the best choice for developing country analysis. The Andhra experience gives one the impression that the consultant has only attractively packaged official social sector targets exogenously determined by the usual target-setting techniques. McKinsey's understanding of issues in these areas appears to be limited. This is apparent in some of the

> 'best practices' chosen from other parts of the world to be followed by Andhra Pradesh. A possible adult literacy model for the state cited is a package used in the US, something so removed from Indian requirements as to be almost laughable.

Similarly, Bandyopadhyay (2001, 900) describes the AP Vision 2020 as "document of dream – a dream dreamt by a hardheaded, hi-tech buff and down-to-earth politician, the Chief Minister of the State."

SMART governance and good governance

Inspired by the good governance, preached by the World Bank, Chandrababu Naidu employed the terms *governance/good governance/SMART governance* to assert his contrasts with his predecessors. As Mooij (2003, 10) specifies, the remarkable characteristic of the AP reform under the TDP government is the highlighting 'governance' as a metaphor for reform. While Vision 2020 dealt primarily with development, nevertheless, it was also about governance. The Vision included a chapter on "people-centered, growth-oriented governance" (Government of Andhra Pradesh 1999, 321). The Vision emphasized that the government should be made "simple, transparent, accountable and responsive and that people should have a strong voice in the governance of the State" (Government of Andhra Pradesh 1999, 3–4).

As a not conventionally charismatic regional leader, Chandrababu Naidu tried to represent himself as an able administrator, the CEO of Andhra Pradesh. This image contrasts with the stereotypical State-level politicians. Influenced by the emerging governance paradigm, Naidu criticized the regional politicians for too much politicking and too little governance. He (Naidu 2000b, 17) differentiated between ruling and governance and specified:

> The Telugu Desam is a regional party with a national outlook. There are three fundamental departures from traditional Indian politics that we are attempting within the party. The first is to recognize that the end of politics is governance, not mere ruling. It has therefore to introduce an element of professionalism.

Naidu's view on governance was profoundly influenced by the World Bank's good governance discourse (Naidu 2000a):

> My Vision 2020 programs embodies Simple, Moral, Accountable, Responsive and Transparent governance. I call it the SMART governance. As per my program, everybody – politicians, bureaucrats, and the people – have to prepare short and long-term plans, and then he or she have to work in that direction. My focus is now not on politics, but on development, the second generation of administrative and economic reforms, information technology and infrastructure projects.

Naidu did not consider good governance as an empty slogan. His government established the Centre for Good Governance. It was a think tank, focusing on governance reforms in the State. The Center aimed to support the realization of the reforms in the AP by initiating projects to assist various departments in pursuing reforms. Naidu's focus on good governance is a deliberate attempt to fade NTR's political heritage in the Party. In the 1980s, N.T. Rama Rao as a charismatic leader introduced himself as a savior of Telugu people from the domination of the corrupt and ineffective Congress and introduced several welfare schemes. In the 'welfarism' and 'populism' of NTR, he portrayed himself as a savior, giving rice to the poor and Sarees to women. According to Mooij (2003, 13), while the policy discourses during NTR's tenure can be described as 'donative' with its focus on hand-outs and welfare schemes provided by a munificent leader, Naidu introduced 'developmentalist' discourse including elements such as development, vision, accountability, transparency, delivery, performance, effectiveness, and governance/good governance. This discourse could efficiently differentiate between a populist leader who has charismatic character and a not conventionally charismatic leader who tried to introduce himself as a skilled administrator.

Naidu presented policy reforms as the necessary condition of Vision 2020 success. The first step was financial reform with several fiscal friendly measures. In the first step, his government increased the price of rice that was distributed in the food security scheme. Moreover, the partial lifting of prohibition could generate more revenues for the state. Naidu also attempted to reduce the number of government employees (Mooij 2013, 403).

The State Government set up a specific Implementation Secretariat (IS) to implement the reforms effectively. As Ramachandraiah and Patnaik (2005, 232) clarify, Naidu established the IS as an autonomous institute, and government pay scales and procedures did not restrict it. As an autonomous and professional body, it tried to recruit the best experts that available in the market, and their salaries had been met from the funds provided by the UK department for international development (DFID).

Competing for private sector investments

As Jenkins (1999) and Rudolph and Rudolph (2013) explicated, after the New Economic Policy (NEP) of the Narasimha Rao Government in 1991, Indian subnational states do not depend exclusively on the public investment by the Center; hence, States consider the private investment as a significant financial resource. After dismantling the licence-permit raj the domestic private sector not only could invest more comfortable in the States but also the liberalized Indian economy opened the gates for transnational corporations to invest in India. Since the 1990s, "the new pattern of the rivalry has emerged among the states, and they compete for domestic and foreign private investment" (see Rudolph and Rudolph 2013). Chief ministers, and their finance, and industries secretaries not only tried to convince the domestic private sector through offering them investment friendly measures, but also, they went abroad, to the U.S., Western Europe, and East and South Asian countries to attract private investors, including NRIs. The greater autonomy for the State, transformation in the State–Center relations and the rise of inter-State competition are echoed in the Chandrababu Naidu's view on India's federalism (Naidu 2000b, 16):

> In the last few years, the newborn competitive spirit in our federal polity has also contributed to this spirit of hope. State governments are now competing with each other to put progressive policies in place, to attract investment, to develop their human resources. They are racing each other to get on to the information technology bandwagon. They are looking around for ideas to bring a fresh approach to the persisting problems of illiteracy, infant mortality, unemployment, and underemployment. They are struggling to fend off the bankruptcy in their exchequers. All said and done; things are happening, not just in my state, but in others as well.

One of the most significant goals of the policy reforms in Andhra Pradesh was to create a business-friendly environment for attracting national and international companies to invest in the State. Naidu realized that he could not remain dependent on State's own income or the Central transfers. Although he tried to improve the relations between the Center and State to convince Central Government and the Planning Commission to allocate more financial resources to the State, he realized that the private sector's investments (by domestic or international companies) would enhance economic growth in the State. He comprehended the new rules of the game in which State–Center confrontation transmuted to inter-States competition.

In addition, Naidu (2000b, 6–7) was aware of the consequences of the collapse of License Raj at the Center and its impact on the political economy of India; as a result, he believed that in the post-reform era States should compete to attract private investments:

> Gone are the days when industrialists had to wait upon the government to get licenses. Today states are competing aggressively with each other to attract industries to their states. We need the jobs, so we try to offer incentives better than those offered by other states … He has to woo industry and sell his State as an attractive investment destination. He has to woo foreign investments. He has to impress upon funding agencies that he can deliver.

Naidu's government encouraged domestic and foreign IT and biotechnology industries to invest in State by numerous incentives and policy initiatives. His business-friendly policies, as well as his public relations, improved the position of Andhra Pradesh in terms of investments. In the Annual *Business Today* survey of CEP perceptions about the States as an investment destination, Andhra Pradesh had substantial progress, and its rank rocketed from twenty-second (out of 26) in 1995 to third in 1999 (quoted in Rudolph and Rudolph 2013, 330).

The number and amount of approved FDIs in India demonstrate the relative success of Andhra Pradesh. From 1991 to 2007, Andhra Pradesh attracted US$4105.73 million that comprised 5.33% of all India's approved FDIs. During the same period, historically more developed States like Maharashtra with 19.3%, Delhi with 11.71%, Tamil Nadu with 8.37%, and Karnataka with 8.28% had the best performance among India's States. Remarkably, Andhra Pradesh as an emerging State had a better performance than the West Bengal (2.71%) and Gujarat (4.33%) (Bhandari, Rahul, and Tiwari 2015, 6).

Hyderabad as the hub for IT-led development

Naidu realized the potentials of information technology (IT) for development in the State. As Chandrababu Naidu clarified, one of the most important reasons that he gave priority to IT industry was the AP's advantage in human resources. Naidu (2000b, 7) also noted 23% of India's IT engineers were from Andhra Pradesh. Moreover, he believed enthusiastically in the role of IT in the development of societies in the twenty-first century. Naidu (2000a) was confident that IT could enhance public administration in the State at different levels and bring accountability, transparency, and more effectiveness. Naidu understood IT as a useful tool in three areas: job generation, poverty eradication and wealth generation As Naidu (1998) states,

> I have emphasized InfoTech because it is the fastest-growing industry in the world. Because of its software talent, India has the potential to capture the global market. So, why should not I capitalize on this opportunity? Andhra Pradesh has also employed InfoTech for better governance, which will bring in major changes in the lives of the common people. We are trying to provide single-network services in areas like transport, employment, and public utilities. These value-added services will be available across the state in a year from now.

Naidu considered the urban centers as the bases for his development strategy. Although most of AP's population live in rural areas, Naidu realized the need for the development of the main urban centers to attract investment into IT industries. Naidu (2004b) clarifies his perception of development and the role of major urban cities:

> I am very clear about my perception of development. If you want to develop a state, you have to make its main cities a showpiece. Hyderabad is the capital of Andhra Pradesh. Naturally, when a foreign investor is coming, if I ask them to go to Warangal, Tirupati or Vijayawada, they may not go. So for the key sectors like information technology, biotechnology, healthcare and various outsourcing services, we had to develop Hyderabad. Then from Hyderabad, we were taking and spreading development to other areas of Andhra Pradesh. We developed Hyderabad and the neighboring areas in districts like Ranga Reddy, Medak and Nalgonda also got automatic progress.

Naidu competed with the other States to attract more investments for development. The famous slogan "Bye-Bye Bangalore, Hello Hyderabad"[4] signifies a severe rivalry between AP and Karnataka. In 1995, the State Government initiated and facilitated the construction of HITEC City[5] as a public–private joint project located 15 kilometers from the center of Hyderabad.

The TDP government invested in Hyderabad infrastructures like roads, airport and electricity network. Moreover, the State Government improved the business environment by the public administration reforms and implementation of several incentives for the investors. To Encourage the national and international IT companies for investing in the State, Naidu's government released the 1999 ICT policy, smoothing and facilitating investment in IT sector in AP. Naidu's government also released a new IT policy for 2002–2005 to improve the previous policy. The State Government granted the substantial incentives to the IT companies such as exemption from inspections under most labor legislation, exemption from statutory power cuts,[6] and permission for three-shift operations. Moreover, the IT companies may also apply for concessional power tariff, reimbursement of stamp duty, and exemption from zoning regulations. Furthermore, the State Government considered the special provisions for extra-large projects, with an investment of Rs 50 crores and above, in which "a special land-pricing scheme will be applicable in respect of land allotted within the HITEC City layout" (see Government of Andhra Pradesh 2002, 3). Consequently, HITEC City has succeeded in attracting domestic and international investments. Most of the major IT companies such as Microsoft, IBM, Dell, and Oracle established their units in 'Cyberabad.' Also, large corporations such as General Electronic, HSBC, Motorola, Wipro, Infosys, Ericson, Toshiba, and Tata Teleservice invested in the State. One of the most significant successes of Naidu was the establishment of Microsoft's first software development center outside of United States in Hyderabad. Chandrababu Naidu convinced Bill Gates to visit Hyderabad and pledge investment in the State; therefore, the investment materialized on 28 February 1999 in HITEC City; therefore, the second largest Microsoft center after its main headquarters were built in Hyderabad. Experiencing a cumulative annual growth rate of 130%, Andhra Pradesh's total IT export rocketed from Rs 2 million in 1992 to Rs 82,700 million in the 2004–2005 financial year (Kapoor and Ahluwalia 2015, 55).

However, Naidu's interest in IT did not remain limited to the development of HITEC City and flow of FDI. Naidu considered IT to be a useful tool to enhance the administrative reforms within the State. Therefore, the Naidu government introduced several e-governance initiatives such as the Computer Aided Administration of Registration Department (CARD), enabling the electronic registration of documents. The CARD accelerated the land registration process in the State via complete computerization of registration of land transactions and tenancy agreements (Mooij 2013). The second major e-governance initiative was 'e-seva centers,' one-stop counters, enabling citizens to pay their electricity, water, and telephone bills, pay property and sale taxes, get birth and death certificates, register and transfer the vehicles, and other similar services. Furthermore, the AP government established e-Procurement for the online tender process. Thirty-two government departments participated in the process in the 2004–2005 financial year. As Kapoor and Ahluwalia (2015, 55) report, in this year the total volume of the transaction was Rs 359 million and the cost of tenders was Rs 243,380 million.

Y.S. Reddy and the rise of new charismatic populism

The Congress government at the Center had introduced the economic reforms in 1991, and the AP Congress government had followed it in the early 1990s; however, the Congress as the main opposition party opposed most of Naidu's reforms in the State between 1995 and 2004. With an alliance with the leftist parties, the Congress launched attacks against the TDP government's initiatives and policies. The Congress under the leadership of Y.S. Rajasekhara Reddy (YSR) opposed the AP Electricity Reform bill and later fought against the hike in electricity tariff. Y.S. Rajasekhara Reddy and the Congress accused Naidu of being closer to the World Bank and the multinational companies than to the rural people in AP.

In May 2003, YSR launched a 1500-kilometer walking campaign and visited several villages. YSR walked and visited several villages while he dressed as a farmer. The *Pada yatra* (foot march) attracted media attention. The AP's rural areas had been affected by three years drought; therefore, the focus of YSR was water scarcity, unemployment, and poverty. The drought and decrease in the subsidies gave YSR opportunities to repeat the Congress's criticisms about Naidu's development priorities and his party's plans for an agricultural revival. He promised free electricity for farmers and full-scale development of irrigation (Price and Srinvas 2014, 220).

YSR accused the TDP government of leading the State into the World Bank's debt trap. Using a semi-leftist tone, YSR described Chandrababu Naidu, an agent of Western donors and financial organizations. He also accused the TDP government of massive corruption. Criticizing privatization of public sector companies, YSR claimed that several public-sector industries were sold out to private parties below their real value. He also criticized the IT-oriented and service-centered development strategy of Naidu, concentrated in Hyderabad (Suri 2005, 163).

During his electoral campaigns, YSR promised free electricity to farmers, subsidies for crop loans, funds for irrigation projects, relief for families of farmers where someone committed suicide, and loans to women self-help groups at 3% interest per annum. YSR also promised2.5 lakh jobs for the youth. Based on Naidu's bureaucratic reforms, the size of bureaucracy should be decreased. Therefore, the Naidu government imposed several limitations on recruitment in government services. Contrarily, YSR pledged to lift the ban. Moreover, he promised to enhance the old age pensions (Mukherji 2014, 163, Suri 2004a, 5495). While YSR displayed a new image of a populist leader in the State, Naidu was reluctant to implement even targeted welfare measures in 2004 election. He believed that his economic performance and the SMART governance help the TDP to be reelected again.

The next significant determining factor in this election was the emergence of 'Telangana Rashtra Samiti' (TRS), which entered the election with a single-point plan of achieving a separate state for the Telangana region. Initially, the TRS was not considered a significant actor in AP politics; nevertheless, TRS entered electoral alliances with the Congress in 2004; as a result, the TRS increased its influence and emerged as a new political actor in AP. The growing popularity of TRS in Telangana region had a clear effect on the TDP's support basis.

One of the most critical factors that contributed to the victory of the Congress and the TRS alliance was the Congress's stance toward a separate Telangana state. The Congress in the election manifesto for 2004 elections asserted:

> The Congress Party recognizes the growing emotions and aspirations of the people in the Telangana region … while respecting the report of the States Reorganization Commission, the Congress Party notes that there are many valid reasons for the formation of separate states in Vidarbha and Telangana … However, the reorganization of existing States raises a large number of issues. The Congress Party feels that the whole matter could be best addressed by another States Reorganization Commission to look into all the issues involved.
>
> (Quoted in Srikrishna et al. 2010, 51)

In contrast to the alliance of Congress and TRS, emphasizing on populism and regionalism, the TDP's entire electoral campaign rotated around Naidu's economic performance. Naidu openly declared that the 2004 election was "a referendum on his nine-year rule" (Srinivasulu 2004, 12). After an unsuccessful assassination attempt by Naxalites on Naidu, the TDP highlighted order and development versus violence. For that reason, the TDP portrayed itself as a "party for development"; on the contrary, the Congress and the TRS were portrayed as the parties who are against development, and their policies cause anarchy. Naidu was sure that the constituents reward his economic reforms again. Moreover, Naidu underrated the TRS and their alliance with the Congress and said:

> They will simply fade away. Like the Congress party, they lack credibility. They make outlandish promises. They promise free power, which they can probably provide for a year. They are cheating the people with these promises. We do not make such promises because at the end of the day we are honest and want to work honestly for the development of the state.
>
> (Naidu 2004a)

Despite Naidu's prediction, the constituents, especially in the rural areas, did not reward the TDP's reforms and Naidu only secured 47 seats in the Assembly. Securing 185 seats out of 290, the Congress could enter again in its citadel in 2004. Suri (2013, 176) attributes the defeat of the TDP in 2004 election to the alienation of party from weaker sections and farmers. Naidu's government was accused of pursuing the policies, which only promote the interests of businesspersons and urban middle class.

As Balasubramanyam and Balasubramanyam (2012, 49) indicate, because of increasing number of landowners that immigrated to cities, the number of tenants or landless laborers increased during the TDP rule. These new tenants had not sufficient cash flows to manage their farms and their debts. Moreover, the TDP government hiked the electricity price and removed the subsidies that are crucial for the agriculture sector. Although power subsidies imposed Rs 10 billion to State's treasury and a decrease in power subsidies provide more financial resources for developmental investments, the TDP became unpopular among rural poor, depending on the rice and power subsidies.

Whereas Naidu tried to pursue growth-enhancing policies in IT sector as well as targeted welfare schemes in favor of selected social groups, YSR, and the Congress effectively mobilized rural masses as well as backward castes against Naidu with the promise of free electricity. According to Mukherji (2014, 164) majority of the poor voters and agricultural workers, scheduled caste (SC) groups, and backward castes voted for the Congress Party and its allies.

Naidu's strategic choice in the vertical game to be part of the NDA had a direct effect on the horizontal game. Muslims did not reward the TDP in the 2004 election, and the TDP lost substantial vote share among the Muslims. While Muslim in the 1994 election voted in favor of the TDP, Naidu's partnership with BJP, coincided with violent events in Gujarat in February 2002, reduced the popularity of the TDP among AP Muslims. The upper castes, Kammas, and emerging middle class voted for a TDP–BJP alliance; nevertheless, Naidu and the TDP could not secure enough seats; as a result, they became the main opposition party.

Y.S. Reddy and the reforms

Most observers in the media and academia described the results of the 2004 election in AP as a manifestation of public disenchantment with Naidu's focus on the development of urban areas and the IT industry. Moreover, the populist slogans of the Congress, its anti-World Bank rhetoric, and YSR's promises to introduce several welfare schemes for rural people mobilized voters to support the Congress.

Before the 2004 election, in the same vein, as NTR did in 1994, the Congress launched a powerful attack on economic reforms. Although the Congress won the 1989 election, it could not revive its golden age before the 1983 election in AP. Finally, by the emergence of YSR as a charismatic leader, the Congress gained a much-needed pro-poor, pro-women, pro-peasant image, something the TDP enjoyed during NTR's era. Hence, the big question mark for the business community and investors was the Congress's real stance toward the reforms. With his rural-oriented policies and anti-globalization tone during the campaign, would YSR undo the economic reforms undertaken by Naidu and focus exclusively on populist welfare schemes?

Although Y.S. Reddy followed NTR's electoral campaign methods and promised to revive and initiate several populist welfare measures in AP, his tenure did not look like NTR's era. In comparison to NTR, YSR had an entirely dissimilar position in the vertical and horizontal games. NTR confronted the Congress at the Center and rejected Rajiv Gandhi's policies in the mid-1980s; however, YSR as a member of Congress cooperated with the Center and Manmohan Sing's economic policies. Whereas NTR pursued the populist welfare measure to preserve the massive support to his rule and confrontation with the Center, YSR's populism was an electoral tactic to attract votes and to defeat Naidu after nine years rule. As a result, not only were his welfare measures not designed to use as a tool to preserve the State's political support in the vertical confrontation, but also were supported by the Center to sustain Congress's rule in the State. Moreover, YSR as a Congress leader cooperated with the reform-oriented UPA government at the Center. In the early 1990s, the Congress in the State followed the Center and implemented the first generation of economic reforms, recommended by P.V. Narasimha Rao, the prime minister, and Manmohan Singh, the finance minister. In the post-2004 election political arrangement, the UPA government declared its commitment to economic reforms and growth-enhancing policies again.

Therefore, while YSR's government implemented several welfare measures to keep the political support of rural people and the poor in the horizontal game with the backing of the Center, he engaged actively in the implementation of the economic reforms, as the Center aimed. YSR's strategic choice includes two elements:

First, cooperation with the Center and implementation of economic reforms as the Center wanted. The cooperation in the vertical game enables YSR to get financial resources and political support from the Center. Second, YSR did not publicize the reforms at State level: hence, he just highlighted his welfare schemes. YSR had 'a Janus–faced' economic policy. The first face that was propagated by his government included several welfare schemes and initiatives. The second face was economic reform and neo-liberal policies, introduced and implemented by stealth.

While YSR in his speeches during his campaign had criticized Naidu's focus on IT sector and urban development, after the election, he adopted a more pragmatist approach toward it. Six months after the 2004 election, when a journalist asked YSR about his idea of attracting more foreign investment and IT companies to Hyderabad, YSR responded,

> That is also my agenda, very much. There is a saying in Telugu: the king's second wife is good does not mean that the elder wife is bad. When I say the focus is on agriculture and irrigation, it does not mean that I do not like to develop Hyderabad.
>
> (Reddy 2004)

As Mooij (2013, 412–413) observed, the Congress government in AP continued to pursue the reform agenda, which had been executed by the TDP. For Instance,

YSR's government promoted Special Economic Zones (SEZs), with a particular focus on the IT and pharmaceutical sectors. Despite expressing fundamental criticism about the position of IT in Naidu's views on development during the electoral competitions, YSR tried to provide a more investor-friendly environment in the State to invest and work in the field of IT. Following the TDP government's IT policy for 2002–2005, the new Congress government issued *Information & Communications Technology (ICT) Policy of the Government of Andhra Pradesh – ICT Policy 2005–2010* one year after the election. In the new policy, the AP government offered more incentives to private investors. In the new policy (Government of Andhra Pradesh 2005), not only did the Congress government continue previous incentives, but also it permitted three shift operations with women working in the night for IT/ITES units. Moreover, the 2005–2010 policy declared "IT/ITES units/companies and non-hazardous hardware manufacturing industry consisting of IT & Electronics as essential service."

According to Kapoor and Ahluwalia (2015, 26), YSR's policies surprised the business community, industrialists, and private investors. He not only left all of Naidu's economic reforms intact but also improved the pace of execution of the projects. Although in his public statements, YSR emphasized on his policies in favor of rural development and peasants, his policies supported industrialists, real estate developers, private sector investors, and contractors (Mooij 2013). YSR continued the growth-friendly policies and tried to transform Andhra Pradesh to an investor-friendly state by deregulation and institutional reforms. The outcome of these efforts and policy orientation is reflected in the result of a survey of 'Economic Freedom of States in India' (Bhandari and Aiyar 2011) that clarifies, between 2005 and 2009, Andhra Pradesh and Gujarat were the two States that showed the most substantial improvements in terms of economic freedom. According to the study of Bhandari and Aiyar (2011), in overall State rankings, Andhra Pradesh moved up from the seventh rank in 2005 to the third position in 2009.

According to Kapoor and Ahluwalia (2015, 56), the export turnover of Andhra Pradesh increased from Rs 82,700 million in 2004 to 325,090 million in 2009. Remarkably, Andhra Pradesh's share of IT/ITES[7] export turnover in India went up from 8.64% in 2004 to 15% in 2009. Moreover, the intensives in IT sector led to a sharp increase in the number of IT companies, which created related jobs. The total number of IT/ITES companies increased from 883 to 1206, and the number of people directly employed in IT/ITES increased from 85,945 in 2004 to 251,786 in 2009.

The reemergence of the Telangana movement

The demand for a separate Telangana state had not appeared in the mainstream political discourse of Andhra Pradesh for more than three decades. Through oppression as well as political accommodation, the Center could sustain the territorial integrity of AP in the1970s. Furthermore, the rise of Telugu subnational identity weakened the Telangana movement. In the 1960s and 1970s, M. Chenna

Reddy, a Congress leader, led the first Telangana movement and formed 'Telangana Praja Samiti' (TPS). Remarkably, in 2001, K. Chandrasekhar Rao (KCR) a rebellious non-Reddy TDP leader led the second movement and formed 'Telangana Rashtra Samiti' (TRS). This party had a single point agenda and demanded separate statehood for the Telangana region:

> I have a one-point program and a single goal – achieving statehood for Telangana ... No force on earth can stop us from achieving a separate Telangana state.
>
> (Rao 2001)

As discussed, the elite strategies at the Center resolved the political insatiability and protests, caused by the first Telangana movement. Responding to the Telangana movement in the late 1960s and 1970s, the Congress government under Indira Gandhi implemented strategies of law and order management, power sharing, and constitutional reforms. Therefore, M. Chenna Reddy not only was appointed as governor of another State, and chief minister of Andhra Pradesh, but also some safeguards for Telangana in the form of the Thirty-Third Amendment of the Constitution were enacted in 1973.

Nevertheless, those measures could not appease KCR. First, he does not belong to Reddy caste that had considerable political power both in the Congress and Telangana region. KCR belongs to the Velma caste, another dominant agricultural caste. Although he started his political life with the youth Congress Party in Medak district, he nevertheless joined the TDP, the first non-Reddy political platform in AP in 1983. As Rothermund (2013, 86) notes, in the late 1980s, K. Chandrasekhar Rao emerged as a regional elite in Telangana region and became a key member of the TDP. He served as a minister in the TDP government and deputy speaker of the assembly. In September 2001, when the TDP officially refused to support a separate Telangana state, KCR resigned from his post and formed his new party. KCR claims that his decision to leave the TDP and the formation of TRS was the result of Naidu's approach toward Telangana in his development vision:

> Since Chandrababu Naidu became the Chief Minister, I have been impressing upon him to give a fair deal to Telangana and not to ignore the interests of its people any longer. When the Vision 2020 document for Andhra Pradesh was drafted by McKinsey & Company, I pointed out to Chandrababu that there was no reference to the development of Telangana as well as Dalits, Harijans, Backward Classes and minorities in the document. I asked him how the state would achieve its goal without the welfare of these sections and the development of Telangana.
>
> (Rao 2001)

Initially, the TRS supported NDA and had an anti-Congress stance; nevertheless, L.K. Advani, the Home Minister at the Center, turned down a demand to create a separate Telangana. Consequently, the TRS became closer to the Congress that promised a separate State of Telangana in the 2004 election. KCR contested in a by-election in a constituency in the Telangana region and returned to the Assembly. In addition, the TRS had a successful performance in the Panchayat Raj elections held in 2001 (Narisetti 2002, 205). Unlike the TDP's Telugu sub-nationalism that assumed all Telugu speakers as a whole and tried to construct the Telugu identity based on the language, the TRS, and its regionalism rejected the main elements of the TDP ideology and emphasized the regional identity, constructed based on the Andhra and Telangana distinction and confrontation. The leaders of a new wave of the Telangana movement believed that the leaders of non-Telangana regions violated 'the gentleman agreement'; therefore, the primary root of backwardness in Telangana is domination of other regions. The leaders of the Telangana movement argued that after independence, especially after the reforms, their region has been relatively deprived and has not benefited from the fruits of development. For example, M. Kodandaram (2007, 93) the chairperson of the all-party Telangana Political Joint Action Committee (T-JAC), describes the relationships between Andhra region and Telangana as colonial relations in which Telangana resources have exploited by other regions:

> Telangana has thus been converted into an internal colony as a result of the economic development process pursued by successive governments. Its resources have been diverted and utilized for the development of other regions. The movement for separate statehood seeks to articulate the demand for a fair share in the resources. It is an outcome of injustice meted out to the region by the successive governments in Andhra Pradesh. Separation is seen as the only answer to these grievances.

Accordingly, the rise of the second wave of Telangana movement can be elucidated by Huntington's theory that has been theorized in influential *Political Order in Changing Societies* (1968). In the same way, Gurr's notion of relative deprivation (1970) clarifies precisely why discontent and deprivation are felt most intensely in areas and among people experiencing rapid change such as rapid economic growth. Combining Huntington and Gurr's model "rapid economic development in societies with inadequate institutional infrastructure can lead to violence, unrest, and loss of legitimacy" (Mitra 1992, 211). Accordingly, there is a linkage between economic development, relative deprivation and the rise of ethnic identity, protest, and political mobilization, and loss of legitimacy.

Based on the 'pluralization model,' although Hyderabad is the main destination of foreign investments and developmental activities located in the heart of Telangana, the Telangana leaders claim that the majority of rural areas in the Telangana region remained undeveloped. The rapid economic growth especially in Hyderabad city, major foreign and domestic investments in the city, and extreme contrast between 'HITECH City' and neighboring rural areas can be seen as the leading causes of relative deprivation emerged among Telangana local elites and masses. After around one decade of economic reforms and the liberalization of the economy in AP, the old cleavage between Telangana and Andhra reappeared in the form of second Telangana movement.

As Srikanth (2013, 40) delineates, ideologues of the second Telangana agitation justify it as a struggle against "domination, exploitation, discrimination, deception, and humiliation." Political leaders of the Telangana movement claim that since the formation of united Andhra Pradesh, leaders of the State, as well as Center, neglected and discriminated against Telangana. Telangana agitation leaders perceived the TDP's government reform as the new tool of domination and discrimination of Andhra and Rayalaseema. For instance, KCR criticizes Naidu's reform-oriented policies and claims that Naidu's reforms harmed Telangana:

> Chandrababu has done more harm to Telangana than any other chief minister. He has given a quiet burial to the six-point formula. The power tariff hike has broken the backbone of the farmers. They are unable to sell their produce at minimum support prices now. Weavers are in distress. The farmers and weavers are committing suicide. All big public- and private-sector industries are closed, affecting thousands of workers. There is a ban on recruitment in government services.
>
> (Rao 2001)

While politicians such as KCR and scholars like Kodandaram (2007) and Srikanth (2013) assert that there is considerable data, validating these claims, the findings of the 'Committee for Consultations on the Situation in Andhra Pradesh' (Srikrishna et al. 2010, 117) suggest although at first glance, "some or all such allegations appear true, when rate of change, growth rate and shares in the state economy is evaluated, nothing unusual emerges." The findings of the Sri Krishna Committee, submitted to the Government of India, reject any meaningful discrimination or unusual negative economic trend in Telangana:

> Telangana excluding Hyderabad currently has a share of 36% in state population and 41% in state land mass. Any development parameter that is consistent with these shares can be considered on par or at parity with the population/share of land mass. Indeed, one finds that at a reference point in the past, such as the census 1961 or 1956 or 1974 since when factual data are available, the shares for Telangana were far too low. In recent years, however, the shares of Telangana for many common development parameters are in league with the share of population/area, often being higher.
>
> (Srikrishna et al. 2010, 117)

The sudden death of the Y.S. Reddy in a helicopter accident only a few months after his victory in the 2009 election was a new turning point in the State politics. Not only did the Congress lost its charismatic leader who could mobilize rural masses in all regions, but also the TRS, annoyed by the Congress delays in forming the new State, intensified the agitation to form a separate Telangana state. After the vacuum of leadership in the Congress, the party witnessed factionalism and rivalries among the politicians from Telangana region and Andhra or Rayalaseema regions. Although the high command in Delhi appointed Konijeti Rosaiah as the new chief minister of state, he could not sustain the orderly rule in the State. Several *bandh*, *rail rook*, and protests interrupted daily life. In this phase, although the State received a higher share from the Center for its developmental expenditure, political instability and the emergence of the sub-regional movement disrupted business climate in the State.

Appointment of another dominant Reddy, Kiran Kumar Reddy, as the successor of Rosaiah could not help the Congress to maintain the orderly rule as well as its power in the State. In February 2011 and September 2011, the TRS with cooperation with T-JAC crippled the State Government with a noncooperation movement and *Sakala Janula Samme* (All people's strike). As a result, not only did the State lost a considerable amount of its revenues, but also faced a massive power cut that affected the IT sector. The massive resignation of Telangana MLAs, MPs, and ministers was the other leverage to press the Center to create a new spate State of Telangana.

The 2012 by-elections for Telangana Assembly seats showed the rising power of TRS, winning four out of five seats. In addition, the rebellious son of Y.S. Reddy with his YSRCP emerged as the new threat to the Congress in Andhra region.

Therefore, just few months before the 2014 election, the UPA government at the Center took the practical steps to form a separate State of Telangana. The result of the late decision on Telangana was echoed in the 2014 election results. Not only unhappy Andhra constituents punished the Congress by voting in favor of the TDP, but also the Telangana constituents gave all credits for the creation of Telangana state to the TRS, not the Congress. The result of the 2014 election displayed how Congress's success in AP after 2005 was dependent on the charismatic leadership of Y.S. Reddy.

Conclusion

After the 'Palace Coup' in 1995, Naidu was supported neither by a strong Reddy caste, possessing a considerable influence on rural masses, nor did he have the charisma of NTR, which could provoke the masses against the Delhi government. In addition, despite the economic power of the Kamma caste, they constitute around 3% of Andhra population, which was not sufficient for winning the election. As a result, Naidu needed to find other plans to run his campaign. In the vertical game, the strategic choice of the TDP leaders was to join NDA, and a have closer relations with the BJP. This choice facilitated the consolidation of non-Congress votes in the State. Moreover, the allocation of financial resources to the State increased, and Naidu had more extensive room to maneuver. Furthermore, effective implementation of the reforms attracted foreign investors and international financial institutions, which enhanced investment and growth. In the horizontal interactions, grassroots institutions like *Janmabhoomi* created initially for development at the local level or the Self Help Groups (SHGs), which had been formed for the empowerment of poor women, played a significant role in activating the grassroots network for the TDP. Also, economic benefits of growth, as well as targeted populist measures, attracted the vote of emerging new middle classes, women and the OBCs to the TDP. Because of reelection as a reward in the horizontal games, Chandrababu Naidu became the longest-serving chief minister of the State. Even during the Reddy Raj era, there is no chief minister, who can serve as the chief minister for more than eight years.[8] Naidu served as the chief minister of Andhra Pradesh for eight years and eight months.

Nevertheless, the emergence of a new form of welfare populism under the electoral campaign of YSR terminated the era of the CEO of Andhra Pradesh. Unhappy rural masses dissatisfied with urban-centered policies of the TDP government voted for the Congress to restore welfare measures in the State based on direct redistribution and subsidies. While public opinion predicted a U-turn in the developmental policies of AP, YSR pursued a Janus-faced policy in the State. Although YSR, as a member of the Congress and loyal politician to the 'high command' in Delhi, tried to implement the economic policies, stressed by Manmohan Singh's government, YSR implemented several welfare schemes to attain rewards in the horizontal game in the form of reelection. The UPA government at the Center also allocated more resources to AP for social spending. The financial reforms and accelerated growth under Naidu helped the new AP government to generate larger revenues, which made welfare schemes and social spending more feasible. Interestingly, conceptualization and implementation of 'SMART Governance,' administrative reforms and experiences such as SHGs in Andhra Pradesh during the TDP government played a significant role in successful implementation of national schemes like Mahatma Gandhi Nation Rural Employment Scheme (MNREGS) in the State during YSR tenure.

Compared to Naidu, YSR had a different political position. Naidu, as a successor to a charismatic leader, needed to publicize his reforms to attain rewards in the horizontal game. Naidu was dependent on international acclaim and success. In contrast, YSR was a State-level politician, supported by the Center. Therefore, he could get political support by implementing several welfare measures and subsidies. In sum, two factors contributed to sustaining these Janus-faced policies without interruption: the political survival of YSR which was dependent on political support in the State in horizontal interactions and his loyalty to 'high command' in Delhi in the vertical interactions.

Notes

1 The BJP emerged as the single largest party in parliament in the 1996 general election; however, it did not have a sufficient majority. Although Vajpayee was sworn in as the 10th Prime Minister of India, the BJP failed to secure enough support from other parties to obtain a majority; therefore, he resigned after 13 days.

2 As Torfing (2010, 565) elaborated, the Trilateral Commission played an important role in the rise of public sector reforms in the mid-1970s. The Trilateral Commission mainly dealt with 'the overload of government' and tried to address this problem. The commission described the overload of the government as the result of limited capacities of public

bureaucracies toward the increasing expectations of citizens. Furthermore, the commission construed 'the ungovernability of society' as the consequence of the 'decline of public-spirited values.' Neo-liberalism responded to the problem of overload government by suggesting some reforms in the public sector (see Kjær 2004, 20–25; Rhodes 2012, 34–35). Reforms like the privatization of public enterprises, contracting out of public services, and deregulation were the translation of neo-liberal recommendation in the Western societies. The New Public Management (NPM) reforms aimed at proliferation of the role of market and corporate management techniques in the public sector (Bevir 2009, 9). Thatcher's government introduced NPM for the first time in Britain in the 1980s. Subsequently, Reagan government implemented it in the US and countries like Australia and New Zealand followed it. According to Bevir (2011, 8), these reforms led to fragmentation of the traditional ways of service delivery, the spread of new managerial practices, and the creation of quasi market and hybrid organizations. These neo-liberal reforms aimed to redefine the role and position of state and advocated the idea of 'rolling state back' (see Suleiman 2005). Criticizing the traditional model of the public sector, NPM targeted the traditional model bureaucracy and tried to remove the obstacles to effective public service delivery by private–public partnership and introducing private sector management into the public sector (Kjær 2004, 25).

3 For example, the growth engines in the Vision 2020 for the agriculture sector were rice, dairy, poultry, horticulture, fisheries, and agro-industry. In the industry sector, the vision considered infrastructure, construction, garments, leather products, and other export-oriented industries, mining, pharmaceuticals and small-scale industries as the engines. Finally, the vision introduced information technology, knowledge-based services, tourism, logistics, small-scale services, healthcare and education as the growth engine in service sector.

4 After the bifurcation of Andhra Pradesh in 2014, it was supposed that Hyderabad would become the capital city of Andhra Pradesh and Telangana for ten years. Then, Hyderabad will be exclusively the capital of Telangana; as a result, Andhra Pradesh must find or build another capital city. Consequently, the TDP government in Andhra Pradesh introduced Amaravati in the Guntur region at the southern banks of the River Krishna as the place for construction of State's new capital. The master plan of the new city was prepared by Singaporean companies. Naidu aims to have Amaravati as the new hub of India's IT industry.

5 The *Hyderabad Information Technology and Engineering Consultancy City*, abbreviated as HITEC City, is a major high-tech business district in Hyderabad, developed mostly under the TDP regime.

6 According to ICT Policy 2002–2005 (Government of Andhra Pradesh 2002),

> IT units are exempt from inspections under the following Acts and the Rules framed there under, barring inspections arising out of specific complaints. The IT units are permitted to file self-certificates, in the prescribed formats.
>
> - The Factories Act 1948
> - The Maternity Benefit Act 1961
> - The AP Shops & Establishments Act 1988
> - The Contract Labor (Regulation & Abolition) Act 1970
> - The Payment of Wages Act 1936
> - The Minimum Wages Act 1948
> - The Employment Exchanges (Compulsory Notification of Vacancies) Act 1959.

7 Information Technology Enabled Services.

8 The longest Congress government in AP belongs to Kasu Brahmananda Reddy who served as chief minister between 21 February 1964 and 30 September 1971.

6 Elite agency and development in Bihar (I)

Confrontation and populism in the era of '*Gharibon Ka Masiha*'

Introduction

The State of Bihar is a notable case for political economy scholars who want to investigate the political roots of development and underdevelopment at the sub-national level. By looking at different economic indicators, Bihar has been one of the poorest States. Not only in terms of per capita NSDP Bihar has been one of the weakest among India's large States, but also indicators such as the human development index imply a gap between India's average and Bihar.

Unlike other less-developed States such as Andhra Pradesh that have achieved a higher level of development and poverty reduction after liberalization, Bihar did not prompt and implement the policies that could enhance development until 2005. Throughout the 1990s, and the first half of the 2000s, not only did Bihar's economy suffer from overall stagnation, but also Bihar was famous for its caste politics and populist economic policies.

The rise of Lalu[1] Prasad Yadav, a popular politician who represents "new type of low-caste social base of mass politics" (Rothermund 2008, 22), ended the continuous power of the Congress Party in the Bihar in the first years of the 1990s. Although he opposed the Congress initially, he became the chief opponent of the NDA government. As a populist leader, he implemented several populist schemes and resisted the reform policies, advocated by the Center.

After the 2005 Assembly election, Nitish Kumar, his successor, and his rival, was elected as the chief minister of Bihar (2005–now), and he adopted entirely opposing policies and implemented the pro-liberalization reforms in the State. While he was a left-wing political elite in the State, he advocated some liberal economic reforms in the State. Influenced by neo-liberal principles of good governance, he started to fight against corruption and political violence in Bihar. Moreover, Nitish Kumar introduced privatization, liberalization, and deregulation by stealth to improve the business environment, attract more central transfers and private sector investments. His policies played a significant role in the considerable economic growth of the State after 2005.

The primary aim of this chapter and the next one is to explore the political roots of the policy shift in Bihar, which transformed Bihar from 'Jungle Raj,' to a fast-growing State after 2005.

Table 6.1 Bihar factsheet

Name	*Bihar*
Capital city	Patna
Established	1912 as Bihar and Orissa Province 1936 as Bihar 2000 Jharkhand region was recognized as a separate State
Population	1991: 64,531,000 2001: 82,998,509 2011: 103,804,637
Rank	Third (2011)
Total area	94, 163 km^2
Rank	Twelfth (2011)
Districts	38 total
Religions	Hinduism: 82.69% Islam: 16.87%, other: less than 1% (2011)
Official languages	Telugu and Urdu
Urbanization	1981: 12.47% 1991: 10.4% 2001: 10.46% 2011: 11.30%
Literacy Rate	1981: 26.2% 1991: 38.5% 2001: 47.5% 2011: 63.82%
HDI rank	21st (2011)

Sources: Census of India (2011), Paul and Sridhar (2015), drawn by the author.

These chapters focus on the shifts in the strategic choice of regional leaders in an underdeveloped State and want to answer this question: Why did the ruling elites in Bihar, especially in RJD resist the reform policies and economic liberalization in the 1990s and early 2000s? Moreover, despite a long historical background of political and economic populism, why did the new leaders in Bihar decide to adopt the economic reforms, accelerating economic development after 2005? Also, what was the political outcome of these shifts?

State profile

Bihar is a significant State in India and located in the eastern part of India. The capital city of the State is Patna. If Bihar were a nation-state, it would have the 14th largest population in the world. However, in terms of annual per capita income, it would be one of the poorest in the world.

Under the British Raj, Bihar was a part the Bengal Presidency until 1911. More than one century ago, the province of Bihar and Orissa was created as a separate province. However, contemporary Bihar is different from what had been carved out from the Bengal Presidency. Orissa became a separate entity with its own capital in 1935.

After independence, Bihar kept its territory until 2000. The borders of Bihar have today been redesigned based on the Bihar Reorganization Act of 2000 that separated Jharkhand from Bihar. The current book is aware of the implications of this separation for the analysis of economic development in the State. Hence, economic data should be considered and used carefully.

As Alakh (1995) asserts, Bihar was viewed as a well-administered, and peaceful State in the first decades after independence. However, Bihar turned into an unstable and poor State, identified with caste and communal riots, factionalism, economic and social economic backwardness, violence, political instability, failure in public service delivery, corruption, and criminality. Consequently, Bihar became an excellent case for cross-State studies, looking at the crisis of governability and governance (see Kohli 1990; Mitra 2006).

Geography

Bihar is a significant historical and cultural part of India and located in the east of the country. Bihar is a landlocked State, bounded by Uttar Pradesh to its west, Nepal to the north, West Bengal to the east and by Jharkhand to the south. Bihar can access the sea through the port of Kolkata. Bihar is the 12th largest State in terms of territorial size with an area of 94,163 km^2.

The climate of Bihar may be described as subtropical with hot summers and cold winters. Rivers are the vital elements in the life and agriculture in the State. Bihar is located on a fertile plain, drained by the famous Ganga River. Nevertheless, devastating floods in the State are also the result of its geographical location.

Bihar is divided into nine divisions and 38 districts. Patna is the capital, and it is the largest city in the State the second largest city in Eastern India after Kolkata.

Before the separation of Jharkhand,[2] there were three distinct regions in Bihar, differing widely in resources and socioeconomic structures. The Northern region of Bihar with a high population density is one of the poorest in India. With a low level of industrialization and urbanization and infrastructural backwardness, North Bihar is one of the least developed regions in the country (Roy 1994, 223).

Population and demography

According to the 2011 Census, the total population of Bihar was 10,380,463. Bihar is the third largest State in terms of population in the country. Noticeably, until the 1991 Census, the State of Bihar was the second most populous state in the country; however, after bifurcation of the State of Bihar and formation of the new State of Jharkhand, the rank of Bihar among India's States has fallen to third.

The population of Bihar as per the 2001 Census was 82,998,509 and was 64,531,000 as per the 1991 Census. While the State's population contributed

8.57% of whole of India's population in 2011, it contributed 8.07% as per the 2001 Census. The official languages of the State are Hindi and Urdu.

Languages spoken by the majority of people are Hindi followed by Bengali and Bihari languages. The literacy rate in Bihar increased from 37.5% in 1991 to 61.8% in 2011, but it is still lower than the all-India figure of 74.04%.

As the Census of India (2011) elaborates, there is a substantial gap in the literacy rate between males and female, rural and urban people, tribal and non-tribal population, and socially backward castes and the upper castes. With 11.29% of the population living in urban areas in 2011, the level of urbanization in Bihar is lower than the national average (31.16%).

According to the Census of India (2011), the Hindus, including the scheduled castes (SCs) and scheduled tribes (ST), constitute 82.69% of the total population. Muslims are ranked second with 16.87%, of the State population. Christians constitute about 0.12% in the State.

Economy

At the initial stages of economic liberalization, as the Reserve Bank of India reports (2006), Bihar was the most impoverished State in India with a per capita income of Rs 3036 in 1994–1995, compared to India's Rs 8070. After ten years, Bihar's NSDP per capita increased by Rs 670 only. In 2003–2004, while India's NSDP average increased to Rs 11,799, Bihar's disappointing performance led to Rs 3707 NSDP per capita. As Figure 6.1 illustrates, after liberalization, while India's per capita NSDP increased steadily, Bihar remained stagnated until 2004.

However, Bihar grew faster after 2005. As Figure 6.2 depicts, while Bihar's per capita NSDP is less than India's average, its rate of growth increased after 2005.

The pattern of growth in Bihar has been different with Andhra Pradesh and India's average. As Figure 6.3 reveals, India's rate of growth did not decrease or

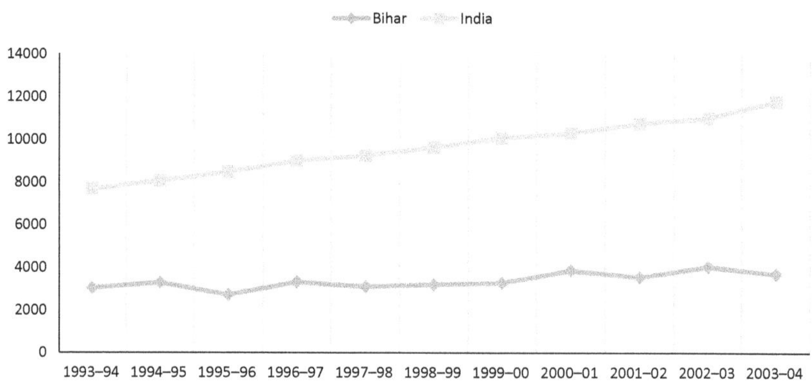

Figure 6.1 Per capita NSDP in Bihar and India 1993–1994 to 2003–2004.

Source: *Handbook of Statistics on Indian Economy 2005–06* (2006), drawn by the author.

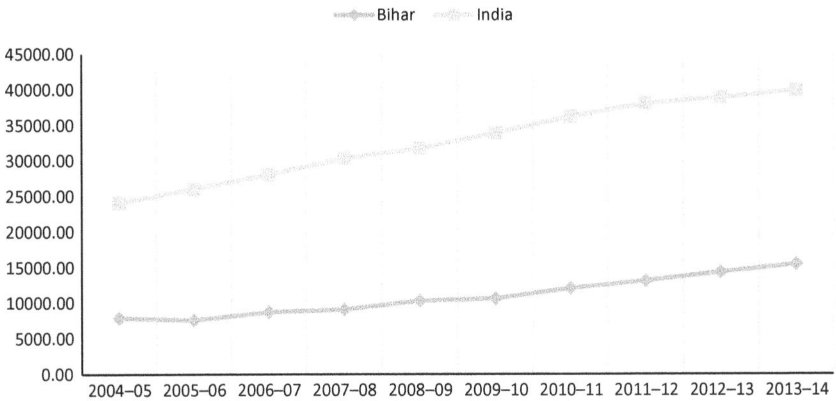

Figure 6.2 Per capita NSDP in Bihar and India 2004–2005 to 2013–2014.

Source: *Handbook of Statistics on Indian Economy 2014–15* (2015), drawn by the author.

increase dramatically after liberalization. In contrast, Bihar's rate of growth was not stable and experienced several rise and falls. Although Bihar frequently faced a minus rate of growth during the RJD rule, this rate has become more stable after the rise of Nitish Kumar.

Bihar had traditionally been an essential agricultural State; nevertheless, the State's service sector is the main contributor to NSDP over the years. Although the share of agriculture in NSDP was 50.29% in 1980–1981, it fell to about 42% in 1990–1991. However, the significant changes took place after the reforms. As Figure 6.4 illustrates, while the share of agriculture in NSDP decreased from 41.97% in 1990–1991 to 22.46% in 2010–2011, services have become the

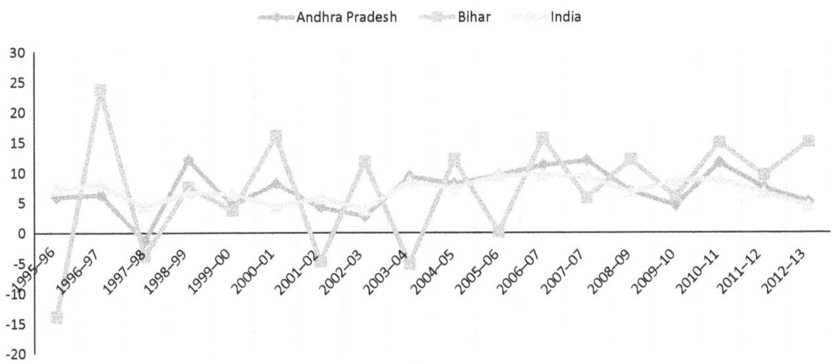

Figure 6.3 Real growth rates of states – GSDP percentage at constant prices, Bihar, Andhra Pradesh, and India.

Source: Planning Commission (2014), drawn by the author.

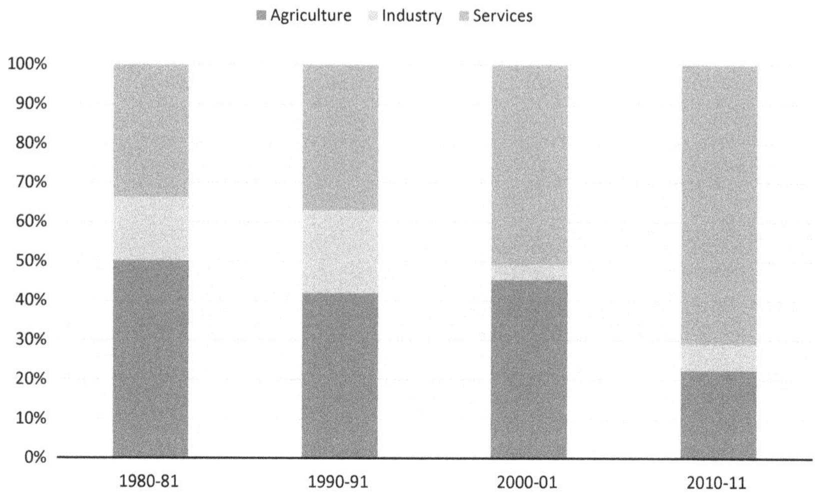

Figure 6.4 Percentage of components of Bihar's NSDP at factor cost by industry of origin (at constant prices).

Sources: *Handbook of Statistics on Indian Economy* (2006) and (2015), drawn by the author.

primary contributor in NSDP over last two decades. The share of the service sector as a whole increased from 33.68% in 1980–1981 to 36.98% in 1990–1991, 50.81% in 2000–2001, and 70.99% in 2010–2011. On the other hand, Industry's share in NSDP is narrow and limited. The proportion of the industry sector in NSDP was 21.05% in 1990–1991 and fell to 3.73% in 2000–2001. However, with a minor increase, this share had been 6.55% in 2010–2011.

Even though the service sector contributes more than 70% of Bihar's NSDP, 74% of the total human resources in the State are engaged in agriculture. This rate is much higher than the national average (Paul and Sridhar 2015, 137). According to *Handbook of Statistics on Indian Economy 2014–15* (2015), Bihar has reported a total NSDP of Rs 1566.71 crores, which work out as Rs 15,506 per capita for the year 2013–2014 at constant prices. Bihar's per capita income has been below national average since the beginning of the 1990s, and this gap increased throughout the 1990s and the first half of the first decade of twenty-first century. This gap has decreased steadily since 2005. When Nitish Kumar started his tenure as the chief minister of Bihar (2005–2006 financial year) the per capita NSDP at a constant price[3] in Bihar was Rs 7588 and it was below the average of Rs 26,015. This rate means that Bihari people had one-third of the average of all Indians per capita NSDP. At the end of his second government (2013–2014 financial year), this amount increased to Rs 15,506, which was half of the national average of Rs 31,863. This trend of growth reveals that although Bihar is still the weakest State in terms of per capita NSDP, it could reduce the gap with the national average after 2005.

The next important issue is the pattern of economic growth in the State. The current study distinguishes two distinct phases of economic performance in the State after liberalization. In the first phase and under Lalu Prasad Yadav, the agriculture and industry sector did not achieve a significant rate of growth. While the share and contribution of these two sectors remained without any considerable change, as Figure 6.5 depicts, service sector grew slightly and became the leading contributor in State's NSDP.

In the second phase, after a persistent stagnation, Bihar's economy has grown faster since 2005 (see Figure 6.6). After the victory of JD (U) in the 2005 election, Nitish Kumar implemented several reform-oriented policies, which enhanced economic growth in the State. The post-2005 growth in the NDSP is

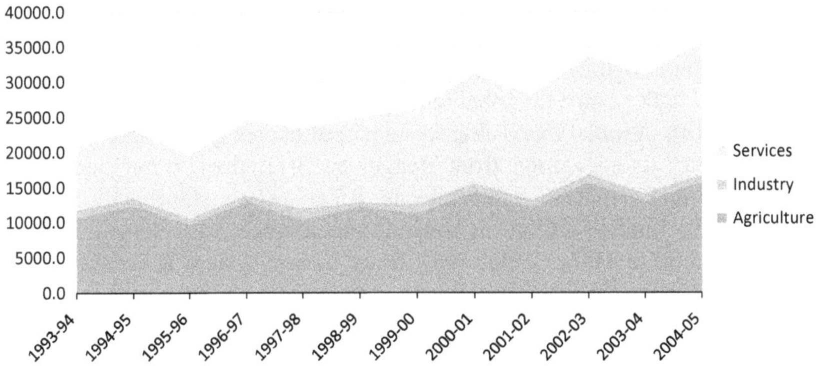

Figure 6.5 Components of Bihar's NSDP at factor cost by industry of origin (at constant prices, the base year 1993–1994) 1993–1994 to 2004–2005.

Source: *Handbook of Statistics on Indian Economy 2005–06* (2006), drawn by the author.

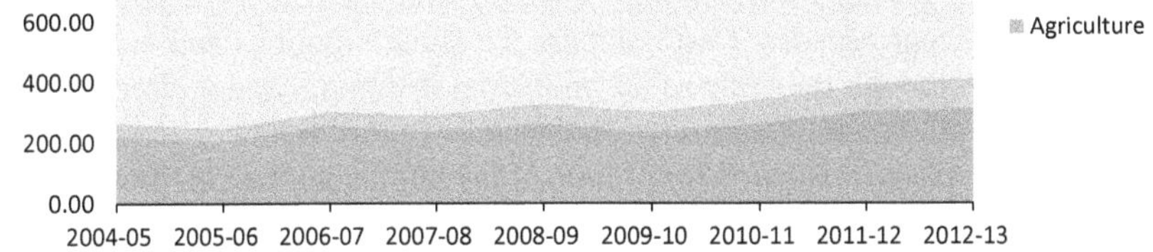

Figure 6.6 Components of Bihar's NSDP at factor cost by industry of origin, 2004–2005 to 2012–2013.

Source: *Handbook of Statistics on Indian Economy 2013–14* (2014).

mainly based on the growth in the service sector. As will be elaborated, the chief economic initiatives in the JD (U) rule concentrated on the service sector.

Pre-1990s politics in Bihar

Historical background

Bihar had been a developed region in ancient India. Mauryans and the Guptas ruled Bihar, and their role transformed it into one of the most significant centers of India's culture and civilization (Kulke and Rothermund 2004). 'Bodh Gaya,' the holiest place for the followers of Buddhism, is located in this State. The term 'Bihar' is derived from the Sanskrit term 'Vihara' meaning monastery. Pataliputra, ancient Patna, was the capital of the Magadha Empire, founded in 490 BC. As Kulke and Rothermund (2004, 11–12) indicated, Pataliputra was a strategic place located on a high bank of the River Ganga and emerged as "a bastion of Magadha in its fight against the tribal republics to the north of the Ganga."

During British Colonial rule, Bihar was a part of the composite State of Bihar and Orissa after its separation from Bengal in 1911; then, Bihar became a separate State in 1931. After independence, Bihar was constitutionally recognized in 1950. Socially, Bihar is entirely fragmented with several Hindu castes. According to Mitra (2006, 106), Bihar's caste system is characterized by "extreme subdivision within the Hindu *varna* scheme." In the next sections, the consequences of this traditional institution on the politics and economy of State will be analyzed.

The Congress Party and upper caste domination

For the period after independence, politics in Bihar cannot be analyzed without considering the role and position of caste in politics. As a result, there is a bulk of literature, investigating caste politics in Bihar in terms of coalitions and sub-coalitions, alignments and counter-alignments and rivalries (see Jha 1970; Blair 1972; Prasad 1979; Verma 1991; Gupta 1992; Roy 1994; Prasad 1997; Kumar 1999; Ojha 2006). Influenced by this reach literature, the current book considers caste as a micro-institutional variable, playing a critical role in the shaping of Bihar's politics. Caste served as an institution with a direct impact on political mobilization and participation, voting behavior, and interest aggregation and articulation in recent decades. Caste matters for Bihar's politics and economic performances. Although the caste as an influential institution had a direct political impact in all Indian States after independence, its political importance became more evident in Bihar. Mitra (2006, 106) highlights the significance of traditional institutions in the shaping of Bihar's post-colonial politics and writes:

> In contrast to the post-Partition history of regional state formation in Punjab and West Bengal, where politics was deeply marked by the influx of refugees, post-independence Bihar was not a new political arena. Hence, no

> dominant theme of identity, corresponding to an expanding thin regional identity, emerged in Bihar's politics at the outset. Instead, old loyalties and a conglomerate of thick identities based on local 'Jati,' or religion in the case of Muslims, and tribal networks for a substantial part of the population became the dominant mode of political organization, working in parallel with modern institutions such as parties, unions, and the ubiquitous bureaucracy.

Similarly, As Verma (1991, 1142) specifies, the voting behavior in Bihar can be understood and analyzed on the basis of caste, religion, and class. Therefore, for analyzing this determinant institution that had a direct effect on a regional leader's strategic choice and constituents, its compositions and structure should be delineated. Ravi provided detailed information about the caste composition in Bihar. His data related to Bihar in 1991; nevertheless, the caste structure in Bihar remained relatively without significant change.

The upper castes in the State include Brahmins and other caste groups such as Bhumihar, Rajput, and Kayastha. However, their number is numerically small.[4] They had better access to the objective sources of power and wealth after the independent because of their better literacy, land-owning, and social capital. As Weiner (2001, 196) indicates, these forward castes dominated universities, colleges, civil service and bureaucracy, military, police, and State and Union Governments. Remarkably, because of their educational and economic privileges, they also engaged in politics and played a vital role in the nationalist movement.

As a result, most leaders of political parties after the independence came from these forward castes. Therefore, despite their small number in Bihar, they were involved actively in politics and their coalitions or competitions influenced the social and political life of the State. In contrast, the Yadav[5] caste and other OBCs are the most significant social groups in the State; nevertheless, after the first decades of independence, they had no strong political influence in the Congress. As Robin (2009, 66) notes, because of a considerable percentage of Yadavs, Bihar is an exception in entire Hindi Belt.

After independence, the Congress was the dominant party in Bihar and ruled until the end of the 1980s. Although two interruptions (1967–1971 and 1977–1979) paused the rule of the Congress, this party remained the most significant political actor in Bihar until the 1990 election. Upper castes, the scheduled castes (SCs), and Muslims were the main supporters of the Congress in Bihar (Roy 1994, 227).

Like Andhra Pradesh, specific castes organized themselves as dominant political players in the Bihar Congress after independence; nevertheless, the rivalries among these social groups existed even before the independence. The Bihar Congress was established in 1908, and national freedom for India was its primary objective. However, as Roy (1966, 707) indicates, the intense rivalry for office in the organization, indiscipline, rebellion as the signs of factionalism became manifest as early as the 1920s when the Bihar Congress decided to participate in elections for local bodies.

As Mitra (2006, 107) notes, three upper caste groups, namely, the Kayasthas, Bhumihars, and Rajputs, had emerged in the Bihar Congress in the 1930s. According to Roy (1994, 226) in the early years of the Bihar Congress, Muslims and Kayasthas emerged as the leaders; nevertheless, other upper caste groups, particularly Bhumihars, Rajputs, and Brahmins – joined the party later and ended their dominance. As Roy (1966, 710) elucidates, two sub-coalitions, composed by Rajputs and the Bhumihars were active in the Bihar Congress until 1946.

Like Andhra Pradesh and others Indian States, the Congress Party emerged as the dominant political party for decades after the independence. The pre-1990s politics in Bihar can be divided into different phases:

The pre-1967 period

In the era of the 'one dominant party system,' the Congress won a majority of seats in the Legislative Assembly elections as well as the Lok Sabha elections. Under the leadership of Jawaharlal Nehru, no other political party could challenge the Congress effectively; as a result, various social and political actors tried to secure political power in the framework of the Congress as the single available political platform. Roy (1994, 225) describes the Congress as "a vehicle for political mobilization and of the satisfaction of mobility aspirations of different socio-economic interests in Bihar." As Mitra (2007, 42) specifies, the Congress maintained the stable percentage of caste composition in all elections and upper caste candidates were the majority in all election except the 1977 election. In this period, the upper castes were dominant in the State politics. Although the leadership of the Congress and majority of the candidates belonged to the upper castes, as Jha (1970) states, there was a rivalry among Brahmins and other upper castes such as 'Kayastha,' 'Bhumihar' and 'Rajput' to secure political power in the party.

Brahmins had a traditional influence on 'backward castes.' This influence supported them socially and politically to become more dominant in the elections and party politics. Contrary to Brahmins in Andhra Pradesh who had only ritual status and did not possess considerable property and land, Bihari Brahmins enjoyed both ritual and property privileges (Satyanarayana 2007, 15–16). Brahmins formed a major part of State's bureaucracy and judiciary after the independence.

As Jha (1970, 341) maintains, Kayasthas were the first group in the State who had an English education and dominated the professional and salaried positions. As Table 6.2 shows, the Kayasthas constitute only a small percentage of the total population of the State. Moreover, their number was even less than other upper caste groups such as Rajputs or Brahmins. Despite their low percentage, Kayasthas have acquired importance in Indian history since the Mughal Empire. Kayasthas learned Urdu (and later English in the colonial period) and secured different positions in Mughals and British colonial administration. As Verma (1991, 1142) specifies, Kayasthas have been politically significant even before independence. Several national leaders during the freedom struggle such as

Sachchidanand Sinha, Rajendra Prasad, and Jai Prakash Narain belonged to this caste. However, the role of this caste in Bihar politics has declined sharply since the 1972 Assembly election.

Jha (1970, 341) introduces Bhumihars as a 'landed aristocracy' in many districts who could afford politics with their properly secured future. Regional leaders such as Sri Krishna Sinha (Dr. S.K. Sinha) who belonged to this caste had a considerable political impact. Not only was he the premier of Bihar from 1937 to 1939 but he also served as the first chief minister of Bihar after independence and remained in this position for more than 15 years. In this period, not only did S.K. Sinha rule the State until his death in 1961 as 'Bhumihars Raj,' but also this caste group became more visible in the bureaucracy, the Congress and even opposition parties such as the CPI (Witsoe 2013, 40).

The Rajputs have also been a land-owning caste, fighting for dominance in the Congress and Bihar politics. As Verma (1991, 1143) mentions, the Congress Party witnessed the struggle between Sri Krishna Sinha as a Bhumihars leader and Anugrah Narain Sinha as a Rajput leader for the leadership of the Congress. The successor of Sri Krishna Sinha was Deep Narain Singh, a Rajput politician. Chief ministers such as Chandrashekhar Singh (14 August 1983–12 March 1985) belonged to this caste.

As Mitra (2006, 109) illustrates, during the first two decades after independence, while there were tense rivalries among upper castes, which caused factionalism in Bihar Congress, the central high command had watchful eyes on Bihar to control the level of confrontations in the State and party. However, unlike Andhra Pradesh that Reddy caste group controlled the Congress, and there was no other real challenge to their dominance in the party, in Bihar, rivalries, and conflicts between Rajputs, Brahmins, Bhumihars, and Kayasthas weakened the position of the party after the death of Nehru. In the mid-sixties, the internal conflicts among the Congress leaders accompanied by the drought, induced famine condition, student unrest, and agitation by non-gazetted government employees. Internal conflicts and inability to cope with these challenges affected performance and capability of the Congress adversely. This condition led to the erosion of voters' support and legitimacy of the State Government. Interestingly, upper castes also dominated the opposition parties in the 1960s and 1970s. For example, in the crucial 1967 election, upper castes were dominant in JKD, PSP and among independent candidates (Mitra 2007).

The period between 1967 and 1972

The first interruption in the dominance of the Congress took place in the 1967 election; however, the erosion of Congress's power can be traced to the developments that occurred in 1963 when Binodanand Jha, the Brahmin chief minister, resigned under the Kamaraj Plan.[6] During his tenure, he restored the Zamindari rights of the Tatas in Jamshedpur. His successor, K.B. Sahay, who was a Kayastha leader, tried to consolidate his power via organizing numerically backward castes such as Ahirs, Koeris, and Kurmis.

As Robin (2009, 70) clarifies, the abolition of the Zamindari system in 1950 was a major legislative success of the Congress government in Bihar. Although the intermediaries were not eliminated entirely, a significant percentage of the tenants of the Zamindars arose as new middle peasants. Therefore, as Witsoe (2013, 41) and Robin (2009, 70) elaborate, after the abolition of the Zamindari system in Bihar, new landlords came from peasant caste backgrounds such as Koeri, Yadav, and Kurmi caste groups. These recently political ascendant castes could be considered as the new political allies in a power struggle among the upper caste leaders in the Congress. K.B. Sahay argued that the backward castes are under-represented in Bihar Congress. So, along with his backward caste ally, Ram Lakhan Singh Yadav demanded a large number of nominations for members of backward castes. Other Congress leaders such as S.N. Sinha, a Rajput leader, were opposed to this idea and perceived it as a challenge to the upper-caste dominance; therefore, they joined the rival camp. As a result, K.B. Sahay became more dependent on backward and lower castes. The needs of dominant upper castes to secure more support from the numerically strong backward and lower castes enhanced their position in State politics indirectly. Also, factionalism and struggles among upper castes in the Congress weaken their position and the Congress. As Mitra (2007, 44) explains, at this moment, backward castes begun to engage actively in the electoral politics. The consequence of these developments is reflected in the 1967 election.

Figure 6.7 illustrates the process of gradual erosion of the Congress's power in Bihar. As we can see the Congress as the dominant party won 239 out of 330

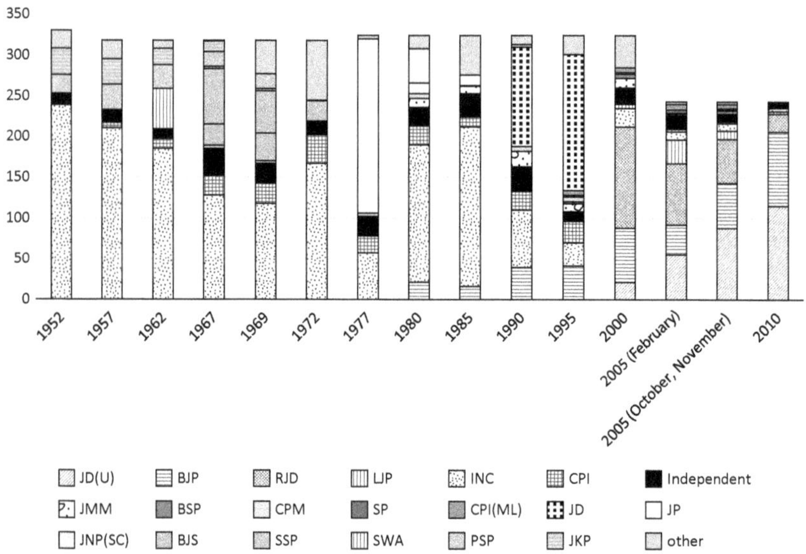

Figure 6.7 Bihar Assembly election results (1952–2010).

Source: Statistical report on general legislative assembly of Bihar series (Election Commission of India 1951–2014).

Legislative Assembly seats in the 1951–1952 election; however, the Congress could secure only 210 seats in 1957 out of 318, and declined to 185 seats in 1962 and 128 seats in 1967.

The 1967 election was a turning point in Bihar politics. Although the Congress won 128 seats out of 318, it was not able to form the government.

Although the Communists could not secure any seats in the 1952 election, they gained 28 seats in 1967. Similarly, the socialist camp improved on their 24 seats in 1952 to 86 seats in 1967. The Sanghata Socialist Party (SSP) with 68 seats and the Praja Socialist Party with 18 seats became the major political players in the State.

The poor performance of the Congress and the rise of other political parties in the 1967 election implied a new phase in the State-level politics in States such as West Bengal, Kerala, and Tamil Nadu. Although regional parties in States like Tamil Nadu or the Leftist parties in Kerala or West Bengal emerged and developed gradually, in Bihar, any significant political actor could fill the vacuum of the Congress's power. The period between 1967 and 1972 included nine coalition governments and three periods of President's rule (Mitra 2007, 44–45). The coalition governments had a short life, and they could sustain their power between a few days to less than one year. Interestingly, the Congress formed three coalition governments in the State and supported two other minority governments. This fact illustrates that although the Congress was weakened considerably, it remained a significant political actor in the State. On the other hand, contrary to other opposition political parties like DMK in Tamil Nadu or CPI in Kerala, the opposition forces in Bihar remained fragmented.

In this period, non-upper caste chief ministers emerged for the first time in the State. Seven chief ministers out of nine belonged to the backward castes or Harijans. Nevertheless, none of them could form a stable government and consolidate their position as a regional leader. As Table 6.2 reveals, whereas all Congress chief ministers between 1946 and 1989 are from the upper caste groups (except one Muslim chief minister), the two interruptions in the Congress's rule paved the road for the backward caste and scheduled caste politicians to be chief ministers of Bihar. However, two interruptions (1967–1972 and 1977–1979) prevented the revitalizing of Congress's power and upper caste's dominance.

The period between 1972 and 1977

After a period of unstable governments, the constituents voted again for the Congress to restore political stability in the State. Like Andhra Pradesh, the victory of the Congress in the 1972 election can be attributed to the leadership of Indira Gandhi and her role both in national and State politics. During this period, the Congress high command appointed three chief ministers in Bihar. Two of them were Brahmin, and the other one was a Muslim; however, the upper caste had a maximum representation in his cabinet. In this period, the State Government became more dependent on Delhi and the high command. As Mitra (2006, 110) asserts, with the close connections to the high politics of the Center, "governance

Table 6.2 Chief ministers of Bihar and their caste background between 1946 and 1989

Name	*Took office*	*Left office*	*Caste background*	*Party*
Krishna Singh	2 April 1946	31 January 1961	Bhumihar	Indian National Congress
Deep Narayan Singh	1 February 1961	18 February 1961	Rajput	
Binodanand Jha	18 February 1961	2 October 1963	Brahmin	
K.B. Sahay	2 October 1963	5 March 1967	Kayastha	
Mahamaya Prasad Sinha	5 March 1967	28 January 1968	Kayastha	Jana Kranti Dal
Satish Prasad Singh	28 January 1968	1 February 1968	Backward caste	Indian National Congress
B.P. Mandal	1 February 1968	2 March 1968	Backward caste	
Bhola Paswan Shastri	22 March 1968	29 June 1968	Scheduled caste	Indian National Congress (O)
Vacant (President's rule)	29 June 1968	26 February 1969	N/A	N/A
Harihar Singh	26 February 1969	22 June 1969	Rajput	Indian National Congress
Bhola Paswan Shastri [2]	22 June 1969	4 July 1969	Scheduled caste	Indian National Congress (O)
Vacant (President's rule)	6 July 1969	16 February 1970	N/A	N/A
Daroga Prasad Rai	16 February 1970	22 December 1970	Backward caste	Indian National Congress
Karpoori Thakur	22 December 1970	2 June 1971	Backward caste	Socialist Party
Bhola Paswan Shastri [3]	2 June 1971	9 January 1972	Scheduled caste	Indian National Congress

Vacant (President's rule)	9 January 1972	19 March 1972	N/A	N/A
Kedar Pandey	19 March 1972	2 July 1973	Brahmin	Indian National Congress
Abdul Gafoor	2 July 1973	11 April 1975	Muslim	
Jagannath Mishra	11 April 1975	30 April 1977	Brahmin	
Vacant (President's rule)	30 April 1977	24 June 1977	N/A	N/A
Karpoori Thakur	24 June 1977	21 April 1979	Backward caste	Janata Party
Ram Sundar Das	21 April 1979	17 February 1980	Brahmin	
Vacant (President's rule)	17 February 1980	8 June 1980	N/A	N/A
Jagannath Mishra	8 June 1980	14 August 1983	Brahmin	Indian National Congress (I)
Chandrashekhar Singh	14 August 1983	12 March 1985	Rajput	
Bindeshwari Dubey	12 March 1985	13 February 1988	Brahmin	
Bhagwat Jha Azad	14 February 1988	10 March 1989	Brahmin	
Satyendra Narayan Sinha	11 March 1989	6 December 1989	Rajput	
Jagannath Mishra [3]	6 December 1989	10 March 1990	Brahmin	

Sources: Jha (1970) and Mitra (2007), drawn by the author.

in Bihar, endogenously unsustainable at the best of times, went into a state of animated suspension from which it is yet to recover."

Continuous manipulations by the Center, corruption, factional infighting in the Congress, worsening economic situation and extreme droughts and floods, contributed to general political discontent. This discontent manifested in the Bihar Movement, targeting the Congress in the State and later became anti-Indira Gandhi. The Bihar Movement was initiated by students at Patna University in 1974 and led by Jayaprakash Narayan, popularly known as JP (Krishna 2011, 120–126). The Patna University Students Union organized a meeting of student leaders from different regions of Bihar. They formed Bihar *Chhatra Sangharsh Samiti (BCSS)* in February 1974 to spearhead the agitation. Lalu Prasad Yadav, a student at the Patna University at that time, was elected to preside over the BCSS (Krishna 2011, 122). Lalu started his political activism with anti-Center and anti-Congress attitudes, and this political background had a direct impact on his political life. Moreover, Nitish Kumar, another student activist, started his political career from this movement. Nitish and Lalu as two friends were two student leaders of Lok Dal. The BCSS also requested Jayprakash Narayan to lead the movement.

Although the movement at the beginning had demands such as to control the prices of foodgrain and other essential goods, lowering of tuition fees and prices of textbooks, better amenities in hostels, a role for elected students in the various decision-making bodies of the colleges and universities (Krishna 2011), the BCSS widened the scope of its requests and demanded the resignation of the Abdul Ghafour government and dissolution of the Legislative Assembly. The BCSS called several times for *agherao*, *Bandh*, and *Satyagraha.* Political unrest crippled everyday life in the State. As Mitra (2006, 110) indicates, the political condition became worse when the army had to be called in to help the civil administration in the State. On the other hand, the movement radicalized and called for 'Total Revolution Movement.' During the wave of political instability and unrest L.N. Mishra, the Central Minister, was killed in a bomb blast at Samastipur in January 1975. Not only Bihar witnessed to political instability and crisis in the order; other States also experienced several challenges. Subsequently, Indira Gandhi asked the President to declare a National Emergency in June 1975. During the emergency, the fundamental rights were suspended, and the general election was postponed for one year. Moreover, numerous opposition politicians, journalists, and political activists were arrested and sent to jail. Mitra (2011, 73) describes the National Emergency as "the first major trial of strength and resilience of India's democracy."

As Kulke and Rothermund (2004, 337) elucidate, an emergency with almost dictatorial powers continued for more than a year; as a result, the political instability in the country decreased, and the economy was geared up. With the higher level of order and fewer strikes, the economy found a better perspective; however, the new political arrange could not sustain very long. Despite Indira Gandhi's hope to win the 1977 election, the public opinion verdict was against her and the Congress. The opposition leaders, both at the national and State level, after their release from the jail, organized the election campaign. The emergency unified the opposition leaders to form the Janata Party; thus, Indira Gandhi lost the 1977 election. While Andhra Pradesh remained as one of the rare strongholds of the Congress in the 1977 election, Bihar like several other States voted for the opposition parties. One of the young candidates who won the 1977 election and was selected as MP was Lalu Prasad Yadav, the student leader at Patna University.

The period between 1977 and 1979

The supremacy of the Congress was interrupted again by the 1977 election; people voted for Janata Party as a reaction to the emergency that Prime Minister Gandhi had imposed in 1975. Jayaprakash Narayan guided the opposition actors to be united under the flag of Janata Party. Opposition parties such as Congress (O), Jana Sangh, BKD, Congress for Democracy, and various socialist parties formed a 'Grand Alliance' (Roy 1994, 229). The Janata Party tried to attract political support from the backward castes and perceived them as a significant political force. During the short time of the opposition rule in Bihar, two chief ministers had the backward caste background (Mitra 2007).

As Mitra (2006, 111) explicates, Karpoori Thakur, the first Janata Party chief minister had promised job reservations for backward castes during the election campaign. After the election, Thakur as a chief minister who belonged to a backward caste group tried to implement his electoral promises; however, upper-caste members of his cabinet opposed these measures. Thakur government issued a notification for the reservation of 20% government jobs for the backward castes on 10 November 1978. Moreover, a 25% job reservation for scheduled castes and scheduled tribes already existed (Mitra 2007, 49). The upper caste members of the cabinet claimed that Ahirs, Koeris, and Kurmis caste groups had progressed financially; as a result, they wanted a fresh examination of the issue. While the chief minister was determined in the implementation of reservation policy, other members of the cabinet and the party opposed him. According to Mitra (2006, 111), the struggle on the reservation policy caused "polarization of backward castes and upper castes" and resulted in violent riots and agitations by upper-caste youth. Ultimately, Karpoori Thakur had to resign in 1979 when he lost the confidence of the Legislative assembly. His successor also could not continue his tenure for more than ten months.

The period between 1980 and 1990

After imposing the fifth President's rule in Bihar, the Lok Sabha and Assembly elections took place in 1980. In the Assembly election, the Janata Party had divided into four groups; therefore, their votes were distributed. Consequently, the Congress came back to power and Jagannath Mishra, a Brahmin politician, became the new chief minister of Bihar. As Mitra (2006, 111) illustrates, Bihar witnessed conflicts between upper castes and backward castes, factional fights, corruption and communal riots during Mishra's rule. However, the power of Mishra depended on the Center and was supported by the high command in Delhi, until they asked him to leave his job.

The Centre also dominated the other chief ministers of Bihar. As Mitra (2007, 50) notes, these chief ministers were appointed at the "sweet will of the high command." Similarly, as Roy (1994, 229) maintains, during these ten years, seven Congress chief ministers were appointed and "were forced to retire."

In this era, the regional leaders were mostly dependent on the Center in the vertical game. While there is no compelling alternative for the Congress in the State, the Congress again transformed into a single political platform that could attract the votes. However, the leadership of Indira Gandhi with her *Gharibi Hatao* could attract voters in the State, and regional upper caste leaders lost their importance gradually in terms of attracting the votes. As a result, the chief ministers relied more on the Center's power than their local popularity. In the vertical game, regional leaders should present their loyalty to the Center to receive more political support. On the other hand, the regional leaders were relatively confident to constituent's support in the horizontal game. Frustrated by 1967–1971 and 1977–1979 opposition rule, constituents voted for Indira Gandhi's populist measures and later Rajiv Gandhi. Varma (1987, 508) asserts that the position of the State chief ministers in Bihar has been considerably denigrated since 1980:

> Gone are the days when there were organized fights between rivals for the leadership of the Congress Legislature Party. New Chief Ministers are imposed from the Centre, and they depend on for their existence on the mercy of the Central Congress (I) leadership. Kedar Pande, Jagannath Mishra, Chandra Shekhar Singh and Bindeshwari Dube, were nominees of the Central High Command, and they seem to glory in this kind of delegated leadership. Not only are such leaders helpless in eliciting more funds from the Centre to the State Exchequer but they also fail to build an aura of statewide leadership around them. Their statements fail to convince the intellectuals and appear like echoes of the voice of the central leadership. This is an unfortunate situation in a federal system of government.

As Mitra (2006, 111) mentions, the Congress Government was not able to enforce the order and law in the State. The inter-castes conflicts found new dimensions by the development of armed bands and protection rackets. Not only law and order were disrupted by the mafia gangs and riots, but also Naxalites with their Maoist ideology committed several violent actions. On the other hand, the power of the Congress was worn out by the internal conflicts and interventions of the Center. The fractious Congress could not manage law and order effectively and became more dependent on the Center.

In sum, as Mitra (2006) clarifies, based on the neo-institutional model of governance, the polarization of castes and the gradual erosion of the Congress's power in the State had a direct negative impact on the orderly rule in the State. Also, because of an intense power struggle among the upper caste elites in the Bihar Congress, the Congress fragmented institutionally, and elite agency at the Central level could not be efficiently implemented at the regional level. Not only was the State Government not able to implement law and order management, but also regional institutional complexities intensified the communal riots, caste-based violence, and Naxalite violence. Caste polarization and mass poverty with an institutionally weakened government prompted a high level of deinstitutionalization and collective violence and further political instability. Following Mitra (2006), this study employs the aggregated indicator of incidents of murder and riots per million to measure orderly rule and the ability of the state to govern. As we can see in Figure 6.8, Bihar had an equal level of political violence to average India in the early years after the independence. However, the first wave of increase in violence took place in the late 1960s and begging of the 1970s. This wave can be attributed to the first interruption in the Congress rule as the most important political party. Interestingly, the first increase of orderly rule in the mid1970s synchronized with the reelection of the Congress. Nevertheless, like another part of India, Bihar experienced a lower level of the orderly rule in the late 1970s because of the after-effects of the Bihar Movement and subsequent emergency. Remarkably, with the rule of the JD and later RJD as the first stable non-Congress parties, the trend reversed and showed a slight decrease. As will be elaborated, this success can be seen a result of Lalu Prasad Yadav's strategies to control the communal riots in the State. However, the level of instability remained higher than the national average.

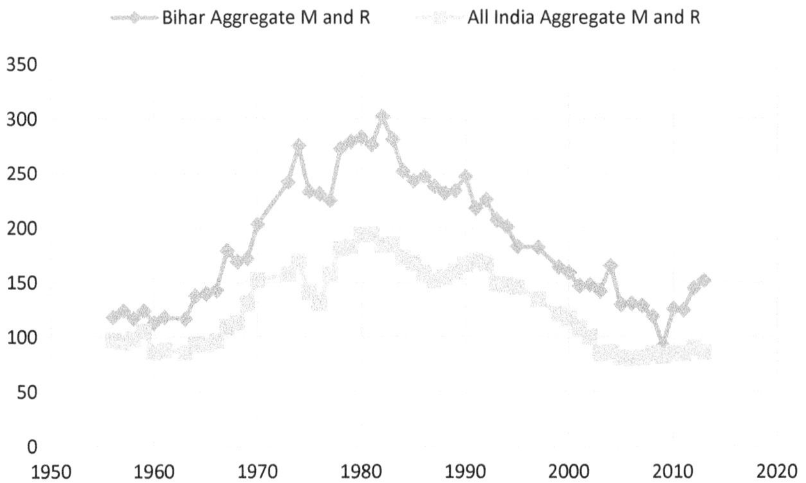

Figure 6.8 Combined index: murder and riots in Bihar and India (number of riots and murders per million population).

Source: *Crime in India* (annual), drawn by the author.

Fall of the Congress, rise of the JD, and lower caste politics

The 1990 election is a significant turning point in Bihar Politics. The political developments at the national level at the end of the 1980s affected domestic politics in the State. The main factor that affected Bihar politics was the rise the Janata Dal (JD, or Dal) as a new anti-Congress force in the ninth general election in India in November 1989. The JD was formed in the same way as Janata Party came into existence in 1977.

Three different political factions formed Janata Dal in October 1988. As Fickett (1993, 1151) elaborates, Chandra Shekhar was the leader of the first faction of the party. This faction reached back to the socialist parties of India and a splinter of the old Congress Party of Morarji Desai. Some of the Congress dissident leaders, such as former Defense Minister Vishwanath Pratap Singh, Arif Mohammed Khan, and Arun Nehru were the main pillars of the second faction of JD. The third wing of the party was rooted in the middle peasantry and 'backward castes' of Bihar and Uttar Pradesh. As was discussed, after a long history of dominance of the upper caste groups in Bihar, the Janata government introduced caste basis reservations. Although this policy could not be implemented successfully in a short time, political action based on caste identity, especially among non-upper caste groups increased. While the forward castes leaders had traditionally been the most important political actors in the State, the leaders of backward and scheduled castes and scheduled tribes have emerged as influential political players (Roy 1994). Although Charan Singh, an old politician and Prime Minister of India during Janata Party rule, had been the leader of this wing, he was, however, not alive when this wing reorganized itself in the form of Janata Dal. The younger generation of regional leaders, engaged in politics as a student leader in the 1970s, such as Lalu Prasad Yadav, emerged as the leaders of this faction. This wing played a vital role in the political and economic future of Bihar.

Born in Phulwaria in 'North Bihar,' in 1988, Lalu Prasad Yadav grew up in a marginal landless cultivator family. They lived at the 'lower end of the feudal system' with severe economic and social restriction (Thakur 2000, 25). This backwardness was echoed in his political life and his populist appeal (Witsoe 2013, 54). As a six-year-old boy, Lalu left the village and stayed with his uncle who was a milkman at Bihar Veterinary College. That is why he had a chance to go to school (Thakur 2000, 28). He was admitted to B.N. College at Patna University; subsequently, Lalu Yadav started his political life as a student leader. He was elected as the first OBC president of the Patna University Students' Union in 1967. He started his political life as an anti-Congress OBC student leader who fought against the upper caste dominance. As noted, he was elected as the chief of all Bihar students' agitation committee in 1974 and led the movement under the supervision of Jayaprakash Narayan. He emerged as a prominent student leader during the Bihar Movement. As an activist in the campaigns against Indira Gandhi's government, he was arrested during the Emergency (1975). He was elected as MP of the Chapra constituency in 1977 on a Janata

Party ticket. In the 1980 and 1989 Assembly elections, he was elected as an MLA from Sonepur. Yadav became the successor of Karpoori Thakur as the leader of opposition in the Assembly. Finally, he became chief minister of Bihar after the success of opposition parties (JD in Bihar).

The Congress lost the ninth general election; as a result, Janata Dal with the cooperation of leftist and regional parties like JMM and TDP played a significant role in the formation of a non-Congress government in the Center. Moreover, the Congress was defeated in the 1990 Bihar Assembly election, and the JD won 122 seats out of 324. Lalu Prasad Yadav assumed the office of chief minister and formed a cabinet with a majority of backward caste group members (Mitra 2007, 49). As both chief minister and as a 'chief minister in shadow,' he had a significant influence on Bihar politics in the 1990s until 2005. Lalu Prasad Yadav and later his wife, Rabri Devi, served as the chief ministers of three consecutive governments in 1990, 1995, and 2000.

According to Robin (2009, 85), implementation of the Mandal Commission Report by the V.P. Singh government, providing reservation for the socially and economically backward classes, polarized India's political scene to pro-Mandal and anti-Mandal. Mandal affairs can be seen as a significant factor that strengthened the emergence of Janata Dal as the secular alternative to the Congress. As Weiner (2001, 197) maintains, the opposition parties gradually learned to build coalitions among the middle and lower castes and attract Muslims who were alarmed by the growth of the BJP in the state to undermine the strength of the Congress in Bihar.

Lalu Prasad Yadav was supported by the OBCs especially the Yadav caste and minorities (mostly Muslims). The numerically strong Yadav caste belonged to the upper layer of OBCs. The new reservation policies benefited Yadavs; therefore, Janata Dal and later Rashtriya Janata Dal (RJD) received tremendous support from this caste group (Kumar 2004, 125). Furthermore, Lalu Yadav tried to control the communal situation in the 1990s. The government of Bihar arrested L.K. Advani after his attempt to pass through that state in the framework of his Ram Rath Yatra. Furthermore, Yadav dealt with Hindu activists firmly after the demolition of the Babri Masjid. These measures made Muslims the principal supporters of JD/RJD rule and created the basis for a stable alliance among backward classes, Harijans, and Muslims (Mitra 2006, 111).

Yadav was the chief minister of Bihar between 1990 and 1997 with a very short interruption by the President's rule in 1995. In 1997, Yadav faced what became known as the 'Fodder Scam.' He was charged with illegal the withdrawal of Rs 9.5 billion from the Animal Husbandry Department (Witsoe 2013, 71). The CBI started the investigation and the police arrested him. Just before surrendering to the police, Yadav resigned as chief minister and asked his party members to support his illiterate wife, Rabri Devi, as the chief minister of Bihar. Moreover, he announced his split from the national Janata Dal to form the 'Rashtriya Janata Dal' (RJD), which literally means National People's Party. Yadav was in prison between 1997 and 1998; however, he ruled the State and the party by cell phone calls to her wife.

Witsoe (2013, 3) describes Bihar as the 'worse-governed State in India' during the RJD rule. The growing political instability, lawlessness, corruption, and erosion of bureaucracy in the State created chaos, known as 'Jungle Raj.' Sinha (2011, 174) describes the political climate after the arrest of Lalu Yadav in Bihar:

> Lalu had relied entirely on his maneuvering to broaden his support base, and with the 1995 'hurricane Lalu' he appeared to have fully convinced himself that he could go further up only that way – the collapse of governance, the takeover of institutions and resources by the corrupt, the epidemic of thuggery and the 'Yadavization' of power counting for nothing in his eye. With Rabri, a traditional housewife till yesterday, in the chief minister's office, and Lalu away, occupied with his fight against CBI prosecution, even the semblance of governance took a long holiday.

Lalu Prasad Yadav as a charismatic leader

Although Lalu Prasad Yadav became a hate figure for many in forward castes, and his leadership style was the theme for fun making in the media, he emerged as a charismatic leader in Bihar. He portrayed himself as the main supporter of backward caste groups in the State. Lalu named himself the *'Gharibon Ka Masiha'* (Messiah of the Poor) who wanted to save lower caste people from domination and exploitation of the upper-castes:

> *Yeh garib dukhiare Lalu Yadav ko bhool nahi sakte, kyonki Lalu hi unka masiha hai. Baki sab bilkul bakwaas* (the poor and oppressed people can never forget Lalu Yadav because only I am their messiah and the rest are useless).
>
> (Yadav 1998a)

Yadav (2004, 5512) designates Lalu Prasad Yadav as the central character in a political drama unfolding on the Bihar stage in the last decade:

> Critics may ridicule him as a clown, but backward sections and the poor look upon him as their chief protagonist. He may rule Bihar by proxy, keeping his semi-literate wife in the gaddi, but people have reposed faith in him.

As Witsoe (2013, 56) reports, after the first victory and the appointment as the chief minister, Lalu Yadav preferred to stay at a shared small room at the Bihar Veterinary College rather than moving into the chief minister's official residence. He ordered to hold the cabinet meetings on the grounds in front of the complex. Although he later moved to the chief minister's official residence, these actions improved his image as a different leader among the poor and lower castes people.

The charisma of Lalu could not be attributed to any spiritual, ideological or cinematic roots. Although he claims that he was a follower of Jai Prakash Narayan and Lohia, he is not a socialist in the ideological sense. Moreover, while he had several performing capabilities, he did not start his political career as a cinema superstar. Corbridge et al. (2005, 237) suggest that Lalu's charisma is attributed to his image among the backward castes:

> Many backward caste men and women support Laloo Yadav precisely because he articulates – and personifies – their aspirations to speak back, to be virile. He is a charismatic leader in the secular and popular sense: not a man who has divinely given talents or powers, but a man who projects and writes into the public culture the fantasies of an oppressed majority.

As a populist leader, Lalu Yadav laid emphasis on a clear distinction between elites and 'the people.' For him, the elites are members of a forward caste who historically had direct access to a source of power and wealth. On the other hand, ordinary people include the OBCs, Harijans, Muslims, and other marginalized sections of the society. His political mobilization was mostly based on stressing the historical confrontation between the elites and people. He portrayed himself as a revolutionary but democratic leader of lower caste people who fights for the poor against the upper caste domination:

> Look at my foot. See, I am missing a toenail…I lost this toenail when I was a poor boy living in my village. We barely had enough to eat, and I used to herd buffalo day, sometimes so late that I would fall asleep on the back of a buffalo on my way home. One day, a buffalo that I was heading stepped my foot, and I lost the toenail … Now, look at what a tall chair I am sitting in (the chief minister's chair). I have proven that ballot boxes are more powerful than machine guns. Voters can decide whether a man will be in the dust or riding in an airplane. I am a true Naxalite from birth, a democratic Naxalite.
>
> (Quoted in Witsoe 2013, 61)

He depicted himself as the member of poorest sections of 'the people.' When Yadav was asked about his government's measures to protect Dalits after the Massacre of *Musahars* (literally means 'rat eaters,' the poorest caste in Bihar), he explicitly introduced himself as a member of this caste group and responded:

> Listen, I know the pulse of the people. In the fields, there is a species of rats known as kronsa. You catch it and burn a small hole in its belly, then pull out all the intestine, etc., stuff it with green chilly and masala and then roast it. All the juices and hair get burnt out, and when it is roasted properly, you just peel off the skin and taste it. Our Musahars eat rats, and I have also done it. That is why I know what they think, how they think.
>
> (Yadav 1999)

With such comments, Yadav distinguished himself from upper caste politicians (both in the Congress and the BJP) and other OBC leaders. He tried to get more political support for the RJD from SCs. Not only did he try to demonstrate that he is close to ordinary people in his interviews, public speeches, and election campaigns, but he also tried to have face-to-face contact with his supporters, promising to revive their *Izzat*[7] (honor, dignity), dismiss upper caste dominance, and provide some reservation and quota for the OBCs and Muslims in public service and education. According to this populist agenda, Lalu as the leader of 'people' protects the ordinary people from a 'pernicious enemy,' namely the upper castes. The famous slogan of RJD was *Bhurabal Hatao*,[8] meaning "get rid of upper castes." Lalu defined his main political goal as giving *Izzat* (honor) to the previously neglected caste majorities:

> These people have oppressed and suffocated you for thousands of years; they have made you labor, and they have kept the fruits for themselves... This government, this power, the state, this is all yours. You have been deprived of your share because those who ruled the state were not bothered about you... However, now your man has captured the establishment ... 'Bhurabal Hatao': wipe out the upper castes.
>
> (Quoted in Thakur 2000, 82–85)

As Witsoe (2013, 62) elaborates, Lalu Prasad Yadav visited several villages in Bihar, using a helicopter. None of the major politicians visited most of these villages. Lalu visited the poorer OBC and scheduled caste areas of villages, instead of visiting the upper-caste sections of villages. These visits strengthen the position of Lalu Yadav among the rural OBSs and scheduled castes. This populist agenda made him a charismatic leader for the OBCs, Muslims, and Dalits.

Srinivas (2009, xxv) focuses on the performing dimension of Yadav's charismatic leadership and compares him with N.T. Rama Rao in Andhra Pradesh. Although Yadav was not a professional cinema actor like NTR, both had a successful performance in the age of the televized election campaigns and assembly proceeding.

As Witsoe (2013, 55) specifies, Lalu earned a reputation for "wit, humor, theatricality, and rustic oratory." Instead of standard Hindi, he gave speeches in the regional Bhojpuri dialect. While Yadav lacks strong socialist ideological foundations, his personal capabilities and skills made him a charisma leader who could attract the votes of marginalized sections of society.

The vertical game: JD/RJD in the State and Congress/BJP in the Center

The JD and later the RJD defined their primary agenda to reduce the influence of upper caste groups in the State. In the beginning, Lalu portrayed the Congress at the State and the Center as the manifestation of domination of the upper castes. Later, after the rise of the BJP as the leading political actor at the Center and formation of the NDA government, the BJP was introduced as the symbol of the upper caste supremacy. Lalu in both phases had a hostile attitude toward the Center and opposed the policies which had been recommended by the Center:

> *O gai charane walon/ O bakri charane walon/ O tadi peene walon/ Vote dena seekho* (O! cattle grazers, O! toddy-drinkers, learn to vote) …*Bihar chala Dilli ki ore* (Bihar has begun its march towards Delhi).
>
> (Lalu Yadav, quoted in Ahmed 1996)

Muslims, the backward castes, and other lower caste supporters rewarded his party with reelection in the Assembly elections. In the first phase of confrontation with the Center (Prime Minister P.V. Narasimha Rao, 21 June 1991–16 May 1996), Lalu Yadav depicted the Congress at the Center as the representation of upper caste dominance. In the second phase of his confrontation with the Center (Prime Minister Atal Bihari Vajpayee, 19 March 1998–22 May 2004), Lalu intensified his hostility toward the Center and projected it as the confrontation between 'secularism and communalism.' The debilitated Congress in State was not a threat to Lalu anymore. Instead, Yadav perceived the BJP as the emerging player who can challenge his power in State. Even before the formation of the NDA government, he started to launch attacks against the BJP. For example, responding to a question about private armies in the State and violence, Yadav stated:

> Private armies like the Ranvir Sena are being funded by one caste in the state. It is being backed by the BJP, which comprises feudal elements and known destabilizers. Killings such as these are being engineered to malign my government. Even though I have banned private armies, it is impossible to control their movements.
>
> (Yadav 1997)

The hostility with the 'Upper Caste Dominated Center' and 'Communal Politics' was the main foundation for political mobilization in the State against the Center during the NDA government. For example, at a political rally on 30 April 2003, the RJD mobilized thousands of villagers to attend Gandhi Maidan, Patna, This event was called 'Lathi Rally' and its slogan was *Bhajpa bhagao, desh bachao*, which can be translated as 'get rid of the BJP and save the country' (Witsoe 2013, 1). When Lalu Yadav was asked about the goal of this rally, he responded:

> The BJP is a communal party. But it is just the *mukhouta* [mask], and the real forces behind it are the RSS, the VHP, and the Shiv Sena. These forces are bent on destroying the country. They have been trying to do this and have succeeded in the attempt to an extent with what they did in Gujarat.
>
> (Ananth 2003)

The Lalu's confrontationist strategy in the vertical game with the Center had its own consequences. Not only was Lalu arrested after the 'Fodder Scam' and forced to resign, but also the Center tried to remove his wife from power. In February 1999, the NDA government dismissed the Rabri Devi government on the charge of 'perpetuating Jungle Raj in Bihar.' The Center had appointed Sundar Singh Bhandari, the ex-vice-president of the BJP, as the governor of Bihar. The Center used Article 356 of the constitution and imposed President's rule and dismissed the RJD government. As a professional politician, Lalu realized that his party and the government had no chance without the support of the other main political players. The reconciliation with the Congress as the main opposition party against the common enemy was a rational choice. Yadav met Sonia Gandhi, the Congress president, to convince her that the reason behind President's rule in Bihar is not the Jungle Raj but the desire of the BJP to expand its political realm. The Congress decided to support the RJD and Devi government, and the NDA became sure that the bill would be defeated in Rajya Sabha; as a result, it withdrew the dismissal order (Thakur 2000, 144).

Yadav has begun a closer relationship with his old enemy since 1999. The Congress leadership recognized that with the rise of lower caste politics, their party with upper caste domination history had no serious chance in Bihar. So, the cooperation with the RJD who can mobilize the OBCs, scheduled castes, and Muslims against the BJP at the Central and regional level is a more pragmatist approach. Lalu also could be sure that the NDA government in the Center could not easily dismiss his wife's government and declare President's rule. When Lalu was questioned about the alliance with the Congress, he answered:

> I had revolted against the policies of the Congress, against emergency. But now the country under the rule of BJP is going nowhere. Our borders are not secure; neither is the Parliament. Big companies are being sold for peanuts; women are unsafe in Delhi. Due to all this, I chose to tie up with a more secular party, the Congress party. I cannot throw my brother-in-law from my house just because he is working hard and is involved in politics.
>
> (Yadav 2003)

Economic populism and identity politics in the RJD regime

As a result of what Rudolph and Rudolph (2013) call, 'federal market economy,' chief ministers have attained more autonomy in economic policymaking since the 1990s, and their decisions have been the key factor for the economic performance of States. The rise of lower-caste politics in Bihar and the emergence of Lalu Yadav was mirrored in Bihar economic policies. Zoya Hasan (2002, 380) distinguishes the pursuit of power as the most remarkable characteristic of lower caste politics. The new OBCs or Dalit leaders in Bihar under the leadership of Yadav faced the challenges, created by the Congress, as well as the BJP at the Center. Therefore, they tried to find a way to establish and maintain the political power. Especially when they confronted with the Center (either the UPA or the NDA), they needed to be sure about the continuity of political support by the constituents. Consequently, these regional leaders tried to increase their groups and other vote banks' share in public life, education, and public employment. In this context, neo-liberal economic reforms, advocated and pursued by the Center, were perceived as the continuity of old upper caste arrangements that should be broken. Therefore, Lalu Prasad Yadav rejected the mainstream economic development discourse, antipoverty schemes, and state planning arrangements. On the other hand, he underlined the short-term welfare measures, targeting the OBCs, SCs, and Muslims. These plans intended to provide more share in economy and education for the potential constituents. Thakur (2000, 86–87) introduced some of the populist measures that the Lalu Yadav government initiated and targeted his 'MY' (Muslims and Yadavs and other OBCs) supporters:

- More than 150 *charvaha* schools were established in rural areas across the state so shepherd boys (mostly Yadavs) could pick up vocational skills while their cattle grazed.
- Tree tax and the *cess* on the sale of toddy was abolished. The measure benefitted thousands of self-employed in the countryside.
- The minimum wage for agricultural workers was raised from Rs 16.50 to Rs 21.50.
- Hundreds of slums in Patna and other towns of the state were regularized and allowance given to milkmen to establish cowsheds almost anywhere they wished.
- Urdu was recognized as an official language in the State. Students could write the state public service commission examinations in Urdu.
- The State Minorities' Commission was given statutory status.
- Violation of rules for reservations in government jobs and educational institutions was made a cognizable offense.

Whereas Lalu Yadav as chief minister implemented these populist measures, he was openly skeptical and reluctant about long-term plans for development. For example, after the rise of Naxalite violence in the State, a journalist asked him "Is radical land reform the answer?" He replied, "The land is not the question. The main question is of dignity" (Yadav 1999).

Yadav interpreted development as the synonym of policies, benefiting upper-caste elites in Bihar. Consequently, he concentrated on the populist initiatives that highlighted the empowerment of OBCs and Muslims to provide him more political support. For example, when Yadav was criticized for lack of development in Bihar under his tenure, he highlighted some populist welfare schemes as developmental activities:

> Right from the time I took over as Chief Minister, I have endeavored for the benefit of the poor and oppressed. That is why I initiated charwaha schools (school for shepherds) so that the children of poor people could progress in life. I have taken the initiative for the housing and welfare benefits of the poor. After all, these people are my strength. I have also

> not allowed congestion in some parts of Patna by clearing away unauthorized structures for shops and business establishments. They have been given alternate arrangements.
>
> (Yadav 1998b)

Bihar as a dysfunctional state

Whereas it was expected that Lalu Yadav employed a redistributive strategy to empower the lower caste poor and promoted investment in health and education, the JD/RJD governments were not successful in pursuing redistributive policies. While Lalu Prasad Yadav and his wife had the longest consecutive terms in the history of Bihar, this opportunity was not translated to the reduction of mass poverty and improvement of literacy or health of the poor lower castes. During his rule, Bihar transformed to a 'Dysfunctional State' whose State Government was not able neither in enforcing the law nor in public service delivery. In the last years of Yadav/Devi rule, Bihar reported the highest incidence of violent crimes accounting for 12.4% (24,432 out of 196,550) in 2003 and 13.4% (28,005 out of 208,736) in 2004 among all Indian States (Crime in India 2004, 2005). Bihar reported 12.4 or 13.4% of total violent crime whereas it has only around 8% of the total population of the country. Bihar was ranked second in terms of highest incidents of murder and attempted to commit murder (mostly murders due to casteism), ranked first in terms of highest incidents culpable homicide (mostly due to property dispute), ranked first in terms of highest incidents of kidnapping and abduction, and ranked first in terms of highest incidents of dacoity and robbery (Crime in India 2004, 2005, 165–173).

The nature of crimes in Bihar suggests a tendency toward human body and life. Therefore, the State Government could not perform its fundamental duty to secure and protect human life. It reflects the severe crisis in governability, as Kohli (1990) mentioned, or governance, as Mitra (2006) defined.

Moreover, the State Government was not able to improve the everyday life of Bihari people. The economic performance of Bihar in terms of conventional economic growth indicators such as NSDP per capita was disappointing. While this rate had been Rs 3037 in 1993–1994, it increased only to Rs 3557 in the 2003–2004 financial year. Other development indicators portray a similar image. For instance, while the Human Development Index (HDI) in Andhra Pradesh increased from 0.30 in 1981 to 0.38 in 1991 and 0.42 in 2001, this indicator remained 0.15 from 1981 to 2001 in Bihar (Banerjee and Kuri 2015, 83). The level of poverty ratio on the Tendulkar methodology in Bihar from 60.5 in 1993/1994 only decreased to 54.4 in 2003/2004. On the other hand, this rate in Andhra Pradesh, which preferred growth rather than redistributive policies, decreased from 49.5% to 33.3% in the same period.

Although the mainstream media and political opponents of Lalu tried to caricature Lalu's policies, as a rational actor in this multilevel game, the purposeful polarization of castes, deinstitutionalization, and crippling the bureaucracy, confrontation with the Center and resistance to economic reforms was the main strategic choices of Lalu Yadav Prasad to be rewarded in the horizontal game by his reelection.

The vertical game and dynamics of reform resistance

Instead of implementation of the economic reforms, Lalu opposed the project of development. He explicitly distanced his government from the economic reforms, because he projected the reforms as the new tool for benefitting the forward castes at the expense of backward classes, castes, and minorities. Not only was he reluctant to implement the economic reforms to enhance development in the State, but he also declared that "development is a foreign and polluting ideology" (quoted in Kumar 2008a, 172). Lalu Yadav depicted the Center (the Congress and P.V. Narasimha Rao's government and the NDA and Atal Bihari Vajpayee's government) as the manifestation of upper-caste dominance. Robin (2009, 88) classified Lalu in the category of politicians who believe development has no electoral value. A popular JD slogan was "*Vikaas nahih, samaan chahiye* (we need dignity, not development)" (quoted in Witsoe 2013, 63).

The alternative for neo-liberal economic reforms was the discourse of lower-caste empowerment. In the absence of policy agenda, pure populism was the substitute for economic reforms in the State. Lalu Yadav promised welfare of the rural poor as the central theme of his election campaign. With an aggressive tone, he described the role of bureaucracy in his government:

> Just as peddlers visit your villages saying, choose what you like for four annas, the officers of my government will come to you with whatever you want. Free sarees, free dhotis. They will camp in your villages. They are your servants. Take what you want.
>
> (Quoted in Hasan 2002, 379)

Whereas in the era of federal market economy (Rudolph and Rudolph 2013), a competition emerged among India's States to attract more investments and implement more economic reforms (Jenkins 2003, 1999), Lalu Prasad Yadav as *de jure* and de facto chief minister of Bihar had a hostile attitude toward the private sector, as a part of the upper-caste dominance, as well as international financial organizations.

Fragmentation of bureaucracy and civil services

Although Lalu Yadav required a powerful bureaucracy to fulfill his electoral promises, his purposeful policies weakened the capacity of bureaucracy to deliver the basic services. As elaborated, Lalu Yadav continuously continued the strategy of confrontation with the forward caste elites as the 'enemy' to keep his electoral base mobilized. One of the major areas of confrontation was the public service employment. Since the upper caste groups had better access to power, wealth and education system, they possessed a major share of jobs in universities, police, civil service and bureaucracy (Weiner 2001, 196). According to Corbridge et al. (2005), instead of developmental goals, the major aim of Lalu Yadav's civil jobs policy was to ensure that members of the forward castes cannot mistreat the backward classes, and lower castes people could attain and sustain their *Izzt*. Yadav avoided the appointment of members of upper castes to civil service jobs; on the contrary, he reserved civil service jobs for people from the castes or communities, supporting his party in the elections (Mathew and Moore 2011, 2015). For example, the key administrative positions in the districts, particularly the influential position of district magistrate, were mostly allocated to the OBC, Muslim, or scheduled caste officers (Witsoe 2013, 88).

Not only did Lalu Prasad Yadav tried to increase the share of the OBCs, Muslims, and Dalits in the public service based on the recommendation of Mandal Commission but he also sought to dismiss the upper-caste civil servants as much as he could. As Jaffrelot (2003, 380) reports, in 1993, Yadav moved to ensure that "an IAS from the scheduled castes replaced a Brahmin as Chief Secretary, and an OBC took over the charge of Director General of Police from another Brahmin." Moreover, he tried to increase the share of the OBCs especially Yadavs in 1427 lecturer positions in Bihar's universities and constituent colleges.

However, as Mathew and Moore (2011, 7) indicate, "these groups were historically so deprived that often it was impossible to find members with sufficient educational qualifications to be appointable even to middle-ranking public sector jobs." Instead of the appointment of suitable candidates from other social groups, Lalu Prasad preferred to leave posts vacant. For example, as Pankaj (2009, 19) reports, 17 out of 19 sanctioned posts of superintendent engineer in the rural engineering department and 64 posts out of 72 sanctioned posts of superintendent engineer in the road construction department remained vacant. Moreover, all three posts of chief engineer and one post of engineer in chief in the rural engineering department as well as 12 posts of chief engineer and all posts of the engineer in chief in road construction department also remained vacant.

The situation in the health and education system was alarming. After the end of Lalu Yadav's tenure, the new government of Bihar published a "White Paper on State Finances and Development" (2006). The White Paper reported a significant number of vacancies in the health system:

> If one takes into account men in position, the situation is very disappointing. The shortage is about 90 percent in a case of doctors and 95 percent in the case of paramedical staff against the norms under the National Health Policy. It can be said that the system of State delivery of Health Care has collapsed.
>
> (Government of Bihar 2006, 32)

The situation in the education system was not different. According to the White Paper (Government of Bihar 2006, 29), only 30,000 elementary school teachers were employed in contrast to the needed 90,000; as a result, the pupil–teacher ratio (PTR), which was already 90:1, worsened to 122:1. Remarkably, as Mathew and Moore (2015, 238) reveal, the Center wanted to pay the salaries of the needed teachers under a scheme called *Sarva Shiksha* (Education for All) as a Centrally sponsored scheme. The aim of the Center was to put pressure on the State Government to start new recruitments. Although the State Government pretended to concede, it changed the recruitment rules in order to recruit teachers from caste and communities, supporting the JD/RJD in the elections. Subsequently, the court suspended this decision. Unsurprisingly, the Bihar government just left the positions vacant.

Not only did the bureaucracy suffer from a human resources crisis, resulting from caste polarization, but also politicization of the transfer of high-level bureaucrats decreased the level of its autonomy and effectiveness. Witsoe (2013, 88) identifies the strategic use of transfers as the vital tool to control the bureaucracy through the JD/RJD rule. Inspired by the idea of the relative autonomy of bureaucracy, it was supposed that governments (both at the Center and State levels) do not have the power to dismiss high-level bureaucrats and have limited disciplinary options. Therefore, frequent transfers instead of dismissing are often used as a tool to control bureaucrats, perceived as hostile to the governments of Yadav/Devi. Pankaj (2009, 20) introduces items such as insecurity of tenure, politically motivated transfers and appointments, and frequent transfers as the factors which negatively affected the effectiveness, capacity, and morale of civil servants.

The weakened bureaucracy and deinstitutionalization of State paved the path for the extensive corruption. Lalu Prasad himself was involved in the 'Fodder Scam,' which forced his resignation. The blameworthy situation of bureaucracy and development machinery of Bihar during the Lalu Raj is echoed in a letter, written by N.C. Saxena, the then Secretary of Rural Development in the Center, to the Chief Secretary of Bihar.

> Without going into the reasons for administrative decadence in Bihar, it is an open fact that the development machinery has nearly collapsed today, more so in the secretariat and central districts, which are prone to caste violence. An unfortunate impression has gained ground that the government is an arena where power and authority should be used for personal gains. Right from the block development officers to many district collectors and often some secretaries are busy making money or collecting money for their political masters. As corruption is on the increase even in the higher echelons of the bureaucracy, the fear in the minds of lower-level officials against taking money has disappeared. Corruption at all levels has become a low-risk, high reward activity… The lower level bureaucracy has no work ethic, no feeling for the public cause, no involvement in the future of the nation … they have only a grasping, mercenary outlook, devoid of competence, integrity, and commitment … During the year 1997–98, Rs 1177 crore was available to Bihar from the Union ministry for rural development for implementing various schemes. Since the number of poor families in Bihar is estimated to be about fifty lakh, allocation per family comes to Rs 2350 per annum, which is a substantial amount, the poor would have been perhaps better off

> if we could send this amount by money order directly to them bypassing the bureaucracy… Not a single rupee has been sanctioned by our department for drinking water schemes year because the Bihar government has not been able procedures for buying pipes for the last one year. The general feeling among field officers in Bihar is that the secretariat is largely dysfunctional.
>
> (Quoted in Thakur 2000, 146–147)

Personalization and centralization of power

The result of a combination of Lalu Yadav's charismatic leadership and dysfunctions of State's institutions was more centralization and personalization of political and administrative power. He was the central character of his party as well as the government. The political success of the JD and RJD in Bihar cannot be imagined without his active role. Even after his arrest, he continued his rule by cellphone calls to his wife, the new chief minister of Bihar. This period has been called the 'Cellphone Raj' era. Lalu Yadav's famous quotation "I am the State"[9] represents the level of centralization of power. The report of the World Bank (2005, 55) on the "Development Strategy of Bihar" introduced "personalized politics that obstructs institutionalized decision-making" as the main characteristic of Bihar's centralized government.

Thakur's (2000, 191) journalistic account below delineates how personalization and centralization of power in Lalu Yadav decreased the autonomy of bureaucracy and led to more deinstitutionalization of the State administration:

> Often the Chief Minister would himself ring up a block or thana-level officials to get work done. He totally disrupted the bureaucracy with his style of functioning, played havoc with the established order of things in the bureaucracy, one of Bihar's topmost serving officers told me, "For one thing, he totally demolished the hierarchy and created chaos. He would ring up block officers and 'darogas' and give them orders on the phone. Having established direct contact with the chief minister, these officials never listened to their superiors in the services; they became part of Lalu Yadav's cadre." … He never let any official feel secure; he kept people on tenterhooks, he bypassed them, overruled them brusquely, insulted them publicly. His methods were totally unconventional and erroneous, but he achieved what he wanted to.

In this centralized model, bureaucrats and civil servants had minor authorities; on the contrary, the major decisions should be made by the cabinet (with the dominant role of the chief minister). The collapse of the State bureaucracy, as well as centralization and personalization of power, crippled the capacity of the State Government to delivers services and sustain orderly rule. Since a considerable number of public sector jobs remained vacant, all main decisions should be made by the leadership of the Party, and the bureaucratic structure was fragmented, the State could not use the considerable transfers from the Center, intended for anti-poverty programs and developmental purposes. Figure 6.9

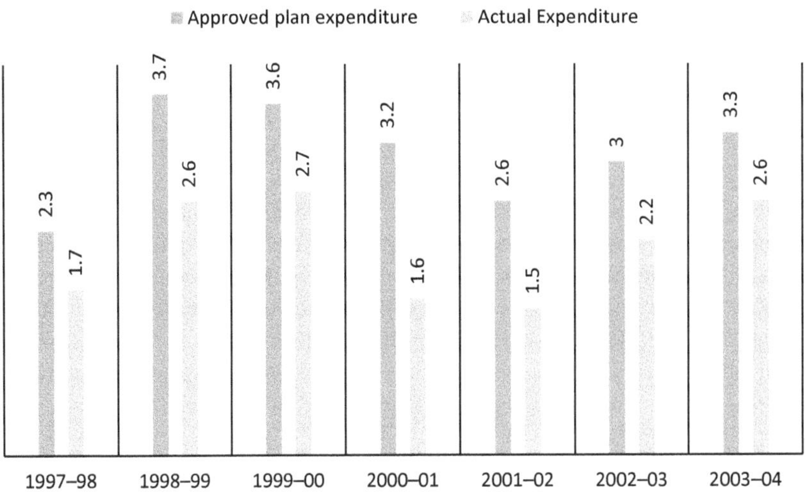

Figure 6.9 Plan expenditure of the Government of Bihar, 1997–2008 to 2003–2004.

Source: Mathew and Moore (2011, 23), drawn by the author.

displays how Bihar under Lalu administration could not spend a significant percentage of the Central transfers because it could not even complete the relevant bureaucratic procedures. As Mukherjee (2010) notes, inflexible and extremely centralized rules of expenditure were mostly responsible for Bihar's incapability to spend.

Similarly, the World Bank (2005, 51) criticized mostly the non-meritocratic bureaucracy of Bihar, which "is compounded by a highly centralized administration with the kind of incentive structure that thwarts decision-making and can cause major delays. This impairs the state's ability to manage public resources and implement projects and programs."

Conclusion

This chapter exemplifies how caste had been one of the critical variables that influenced the voting behavior in Bihar. However, after the emergence of 'lower-caste politics,' this factor became the primary explanatory variable for understanding and analyzing the post-1990 election. Prasad (1997, 3027) explains how regional political elites do not expect to gain reelection through their development agenda but expect to be rewarded by the voter they only focus on the Caste politics in the 1990s:

> Caste and social factions continue to play a major role in the elections in Bihar. What reinforces this pattern further is that the voters, who have largely turned cynical about the electoral political system, don't expect

> anything positive from their elected representatives. In the absence of any concrete agenda offered by the candidates or any sincere promise to fulfill them, elections have become just a means of establishing a phony social dominance by one group of castes over others.

Lalu Yadav and his party leaders as a rational regional political elite expected the most gain (reelection) from confrontational rhetoric and behavior against the upper caste dominance in the State as well as Central Government; as a result, they employed the anti-Center rhetoric (against both the Congress in the early 1990s and later the BJP) and took some populist welfare measures in favor of the OBCs, Dalits, and Muslims to keep them satisfied. Kumar (1999, 2474) delineates how the identity-based caste politics with its focus on *Azadi* (liberty, freedom) and *Izzat* (honor, dignity) of the poor and lower castes overshadowed the development as the expected performance of the government:

> The biggest surprise was that even though Lalu Yadav has been constantly blamed for neglecting developmental work, he still drew large support from the largest sections of society. If one takes a deeper look into the functioning of the Lalu government, during the past five years, one can understand why the poor and the Dalits have voted for the Janata Dal. The Dalits in general overwhelmingly supported Lalu Yadav. They were not satisfied with his performance for, besides constructing some houses under the Indira Awas Yojana for the Musahars, the poorest among the poor Dalits, nothing much has been done for them. But for many, it was the only occasion in their lifetime when they could vote. They reiterated that for them 'Azadi' came only during Lalu 's regime as now they enjoy a sense of self-pride and that upper-caste people do not encroach upon their independence now.

In three consecutive elections, Lalu was rewarded by the OBCs, Dalits, and Muslims because of his emphasis on *Izzat* of the poor. Laloo Yadav asserted that the mass poverty in Bihar is not a great concern; on the other hand, what matters, and what has driven his politics, is a search for *Izzat* of backward classes and castes. Corbridge et al. (2005, 237) elucidate how *Izzat* idea overshadowed developmental performances of government during the JD/RJD rule:

> Instead of an emphasis on jobs and services, he has emphasized the issue of social exclusion and a person's sense of self-worth or honor (Izzat). And in this specific respect, his politics can be judged a success. Poorer men and women in Bihar might not expect to gain much from the state, but some of them at least (perhaps the members of the 'creamy layers') no longer expect to be treated with disdain, or abusively. In any case, for the Yadavs and Kurmis, especially, many of the people they now see in the state are members of their own communities.

Lalu Yadav as a rational actor (egoistic player and maximizer of his interest) realized that the majority of the OBCs, Dalits, Muslims, and other marginalized constituents would reward him if he continues his *Izzat* rhetoric, confrontation with the Center (particularly with the NDA government) and some populist welfare measures. For these constituents, economic growth was less critical than *Izzat*. As Thakur (2000, 215) states:

> [Lalu] got away without governance for so long because to his deprived constituency, governance and development were strange concepts, concepts that hadn't mattered to their lives.

Notes

1 Lalu had been spelled 'Laloo' until 2004. In 2004, Lalu Prasad Yadav claimed that his opponents made Laloo popular instead of Lalu. Laloo could be mistaken for the Hindi word Lalloo, meaning fool (Witsoe 2013, 205). Therefore, the current book uses Lalu as the routine spelling.

2 Jharkhand is a state in eastern India, carved out of the southern part of Bihar on 15 November 2000.

3 Base year 2004–2005.

4 In 1991, Brahmin, Bhumihar, Rajput and Kayastha caste groups constituted 4.6%, 2.8%, 4.5% and 1.3% of the population of Bihar (Ravi Yadav 2004, 17).

5 Yadavs were the largest single caste group in Bihar with 13.8% of total population in 1991 (Ravi Yadav 2004, 17).

6 Kamraj plan was an initiative by K. Kamaraj, the chief minister of Tamil Nadu in order to rebuild the Congress Party at the grassroots level. He called for the voluntary resignations of high-level national and state officials in order to devote their efforts and energy to the re-vitalization of the Congress.

7 Izzat is an Arabic term, meaning honor and dignity. The term is used both in Persian and Hindi.

8 Bhurabal is a Hindi acronym for the four upper-caste groups in Bihar: Bhumihars, Rajputs, Brahmans, and Lalas (Kayasthas). Bhurabal Hatao was made based on Indira Gandhi's famous slogan, Gharibi Hatao (get rid of poverty).

9 This quotation is taken from the title of first chapter of Sankarshan Thakur's (2000) biography of Lalu Prasad Yadav (The Making of Laloo Yadav: The Unmaking of Bihar).

7 Elite agency and development in Bihar (II)

Pragmatism, cooperation, and reforms in the era of *Sushasan Babu*

Introduction

This chapter is all about the causes of a rapid policy shift in Bihar after 2005, which boosted the rate of growth and decreased the political disorder within the State. The chapter argues that without understanding and analyzing the political environment, which shaped the strategic choices of Nitish Kumar as a rational actor in his vertical and horizontal interactions, the remarkable policy shift in the State is not explicable. This chapter begins with tracing the political process, which led to the end of the so-called 'Jungle Raj' in Bihar. Then, after a short political biography of Nitish Kumar, explaining a journey from being a socialist to an advocate of 'good governance,' the chapter provides a clear analysis about the relationship between the chief minister, voters and the regional institutions in the horizontal game and the State–Center relations in the vertical game. The chapter illustrates how political determinants at both levels, encouraged the regional leader to opt for the subnational developmental strategies. Moreover, the chapter discusses how these necessities paved the path to choose a collaborative attitude toward the Center despite political differences. Moreover, the chapter delineates how the regional leader could generate new finical resources for the State not only by increasing the central transfers but also through cooperation with international financial organizations and the private sector.

The historical evidence presented here shows that Kumar could maximize his political benefits (reelection) by a skillful combination of the growth through State-led investment in infrastructure, reconstruction of the State bureaucracy and strengthening law and order in the State.

The end of 'Jungle Raj' and the rise of Nitish Kumar

The 2005 general and assembly election is the second turning point in the post-1990 politics in Bihar. After 15 years, Janata Dal (United) with the support of the NDA under the leadership of Nitish Kumar ended the rule of JD/RJD government and the dominance of the lower caste empowerment discourse.

However, the decline of Lalu Raj did not occur all at once. The 1998 general election was the first sign of erosion of Lalu and Devi's power in the State.

Nitish Kumar as the leader of the opposition party tried to effect a reconciliation between Janata Dal and Samta Party in the State. In the framework of the NDA, the BJP and the SP won 20 and 10 seats out of 54 respectively; while RJD secured only 17 seats. As the leader of the opposition, Nitish Kumar was rewarded with the critical Ministry of Rail Way in Vajpayee's government. As Figure 7.1 illustrates, the share of JD/RJD votes in Bihar has decreased since the 1998 Lok Sabha election. However, Nitish Kumar could not win the Assembly election until 2005. The 2005 Assembly election finally paved the path to form a new government and cleavage from the old lower caste empowerment discourse.

Lalu Yadav Prasad was not the only active student leader during the Bihar Movement in the 1970s. Nitish Kumar also has engaged in politics since the Movement. Like Lalu Prasad Yadav, Nitish Kumar was inspired by Jayaprakash Narayan' views on 'social justice.' Born on 1 March 1951, he grew up in a Kurmi family who has political experience. His father, Ramlakhan Singh, participated actively in the freedom movement and was a regional Congress activist. As Sinha (2011, 14–15) notes, despite his active participation in the Congress, the party had denied the nomination to Kumar's father, Ramlakhan Singh, from Bakhtiyarpur in 1952 as well as in the 1957 elections. Singh became unhappy with the Congress's decision; therefore, he left the Congress and fought against it under the flag of the Janata Party. With such anti-Congress mood, Singh's son Nitish Kumar started his political activities during his study at Patna University (1965–1973). Like Lalu Yadav Prasad, Nitish Kumar emerged as a student leader in the 1970s and was jailed during the Emergency. However, he was not as successful Lalu at the beginning of his political career. He lost the Assembly poll as a Janata Party candidate in the 1977 and 1980 elections. His first success in the election took place in the 1985 Assembly election, selected as an MLA from Harnaut in Nalanda. After the first success, he proved his abilities in a

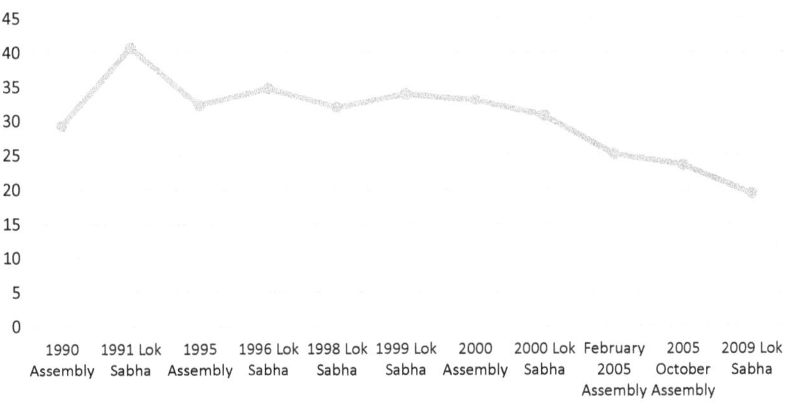

Figure 7.1 Vote share of JD/RJD in the elections (1990–2009) in divided Bihar.

Source: Statistical report on the General and Legislative Assembly of Bihar Elections, drawn by the author.

political career and progressed swiftly. Not only was he appointed as Bihar Janata Dal Secretary-General, but also, he won Barh Lok Sabha seat as Janata Dal candidate. He also served as Junior Agriculture Minister in the V.P. Singh government at the Center. However, he split from Lalu Prasad Yadav and formed the Samta Party with George Fernandes in 1994 (Thakur 2014, ix). He was elected as MP in the 1998 and 1999 general elections and became a close ally of the BJP in the framework of the NDA government. He had served as Minister of Agriculture in Vajpayee's government between May 2000 and March 2001, then appointed as Minister of Railway until 2004. Along with George Fernandes, the Defense Minister, Nitish Kumar played an active role in the foundation of Janata Dal (United), formed by the combination of a faction of the Janata Dal, the Lokshakti Party, and the Samta Party.

The 2005 Assembly election was the first election after the separation of Jharkhand and creation of a new State. Lalu Prasad Yadav, after long supremacy in the State's politics, realized that it would not be a smooth election. Not only did Yadav tried to strengthen his relationship with the Congress as a member of the UPA, but he also employed several other populist measures to provoke lower castes and Muslims against 'communalism' of the BJP. However, the alliance between the Congress, the RJD and the Lok Janshakti Party (LJP) broke up, and the RJD remained excluded (Robin 2009, 91). Moreover, as Ananth (2005, 13) claims, Lalu Yadav "was 'found,' distributing money to some poor people near Patna." These allegations also discredited Lalu more than ever.

In the first round of the election in February 2005, while the NDA coalition led by JD (U) won 92 seats, the RJD secured 72 seats; nevertheless, both sides were far from the 122 seats required to form a government. As a result, for the eighth time after independence, Bihar came under President's rule.

The Assembly election was held for the second time in November 2005. For the first time, the NDA coalition won 144 seats out of 243 seats, and formed a new government. As Robin (2009, 94) indicates, whereas Nitish Kumar decreased the share of Muslims, scheduled castes, and backward castes in his cabinet, he increased the proportion of the upper castes and extremely backward castes.

Nitish Kumar and the new developmental paradigm: change in the horizontal game

As Kumar (2013b, 112) maintains, Nitish Kumar's electoral success cannot be attributed to the "Bihar way of managing the polls." Not only did he not benefit from "the help of money and musclemen (bahubalis)," but also, he did not project himself as a leader for the lower castes. The electoral success of Nitish Kumar can be analyzed by considering several factors:

First, he did not depend on a specific caste group. Although his caste group, Kurmis, had a significant position among the OBCs, unlike Yadavs, they do not enjoy the demographic weight. Contrary to Lalu, who was dependent predominantly on MY (Muslim and Yadavs) as vote banks, Nitish tried to bring together a coalition of Kurmis, Koeris, the EBCs, lower Muslims, and the upper-caste and business community (Jha and Pushpendra 2015). While Lalu had polarized Bihar society by activating the cleavages between upper castes and other lower castes and classes, Nitish sought to form his political agenda based on social convergence. In his election campaign, Nitish Kumar tried to build a sense of Bihari identity instead of caste or religion identities among the voters. During Yadav/Devi rule, caste identity had become the essential identity of most Bihari people. While caste polarization led to an increase in communal conflicts, lawlessness, and violence, Lalu Yadav used it as the main source of his political power. Therefore, Nitish Kumar focused on the unification of all castes under the umbrella of 'Bihari Identity.' Kumar glorified the history of Bihar described Bihar people as "talented and industrious" (Sinha 2011, 217). Nitish Kumar asserted that a State, divided by caste identity, would not develop. Thus, he emphasized the role of Bihari subnationalism and stated:

> We have tried to move away from these categories (Religion and caste), and create an identity of subnationalism. To strengthen the country, you have to strengthen all regions. Only if all regions progress, there will be stability and growth in the country. These identities will not cease to exist but will get weaker. Here, we have tried to instill a sense of Bihari pride, and that has weakened caste and religious identity to some extent. But there is an orchestrated move to revive the other identities. But the good sign is that there is an inherent national identity in the consciousness of people, and sub-nationalism will become stronger. People will come together for different causes. Other identities will get subsumed within that. We connected the struggle for Bihar's rights with pride.
>
> (Kumar 2013a)

Second, Nitish Kumar promised restoration of law and order and implementation of a highly ambitious development agenda in his election campaign. Nitish Kumar declared his priority would be "to restore the rule of law within three months of coming to power" when he released the JD (U)-BJP manifesto for the second election in 2005 (Thakur 2014, 193). Nitish Kumar introduced 'Lalu Raj' as responsible for political instability, violence, and mass poverty in State. The central slogan JD (U)-BJP coalition was *Lalu Hatao*, referring to Lalu's confrontationist slogan, *Bhurabal Hatao*. As Sinha (2011, 197) clarifies, Nitish Kumar's electoral campaign did not only stress the negative aspects of Lalu Yadav's reign such as the collapse of bureaucracy or lawlessness; on the contrary, he invested much time in his speeches to his promises for development. Nitish's elections campaign highlighted his developmental orientation, providing *Sushasan* (good governance) by replacing *kushasan* (bad governance) of the Yadav/Devi regime. Nitish Kumar sought to differentiate himself with a good governance slogan from Lalu's lower caste empowerment agenda. Instead of being '*Gharibon Ka Masiha*,' his strategic choice was to highlight his image as a performance-oriented politician who had a successful experience as a minister at the Center.

As Sinha (2011, 217) asserts, "The advantage he (Nitish Kumar) enjoys was that people – even those who idolized Lalu – desired development." The JD (U) and its allies won the 2005 and 2010 State elections and 2009 general election using the slogan of *Sushasan* and development. The majority of constituents in Bihar did not reward the confrontation and polarization in the name of caste and social justice anymore. On the other hand, the promises for development and reforms were rewarded. As Kumar and Ranjan (2009, 23) observe:

> The common perception was that elections in Bihar are associated only with the caste factor, the results of the 2009 Lok Sabha elections may be seen as a rebuttal to that. If people in Bihar voted only on caste considerations, the Rashtriya Janata Dal (RJD) and Lok Janshakti Party (LJP) should have done fairly well in the state.

Bihar as a developmental (subnational) state under the JD (U) rule

The beginning of the 1990s was a turning point in the development trajectory of India as a whole and its subnational states. With the end of Congress era and the rise of other regional and national parties as well as coalition politics at the Center, the States secured more autonomy in economic decision-making. According to Jenkins (1999, 2003), Mitra (2011) and Kennedy (2004, 2014), the liberalization of economy and globalization played a significant role in more autonomy of States In the era of post-Congress era polity and dismantling of the Center-led development model, Bihar also attained more autonomy in terms of economic planning. However, with the rise of lower caste politics, and anti-development attitude of Lalu Yadav, this relative autonomy of Bihar was not translated into a more efficient policymaking. The strategic choice of Lalu Yadav such as anti-Center and upper caste policies crippled the State bureaucracy and administration.

Unlike the 'Lalu Raj' era, subjugated by the economic and financial consequences of confrontation with the Center and caste polarization, Nitish Kumar realized that confrontation with the Center and caste politics cannot enhance economic development; as a result, he tried reconstruction of bureaucracy, restoration of law and order, and creating a business-friendly environment to attract private domestic and foreign investments.

Under Nitish Kumar, Bihar transformed from one of the slowest-growing States to a fast-growing State, whose rate of growth could be compared with Gujarat. After several fluctuations in the rate of growth during the JD/RJD rule, the post-2005 growth process of Bihar's economy has more stability and continuity. In the new era, Bihar's growth rate was one of the highest among all States. According to recent data (Government of Bihar 2015), in the first five years rule of Nitish Kumar (2005–2006 to 2009–2010), the annual average of growth rate was 10.2%. This rate increased in the second term of the JD(U) rule (2010–2011 to 2013–2014) and reached 10.4%. As the Reserve Bank of India reports (2015), the NSDP of Bihar in 2004–2005 was Rs 701.67 billion at constant prices, yielding a per capita income of Rs 7914. The NSDP at constant prices in 2014–2015 is Rs 1718.02 billion, implying a per capita income of Rs 16,801.

Developmental elite at the state level: Nitish Kumar as *Sushasan Babu*

As aforementioned, Leftwich (1995, 405–407, 2000, 152–196) identifies 'determined developmental elite' as one of the most substantial and compulsory factors for the emergence of developmental states. After a long history of caste politics, violence, and stagnation, and dominance of politicians who had corruption or criminal background, Nitish Kumar with his emphasis on the development of Bihar emerged as the new style of leadership in the State.

In the horizontal game, Nitish Kumar, as a rational actor, witnessed the caste/community vote banks of Lalu (MY and other lower castes) who rewarded him for his *Izzat* promises, despite his poor performance at the State level. Moreover, Lalu Yadav with his humor, theatricality, and rustic oratory was an attractive character for the rural masses. When Lalu was elected as the MP in the 1977 elections, Nitish could not be elected as an MLA. Nitish also could not compete successfully with Lalu in the 1990s. Lalu was a professional leader who could use the caste politics weapon against his opponents; as a result, Nitish required another tool to challenge the RJD in the State. Nitish Kumar used 'development' and 'law and order' as an instrument for political mobilization against Lalu in his election campaign.

His most famous slogan was *Nyaya ke saath vikas ka wada*, translated as 'promise of justice with development' (Jha and Pushpendra 2015). He sought to bridge between votes of forward caste elites as well as the OBS, EBCs, Dalits, and Muslims. Not only upper caste who dominated business community, as well as bureaucracy, responded positively to the new manifesto but also Dalits, EBCs and some section of OBCs, frustrated by lawlessness and stagnation, rewarded Nitish with their vote.

Nitish Kumar realized that securing and sustaining political power in Bihar is not possible anymore through populism, polarization, and confrontation with the Center. On the other hand, the constituents would reward him if he demonstrated his performance to deliver more services and enforce the rule of law. Therefore, development of State became the central goal of his government.

Nitish Kumar as an experienced minister in the Central Government was aware of the ongoing rivalries among the Indian States to attract more financial transfer from the Center. Moreover, Kumar had a clear image of the inter-state competition to attract private national or international investors. He tried by the implementation of measures for law and order management as well as economic and administrative reforms to encourage the private investors as well as international aid agencies to consider Bihar as the new destination for investments. Like regional leaders such as Chandrababu Naidu, Nitish Kumar belongs to a new generation of Indian politicians who possess a neo-liberal developmental perspective and techno-managerial approach.

Nitish Kumar was the main character on the reform stage. He pushed his cabinet and the State bureaucracy to formulate and implement the reform agenda. His government had sufficient legislative support and could enact the required acts to strengthen the legal framework for reform. Although the program for reform in Bihar could not be implemented without political backing from the Center and social support in the State and bureaucracy, the reforms could not be imagined without Kumar's leadership and his strategic choices. As Mukherjee's (2010) interviews with the major players in State Government reveal, the reforms in Bihar were "driven from the top, the Chief Minister's Office." That is why he called the reform in Bihar 'one-man effort.'

Sushasan as the symbol of change

Nitish Kumar gradually changed the political agenda of State from 'lower caste empowerment' to 'development.' Although Nitish Kumar began his political life with a socialist perspective and focused on social justice, he gradually became closer to more liberal economic views especially after his alliance with the BJP. Whereas the keyword of Lalu's political discourse was *Izzat* and social justice, Nitish Kumar's keyword was *Sushasan* (good governance), implying the influence of the neo-liberal discourse. As a socialist who transformed to a neo-liberal developmental-oriented leader, Kumar saw pro-business policies as a tool for enhancing economic development and reduction of mass poverty.

On account of the fact that Nitish Kumar emphasized 'good governance' in his policy agenda, the media nicknamed him *Sushasan Babu*, the man of good governance (Sinha 2011, 7). Influenced by the neo-liberal idea of 'good governance is a prerequisite for the development,' Nitish Kumar emphasized the idea of 'development with social justice' through *Sushasan* (good governance) that would lead to a 'Resurgent Bihar' (Gupta 2013, 177). The *Sushasan* included a set of general approaches. ADRI (2007) introduces these approaches:

- Minimum function of the state: A functioning government through the introduction of initiatives in the fields of law and order, administrative reforms, and fiscal management.
- Growth: Stimulate growth in the agricultural and industrial sectors through the introduction of new agricultural and industrial policies.
- Growth in human development: Facilitate growth in human development through improvements in service delivery of health and education.
- Infrastructure development: Focus on basic infrastructure development including road construction, power generation, and urban development.
- Empowerment: Efforts to empower marginalized classes at the panchayat level.

The Center also encouraged the State Government to implement policies based on a 'good governance' agenda. In the first step, the 'Report of Special Task Force on Bihar' (2007, 12) recommended that the State Government should launch a Centre for Good Governance, similar to Andhra Pradesh, "with an Executive Agency staffed by experts and headed by a professional who is a domain expert and give it a comparable role in designing good governance initiatives." Four years later, the Government of Bihar set up The Centre for Good Governance Society (CGGS) with the objective of providing high-quality policy, managerial and capacity building support to Government Departments and its officials.

The *Sushasan* as a political term finds the symbolic position in the history of Bihar. The term implies the post-Lalu era and differentiates between the new era and 15 years of the JD/RJD rule. Lalu Yadav realized the importance of this term in the public opinion. Nitish Kumar could defeat him with the slogan of *Sushasan*; as a result, Lalu Yadav several times tried to nullify Nitish Kumar's usage of the term in his political agenda:

> *Yeh shasan hai Maharaj Sushasan ka/ Khel ho raha hai kushasan ka/ Barh, sukhar sejanata to rulayenge/RSS ki goad mein baith kar secular kahlayenge.* (Bad governance characterizes the regime of Lord Good Governance/ People hit by drought and floods cry in misery/ Mr. Good Governance claims to be secular while being a puppet in the hands of the RSS.)
>
> (Sinha 2011, 6)

Policy reforms and initiatives in Bihar

A World Bank report, titled *Bihar: Towards a Development Strategy* (2005) recognized three challenges for the development of Bihar: first, the problem of improving growth performance, second, the challenge of improving the social service delivery, and third, the challenge of strengthening the public administration and governance.

Unsurprisingly, after the victory, Nitish Kumar realized that revival and strengthening of State institutions, improving the law and order situation, fiscal management, improving the business climate, investment in infrastructures and introduction of new schemes and measures for public service delivery should be his first priorities. The NDA government policy reforms and initiatives in Bihar rotate around the three core recommendations of the World Bank:

Fiscal management and resource utilization

Improving the performance of the State in terms of growth needed effective fiscal management. Erosion of State bureaucracy, confrontations with the Center, and lack of investments caused a critical condition in the State finance, including high debt with increasing pension and interest payment burden. According to the *White Paper on State Finances and Development* (Government of Bihar 2006, 5–7), the requirement for the committed non-developmental expenditure (pensions, salaries, loan repayment, interest payments, and maintenance) of the State Government was Rs 16,582 crores, whereas the income of the State Government was Rs 12,882 crores. The gap should be filled by the loans from the Central Government or the market. The State Government already had a debt liability of Rs 42,483 crores. In the 2004–2005 financial year, the State Government paid Rs 3474 crores on account of interest, which constituted almost 29.2% of its income excluding Central Government grants. Moreover, the pension to retired State Government employees constituted 18%, salary payment 37.3%, and debt repayment 24% of the State Government's income. The report concluded with the following sentence:

> The State Government hardly spent anything on development from its own income. Whatever was spent on development was either from the grants-in-aid from the Central Government or from a loan from the market.
>
> (Government of Bihar 2006, 7)

As the first priority of State Government, it approved its own 'Fiscal Responsibility and Budget Management' (FRBM) Act in February 2006 as a positive response to the national FRBM Act. Based on these acts, the State Government committed to lowering the overall fiscal deficit to less than 3% of GSDP. With the passing of the FRBM Act, the focus of the State Government was to find ways to finance the existing deficit through appropriate debt management, expenditure rationalization, and tax mobilization measures (Government of Bihar 2007, 10).

Moreover, Nitish Kumar – as a member of the NDA – did not adopt a confrontational strategy toward the Center, which was ruled by the UPA coalition. Both State and the Center in the framework of a neo-liberal consensus believed in the significance of the economic reforms. Therefore, despite political differences, the Center approved and supported the development agenda of Nitish Kumar and increased the transfers to the State.

The target of the FRBM Act was achieved in the 2008–2009 financial year, and a fiscal deficit of the State limited to less than 3%. Figure 7.2 illustrates how fiscal reforms in Bihar and financial discipline and financial support of the Center led to a meaningful positive change in developmental expenditures of the State Government after 2005.

Depoliticization of the state bureaucracy

Mukherjee (2010, 2) identifies three of Kumar's administrative reforms: "first, to restore the physical infrastructure and procedural foundations of the State; second, to delegate authority within administrative hierarchies, particularly with regard to financial expenditures; and third, to bring government closer to the people."

The first strategic move of Nitish Kumar was a reconstruction of the State bureaucracy and strengthening its human capital. Whereas Lalu Yadav preferred to appoint the OBCs or Muslims in the crucial posts or keep them vacant, Nitish Kumar needed to reconstruct the State bureaucracy, based on meritocracy. As a result, after one decade and a half of the anti-upper caste approach of the State

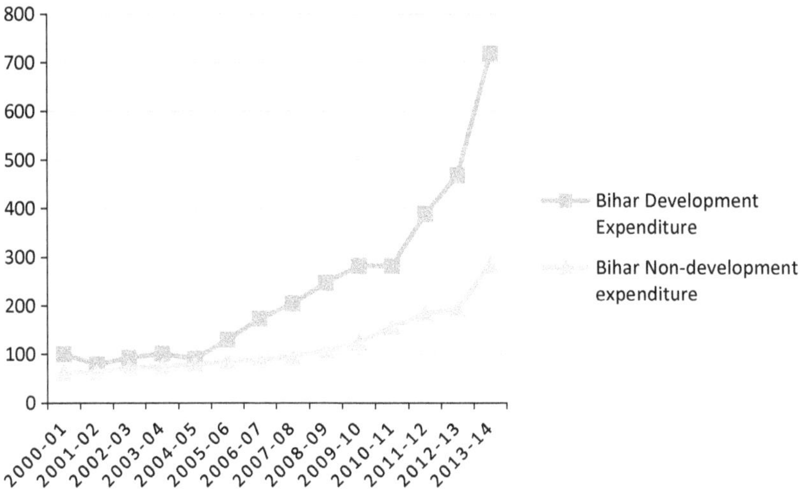

Figure 7.2 Bihar's development expenditure and non-development expenditure between 2000-2001 and 2013–2014.

Source: *State Finances: A Study of Budgets* (Reserve Bank of India 2015), drawn by the author.

Government, Nitish Kumar needed to use the employees from other castes and social groups. The first likely candidates were the upper caste members who already supported the NDA coalition in the election. The upper caste representation in the government increased to 37% (Robin 2009, 94). As Jha and Pushpendra (2015, 192) illustrate, the most prominent share of government posts was allocated to Bhumihar, who were traditionally dominant in the Congress era. However, the victory of the NDA coalition was not synonym to the domination of upper caste politicians, organized mostly in the BJP.

Although the upper castes played a crucial role in the victory of Nitish Kumar, relying on them could create a critical challenge for him. Some of the BJP members and other groups such as RSS were involved in criminal activities (Witsoe 2013). If these politicians had been appointed as ministers or other significant posts in the State bureaucracy, it would be tough to restore law and order in the State. Not only was the appointment of politicians affiliated with criminal groups a green light to other caste militias, but also Nitish Kumar would lose the support of Muslims, and increase the possibility of communal riots.

Nitish Kumar mollified the upper castes by measures such as disbanding the Amir Das Commission (which had been established to examine the political links and role of the Ranvir Sena, a Bhumihar caste militia, in spreading caste violence) or deciding to not implement the recommendations of the Bihar Land Reforms Commission in favor of upper caste groups (Jha and Pushpendra 2015, 193). Nevertheless, Nitish Kumar shifted the power from elected (mostly upper caste) politicians to recruited officials in the State bureaucracy. As Witsoe (2013, 303) reports, although Nitish Kumar centralized power in the post of chief minister, he almost avoided the caste consideration for the appointments in the bureaucracy:

> Nitish sought to revive the bureaucracy by operating through a 'core team' of senior IAS officers. In crucial departments, while Nitish distributed ministerial posts out of political compulsion, corrupt ministers were teamed with secretaries with honest reputations, undermining the influence of the former. Circulars instructed officials at all levels, including police thanas and block offices, to resist interference from politicians, including those from the ruling party. The government threatened politicians caught unduly influencing administration, including those from the ruling party, with being charge-sheeted and arrested. As we would expect, a broad governing alliance enjoying both upper-caste, as well as lower-caste support, resulted in higher cooperation and cohesion between different state institutions.

As Mukherjee (2010, 4) reports, instead of the appointment of the aforementioned politicians, the chief minister's office called several Bihari IAS officers who were serving in the different departments at the Center or living abroad to come back to Bihar. Therefore, after seven years high-ranking bureaucrats such as Navin Kumar came back to serve as the principal secretary of the Finance Department.

The next step was fighting against corruption among the civil servants. The State Government used the services of retired CBI officers to form a special vigilance unit in the Vigilance Department. The investigation into the bribery cases or whom cases have been filed on assets disproportionate to their known sources of income was the primary task of this particular unit (Government of Bihar 2007, 12).

Law and order management

The first precondition for attracting private companies, investors, entrepreneurs, and tourists is a secure and stable physical environment. The first move of Nitish Kumar government to manage law and order was the creation of the 'State Auxiliary Police' (SAP) force (Government of Bihar 2007, 11). This force was staffed entirely by 5000 ex-army employees in the State. This staff had been trained to conducting warfare; thus; they were better trained than the State Police to fight criminals and Naxalites and caste militias (Mukherji and Mukherji 2015, 179).

Although the SAP had primary responsibility for restoring order in the State, the government did not neglect the police and used a contingency fund for structural strengthening of police administration and its modernization. Also, new posts in the police forces were sanctioned and filled to ensure more efficiency (Government of Bihar 2007, 12). Sinha (2011, 242) interviewed a policeman about the results of the SAP operations:

> Between 2005 and 2009 there were 118 encounters between police and extremists in which 62 extremists were killed. A total of 835 illegal fire arms, including 66 looted from police, 365 landmines/bombs, 116 hand grenades and 41,462 cartridges were recovered from them.

Furthermore, the long judicial process was the second major problem in the restoration of order in the State. The Legislative Assembly passed the 'Bihar Special Courts Bill' in 2009 in order to accelerate convictions for hardened criminals. Under the Bihar Special Courts Bill, several notorious political and non-political criminals were investigated and prosecuted.

Enhancing the service delivery system

The deinstitutionalization of State and fragmentation of public services during the RJD rule forced Nitish Kumar to invest a lot of time and energy in the reconstruction of a basic public service delivery system, social sectors such as health, education, and infrastructural sectors like power and roads.

By implementing the Right to Information Act (RTI), Kumar's government introduced *Jankari*, an e-governance program, allowing anyone to call up and file an RTI request on public services on the phone. This initiative quickly caused a degree of transparency in the State Government decision-making and more accountability. This program and other RTI initiatives controlled some corruptions, decreased abuses of power and consequently improved public confidence.

The fiscal discipline and the higher amount of the central transfers facilitated social expenditures of the State Government. There was a steady rising trend of Per Capita Development Expenditure (PCDE) of Bihar during the 2001–2002 to 2010–2011 financial years. While the PCDE of Bihar hsd been Rs 930 in 2001–2002, it rocketed to Rs 3467 in 2010–2011. While the PCDE of India grew at an annual rate of 13.6%, the PCDE growth rate of Bihar was 17.1%. Moreover, the social sector spending improved from 18.9% in 2001–2002 to 31.9% in 2010–2011 in Bihar (Government of Bihar 2012, xxix).

The collapse of the education system was the major challenge to the State. While the literacy rate in Bihar it was 47.0% in 2001, this rate was 65.4% in India. Moreover, the female literacy rate was much lower at 33.6%, as against a national average of 54.2% (Census of India 2011). As mentioned previously, despite relatively high salaries, the public school teachers had been notorious for their high absenteeism. Kumar's government employed more than 200,000 teachers through an innovative decentralized reform, to revive schools across the villages.

Since the State Government had no sufficient financial resources to employ official state-level teachers, Nitish Kumar decided to involve Panchayats to recruit the new teachers at low, market-related wages (Aiyar 2013, 55). This policy accelerated the expansion of elementary education at low cost. On account the fact that the quality of these recently hired teachers was low, Kumar's government tried to improve their skills through teacher training plans.

The remarkable investments of Kumar's government in the education and his policy initiatives improved the education indicators in the State. For instance, total enrollment in elementary classes increased at an annual rate of 8.2%. Furthermore, the rate of total enrollment in upper primary classes grew at an annual rate of 19.1% from 2002–2003 to 2009–2010 (Government of Bihar 2012, xxix). Consequently, Bihar's literacy rate improved from 48% in 2001 to 63.8% by 2011; the fastest among all States. Furthermore, the gap between literacy rate of Bihar and the national average decreased from 17% in 2001 to 10.2% in 2011(Census of India 2011).

The road (highways as well as rural roads) as the basic economic infrastructure became the top priority for the State Government agenda. Supported by the approved expenditure, the State Government introduced the aggressive road construction schemes like *Mukhya Mantri Gram Sadak Yojana* (Chief Minister's Rural Roads Program).

The State Government allocated a considerable amount of its development expenditure to road construction. While the State Government spent Rs 263.22 crore in 2005–2006, the expenditure on roads has reached Rs 2489.15 crore in 2008–2009 (Government of Bihar 2010, xxv). According to Mukherji and Mukherji (2015, 187), there has been an increase of almost 25% in the total length of roads from 2007 to 2010. This agenda increased the Bihar highway network from 3021 km to 3787 km. As Witsoe (2013, 194) reveals, aggressive road building schemes played a significant role in enhancing Bihar's economic growth rate from 2005 to 2011.

Reconstruction of the State bureaucracy, restoration of public order and an increase in the central transfers paved the path for an increase in the rate of economic growth as well as human development indicators. The reappearance of safety, the rapid expansion of the road network and government sponsored investment in education, health, and other infrastructure all created new economic opportunities. These policies enhanced economic growth and attracted the attention of international financial organizations to the State.

A subnational state and international aid agencies: Bihar and the World Bank

While Bihar with its notorious records of violence, erosion of public services, and corruption had deprived of international cooperation and investments during 'Lalu Raj,' Nitish Kumar's aggressive development agenda attracted the attention of international financial organizations. The World Bank in its report "Bihar: Towards a Development Strategy" (World Bank 2005) provided the policy recommendations for the new chief minister of Bihar.

Nitish Kumar's initial reforms were mostly based on the World Bank's recommendation. Impressed by Nitish Kumar's obligation to neo-liberal economic reforms, the World Bank began the cooperation with the State and allocated a considerable amount of loans and aids to Bihar. As Kirk (2011, 130) elaborates, the World Bank committed to a Rural Livelihood Project

Loan of US$63 million and a Development Policy Loan (DPL) of US$225 million in 2007.

Not only the World Bank, but also other donors such as the ADB, DFID, and Japan's Official Development Assistance (ODA) have coordinated with the Bank on a joint strategy for Bihar.

Nitish Kumar and the Center: the vertical game

When Nitish Kumar began his tenure, Bihar's own revenue, tax, and non-tax combined, hardly met 20% of its total expenditure, and the rest should have been provided by the Central Government.

According to *Economic Survey, 2006–07* (Government of Bihar 2007) the share of the State's own tax revenue in total tax revenue has remained between 22 and 28% between 2001 and 2007. The own non-tax revenue of the State has also remained approximately constant during this period except for an increase in the 2006–2007 budget estimates.

According to the report, published by Government of Bihar (2007, 180), the massive transfer of resources including the State's share of Central taxes, grants-in-aid from the Centre, as well as loans increased steadily from 38% to as much as 72% of the aggregate disbursements, excluding the Central loans. More than 80% of the gross amounts for transfer to the State came from its share of Central taxes and the rest from grants and loans. The reports conclude that "The state remains absolutely dependent on the Centre, making it financially vulnerable."

While the State depends extensively on the Central transfers, Lalu Prasad Yadav implemented a confrontational strategy against the Center as the primary tool for sustaining his power. Nevertheless, Nitish Kumar with his promises to restore law and order and economic development needed a more financial transfer from the Center.

Although he won the 2005 election as part of the NDA, he did not implement a confrontational strategy against the UPA government at the Center. As a pragmatist political leader, he tried to find the way to cooperate with the Center and appease them to allocate more financial resources to the State:

> I want money… I am ready to give anyone any concession so long as they fill my treasury.
>
> (Kumar 2006)

The nature of relations between the Center and the State Government has been transformed from the confrontation based on lower caste politics to partial cooperation mainly in the field of economic development and public services. Even the conflicts between the State Government and the Center were mainly about the State's share of the national funds. For instance, Nitish Kumar (2007) asked the Center to invest more in the Bihar education system:

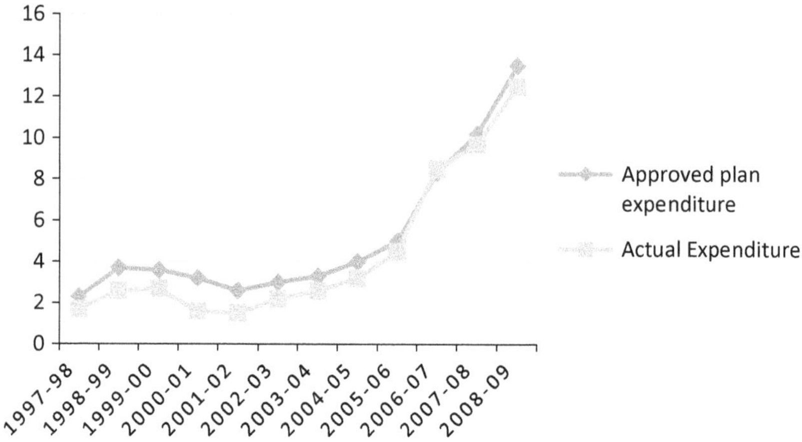

Figure 7.3 Plan expenditure of the Government of Bihar, 1997–1998 to 2008–2009.

Source: Government of Bihar (Economic Survey, 2007, 2010, 2012), drawn by the author.

> There is a shortage of good-quality centers of higher education in Bihar. We do not have any IIT [Indian Institute of Technology] here. In the field of education, Bihar needs a lot of assistance from the Centre. Of course, we have initiated moves with our own resources. But we also need help. We have initiated a massive enrollment of teachers in schools. But we also need to improve the infrastructure in schools. We need more classrooms in schools, and although the Centre is providing a portion of the funds for these, we have to invest substantial amounts on our own. We have also asked the Centre when it plans to proceed with making the idea of common [neighborhood] schools a reality.

Inspired by his obligation to the development of State and his attitude toward the Center, the Central Government rewarded the Nitish Kumar Government by approving a considerable number of plan outlays. Figure 7.3 depicts how after the rise of Nitish Kumar in the State, he could successfully attract a higher amount of approved plan expenditure and also used it for developmental purposes.

Conclusion

The interaction perspective developed in Chapters 6 and 7 urges attention to regional institutions – formal (for example bureaucracy) or informal (for example caste), subnational leaders (both Lalu Yadav and Nitish Kumar), and their strategic calculations based on local political conditions and national level political environment that affect the State Government response toward the economic reforms, supported by the Center.

Interestingly, despite studies suggesting there is a positive correlation between democratic regimes and economic performance, the case of Bihar in the age of Lalu indicates that the subnational democratic competition makes the reelection the main incentive for a regional leader to decide on more confrontational and aggressive attitudes that can stall the implementation of the economic reforms. The findings of these chapters suggest that it is likely in a pluralist democratic system, where local incentives produce rewards for confrontation (in the case of Bihar, caste politics), that the regional leaders will intensify the tension between Center and State.

Nevertheless, when there is no expected reward for confrontation, there is more likelihood to opt for more cooperation and implement the economic policies suggested by the Center. In the case of Nitish Kumar, the voters including the upper castes, Non-Yadav OBCs and/or EBCs, and backward Muslims did not reward caste polarization or anti-Center rhetoric. Rather, they rewarded slogans such as maintaining law and order and good governance. That is why Kumar as a democratic regional ruler also pursued cooperation with the Center to get more financial resources to ensure fulfillment of electoral promises.

8 Conclusion

A transformed institutional arrangement, rational regional leaders, and development

The problem restated

Multiple subnational trajectories of development within a state after the implementation of economic reforms is the problem studied in this book. The discovery of different developmental pathways within India cannot be explicated by both neo-liberal and neo-statist approaches which mostly concentrate on the Center. This study suggests that attention should not be paid solely to macro-allocation institutions (state versus markets); rather micro 'causal mechanisms' are significant too. Accordingly, the central question of this study was why have Andhra Pradesh, and Bihar showed a significant divergence in political and development trajectory after liberalization? Noticeably, both States operated under the same political structure and possessed comparatively similar initial economic conditions after independence. Moreover, they experienced strong subnational movement, which ended the hegemony of the Congress Party in both States.

My study of the puzzle of various subnational development trajectories engages the debate on the political economy of India at a time when governance research as a whole has emerged as a new perspective in development studies and political economy. The international financial organizations such as the World Bank, from their earlier emphasis on economic conditionalities, particularly in the wake of post-Soviet Union Era, have moved on to political conditionalities by introducing of *good governance* as a precondition for development. Unlike studies based on good governance with their emphasis on voice and accountability, electoral democracy and lack of corruption, this book locates itself in the framework of the comparative political economy in which analytical power has been enriched by rational choice institutionalism, subnational comparative method, and analytic narrative. Instead of opting for a normative approach with a predesignated definition of *good* governance, I have argued in this book in favor of governance as an analytical term that can capture and delineate the relations between state and society, the Center and States, interactions between regional, national and international levels, and elite agency and institutional determinants. This book deals with governance as the institutional arrangements that form the pattern of the exercise of power in society and its impact on the economic development. The central claim of this book is the change in these institutional arrangements in India after the end of one dominant party system, and later the beginning of the liberalization created room to maneuver for the chief ministers. Although scholars like Rudolph and Rudolph (2013) or Wyatt (2017), recognized the effect of this institutional transformation, they did not offer a model to explicate the causes of different strategic choices of the chief ministers.

The methodological innovation of this work is the unpacking of the internal architecture of the state in India with a focus on delimiting the State–Center relations. This book has used a simple two-level game model that depicts the choices that chief ministers go through in real-life situations when deciding between the options with regard to the rules of the game. The chief ministers are faced with vertical and horizontal games. They abide by the rules because doing otherwise would be costly in terms of the sanctions that are likely to follow, or because they can maximize their political interest (reelection or getting a higher position at the Center). Also, the chief ministers rebel when obeying the rules of the game cannot provide the expected reward.

This final chapter tries to address the puzzle; therefore, based on the model and findings of our empirical chapters, four hypotheses are recalled. In the following sections, each conjecture has been discussed and analyzed.

The post-reform era in Bihar and Andhra Pradesh

H1: *If the political power of the dominant political party at the Center declines, the new room to maneuver of regional political elites makes their strategic choices (in order to gain reelection) the core determinants of economic policies in the states.*

Bihar and Andhra Pradesh were the significant strongholds of the Congress Party in the pre-liberalization era. In both States, the Congress emerged as the most important political actor after independence. In the 'one dominant party system' and dominance of the Congress in the Central Government as well as the State Governments, the main economic decisions were made at the Center and the high command in Delhi. India's Five-Year Plans, especially in the 1950s and 1960s with the central role of the Planning Commission, exemplify a centralized planned economy model. In the centralized planned economy model, the top-down process of economic policymaking and financial allocation with the vital role of the Prime Minister (Nehru, later Indira Gandhi) and other 'high commands' in Delhi, institutions like Planning Commission and India's Five-Year Plans limited the role of the chief ministers in both States.

The regional leaders, organized in the framework of the Congress, implemented the Center's recommended policies despite their internal factionalism and rivalries. Figure 8.1 illustrates the basic interactions between regional leaders and the Center in a cooperational two-level game model in the Congress era in both States.

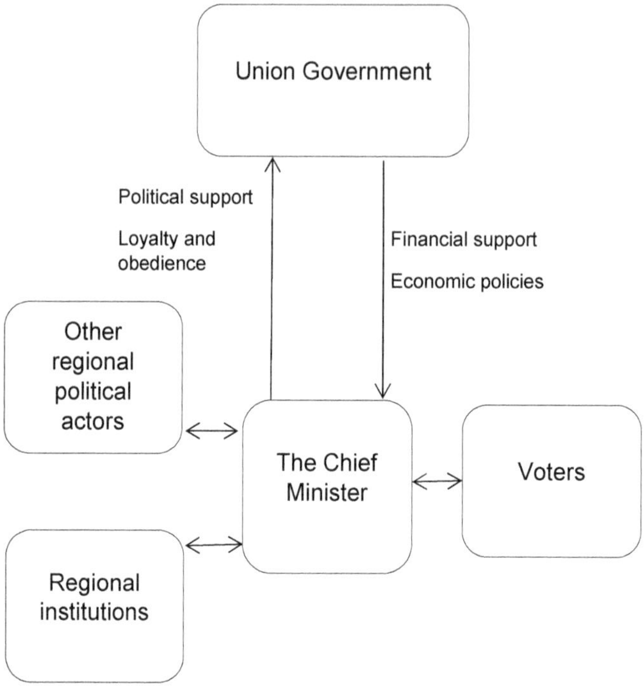

Figure 8.1 Cooperationist two-level game model, the Congress era.

Source: Drawn by the author.

However, the power of the Congress Party declined in both States and two different parties challenged the longstanding supremacy of the Congress. The erosion of the Congress system in Bihar and Andhra Pradesh could not be analyzed without considering the regional institutional variations. Although the dominant caste groups led the Congress after independence in both States, different caste structure caused a difference in the structure and capabilities of the Congress at the State level.

In Bihar, the upper caste politicians who came from Brahmin, Bhumihar, Rajput, or Kayastha castes dominated the Congress. These historically more privileged castes had better access to education, wealth, and power resources during the colonial era and the freedom movement. Accordingly, they emerged as the dominant political actors after the independence in Bihar. However, the differences in the caste background caused internal rivalries and power struggles among the Congress leaders within the party. The factionalism among the regional leaders gradually weakened the Congress in Bihar.

In contrast, the Reddy community, a dominant peasant caste, emerged as the principal political actor in the Congress in Andhra Pradesh. Although it was expected that Brahmins as the top of the pyramid of the caste system had more opportunity to organize themselves in the form of Congress, Reddy caste politicians attain most of the positions in the Party. Demographically, the dominant upper caste groups such as Brahmin constitute a minor percentage in Andhra Pradesh. Moreover, there was a clear cut between Brahmins' ritual status and economic position in Telangana region. While Brahmins in Bihar enjoyed both ritual and property privileges, Brahmins in Telangana had only ritual status and did not possess the significant landed properties. In Telangana, Brahmins should lease the lands from other agriculture upper castes such as Reddy. Therefore, Reddy and Kamma castes, possessing land and engaging more with the lower castes, had the potential to reach a better political position after independence. Therefore, the Reddy caste politicians without any internal challenge dominated the Congress in AP. While the emergence of alternative political parties that could end the one dominant party system began in several subnational states in 1967, 1971 or 1977 elections, Andhra Pradesh remained under 'Reddy Raj' of the Congress under until 1983.

The factionalism and internal conflicts among dominant caste groups in the party deteriorated the Congress position in Bihar, and it was defeated in the 1967 and the 1977 elections. Nevertheless, no strong alternative political party rose in the 1967 or 1977 elections that can consolidate its power. After these two short interruptions, the Congress as the only possible and accessible political platform came back to power.

In Andhra Pradesh, the TDP ended the Congress's supremacy in 1983 as the representation of Telugu subnationalism; however, the Congress came back to the power in the 1989 election. In Bihar, the 'Bihar Movement' for the first time challenged the dominance of the Congress. After the end of the emergency, Janata Party defeated the Congress in the 1977 election; however, the Congress came back to power again and ruled the State until 1990.

In the first years after the liberalization and economic reforms, introduced by P.V. Narasimha Rao's government, the opposition parties governed both States. Lalu Prasad Yadav who represented and led new anti-Congress forces in Bihar (Janata Dal), became the chief minister of Bihar in 1991; similarly, the TDP as the main opposition party in Andhra Pradesh won the 1994 election and N.T. Rama Rao became the new chief minister of Andhra Pradesh. Since the 'centrally planned economy' model was abolished, and the 'one dominant party model' transformed to a coalition politics model at the Center with a higher role for the regional parties at the State level, the strategic choices of these regional leaders in both States have become the core determinants for the way of implementation of economic policies.

Two new chief ministers opposed explicitly the economic liberalization, which had been adopted and recommended by the Center. The confrontation with the Center and rejecting the reform agenda were not the result of the political backwardness of these leaders; on the contrary, it can be seen as their strategy in a two-level game, aiming to maximize their interest (to gain reelection). These strategies are the core determents of economic policies in the States. Table 8.1 summarizes and compares the key features of Congress and the early post-Congress era in both States.

Table 8.1 Characteristics of the Congress and the early post-Congress era in both States

	Andhra Pradesh	*Bihar*
Dominant caste/in the Congress Party in the 'One dominant party' era	A dominant peasant caste: Reddy	Upper castes: Brahmin Bhumihar Rajput Kayastha
Characteristics of the Congress in the State	Remained undamaged even after the first Telangana movement, mostly dominated by the Reddy leaders	Fragmented by rivalries among the upper caste politician and factionalism
Pre-1990 political movements	Telangana movement Jai Andhra movement	Bihar movement
The defeats of the Congress in the pre-1990s election	Only 1983	1967 1977
The main challenger to dominance of the Congress in the State	TDP (the 1980s onward)	JP (the 1970s) JD/RJD (in the 1990s)
Party system after end of one dominant party system	Two-party system (rivalry between the Congress and TDP)	Absolute decline of the Congress/dominance of the regional parties
Charismatic leader of anti-Congress movement	N.T. Rama Rao (1983–1989) (1994–1995)	Lalu Prasad Yadav (1990–2005)
Caste background	Leadership: Kamma (local dominant peasant caste) Support: massive support especially from the OBCs and growing bourgeoisie	Leadership: Yadav (OBC) Support: the OBCs, Muslims, and SCs

Source: Drawn by the author.

The strategic choice of regional leaders: populist economic policies in the horizontal game and confrontation with the Center in the vertical game

H2: *If regional political elites expect the most gain (reelection) from confrontational rhetoric and behavior against the Central Government, they will opt for populist economic policies (handouts) – rather than implementing the reform agenda of the Central Government.*

In both States, the Congress Party's domination was broken by the regional leaders who were rewarded by constituents because of their anti-Center attitudes.

In both States, the non-Congress charismatic leaders led the anti-Center and anti-Congress movements.

The leader of the TDP, N.T. Rama Rao, a charismatic cinema superstar, led the anti-Congress movement by the slogan of self-respect for Telugu people *(Telugu Atma Gowrawam)*. He criticized the local Congress leaders who undermined the 'self-esteem' of Telugu people. The Telugu Desam Party as the manifestation of Telugu identity movement claimed that it fought against the corrupt Congress politicians in the State and their supporter in the Center. TDP introduced them as responsible for the backwardness of Telugu people.

As a populist leader, N.T. Rama Rao emphasized mainly the regional Telugu identity; nonetheless, the TDP was never a separatist party and remained loyal to India's federalism. One account of the fact that his strategic choice in the vertical game was the confrontation with the Center, he needed more political and social support within the State. Through the implementation of several welfare schemes and an increase in the subsidies, NTR tried to prove that his government could deliver services better than the Congress especially to the poor and backward castes and classes. In NTR's rhetoric, the Congress in the State was synonymous with the corrupt and greedy politicians, following Delhi's rule and forgetting the interest of poor Telugu people. Accordingly, NTR as a hero wants to rescue the Telugu people, revive their dignity and fight against the poverty. Therefore, the short-term welfare populist policies with tangible outcomes were more favorable than the economic policies pursued by the Center during Indira/Rajiv Gandhi's tenure and Narasimha Rao' liberalization.

In a similar pattern, the Congress was defeated by a charismatic leader, Lalu Prasad Yadav, in Bihar with the slogan of the revival of *Izzat* (honor, self-pride) of the OBCs, SCs, and minorities. As an apparent manifestation of lower caste politics, the JD and later RJD defined their core agenda to fight against the influence of the upper caste groups in the State. Lalu Yadav emphasized the caste politics and lower caste empowerment. Therefore, he portrayed the Congress Party, both at the State and the Center, as the manifestation of domination of the upper castes. As a result, the confrontation with the upper castes-dominated Congress was described as the pre-requisite for the emancipation of lower caste people. The constituents had also rewarded the hostility with the 'Upper Caste Dominated Center' during the NDA government. Lalu Prasad Yadav portrayed the reform agenda and the economic liberalization as an instrument that benefits the upper caste-dominated business community rather than backward caste people. Therefore, he preferred the short-term welfare populist policies with clear outcomes in favor of targeted caste or community groups instead of following the economic reform agenda.

Figure 8.2 exposes the strategic choices of these two regional leaders when they were elected in the regional elections, and the Congress was ruling at the Center. The findings of this study suggest that in both States, N.T. Rama Rao, as well as Lalu Prasad Yadav as the rational regional political actors, expected the most gain (reelection) from confrontational rhetoric and behavior against the Central Government. For that reason, both employed the anti-center rhetoric (against the Congress in the 1980s and early 1990s by N.T. Rama Rao and against the Congress at the

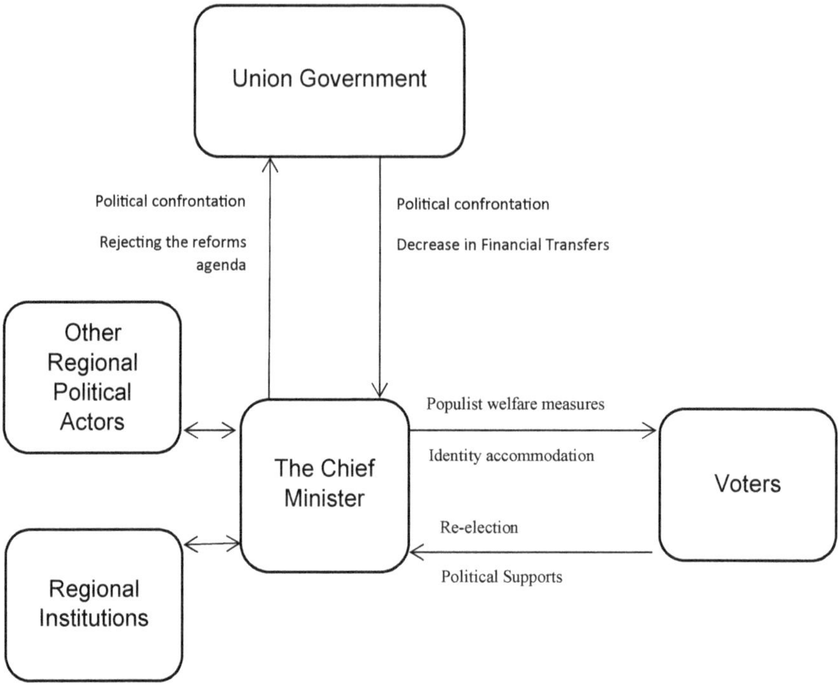

Figure 8.2 Confrontational game model, the post-Congress era.

Source: Drawn by the author.

beginning of the 1990s and the NDA between 1998 and 2004). Both leaders needed to sustain the constituent's political support; especially when they were threatened by the Center (through tools such as the President's rule or reducing the central transfers). The short-term populist welfare measures with the clear outcomes are the similar strategy in the horizontal game. The populist policies such as the Rs 2 a kilo rice scheme, *Janata* cloth scheme or subsidized housing for the poor in Andhra Pradesh and *Arvada* schools for shepherd boys, declaring hundreds of slums in Patna and other towns as regularized, and several job reservations for the OBCs and minorities in Bihar are the most significant examples of these strategic choices in the horizontal game. Being '*Gharibon Ka Masihai* (Messiah of the Poor) or *Anna* of Telugus provided more political support for these leaders in their confrontation with the Center.

The characteristics of anti-Congress movements in each State played different roles in the vital strategic choices of regional leader in the horizontal game. While N.T. Rama Rao tried to unify all Telugus regardless of their caste and community based on Telugu subnational identity and mobilized them against the Congress rule, Yadav's lower caste politics rhetoric was based on the polarization of castes.

In Andhra Pradesh, the emergence of Telugu-sub nationalism with its focus on the unity and self-pride of 'all Telugu' people reduced the intensity of regional movements like the Telangana movement. N.T. Rama Rao required the State bureaucracy to deliver effective services to the 'deprived Telugu people.' Therefore, he never tried to weaken the State bureaucracy and public service delivery system.

On the contrary, Lalu Yadav perceived the State bureaucracy as one of the most powerful citadels of upper castes in the State. He adopted a confrontational strategy both in the horizontal and vertical game. The famous slogan of RJD was *Bhurabal Hatao* implies the confrontation with the Center as well as dismissing the upper caste bureaucrats and weakening of the State bureaucracy, which had been perceived as the instrument of the upper caste dominance.

Table 8.2 Main characteristic of anti-Center political actors in both States

The main characteristics of anti-Center Political Actors	*Telugu sub-nationalism in Andhra Pradesh*	*Lowercaste politics in Bihar*
Main political actors	The TDP under N.T. Rama Rao (1983–1989 and 1994–1995) as the Chief Minister of Andhra Pradesh	The JD/and RJD under leadership of Lalu Prasad Yadav as *de jure* and *de facto* Chief Minister of Bihar (1991–2005)
Background of the opposition party	Subnational identity (Telugu identity) against the Center and their representatives in the State	Caste identity (the OBC castes) against upper castes
Caste background of the dominant regional political Party	Coalition between Kamma community and OBCs against Reddies, which had been organized in the Congress	Coalition between the OBCs (mainly Yadav), SCs and Muslims against upper castes in the Congress and BJP
Strategic choice of the leader in the vertical game	Confrontation with the Center	Confrontation with the Center
Strategic choice of the leader in the horizontal game	Unification of all Telugus regardless of their caste and community Comprehensive welfare schemes	Confrontation with upper castes in the State Targeted welfare schemes to specific caste groups or communities
Economic policies	Economic populism in the name of service delivery to Telugu people	Economic populism Deinstitutionalization in the name of fighting against the upper castes

Source: Drawn by the author.

My findings reveal that while the State bureaucracy remained relatively autonomous during the TDP government under NTR in AP, and it was used to implement the populist welfare schemes, the purposeful strategy of Lalu Yadav weakened the State bureaucracy in Bihar; therefore, it became more dependent on the politicians. Table 8.2 compares the critical features of anti-Center/Congress political actors in two States.

The findings of this study suggest that unlike the image of Lalu Yadav in the media and some scholarly works as a simple, unskillful and incompetent leader, who ruled Bihar wrongly, he was a rational actor (power and interest maximizer) who tried to balance his horizontal and vertical interactions to sustain his political power in the State. Although the result of his strategic choices was disastrous and tragic for Bihar and made Bihar's economy stagnated, he could break the record for the longest tenure as chief minister of Bihar (de jure and de facto). His successful experience as the railways minister in the Central Government between 2004 and 2009 implies Lalu's potential to be a successful reformer; however, he had realized that gaining more interests in State politics needed intensification of caste polarization instead of reforms.

The strategic choice of regional leaders: cooperation with the Center implementation of reform agenda

H3: *If regional political elites do not expect to gain reelection through confrontational behavior against the Center but expect to be rewarded by the voter if their economic performance is convincing, they will opt for gaining access to funds from the Center and international agents and adopt reform-oriented policies.*

While the charismatic leadership of Lalu Prasad Yadav and his populist and confrontational strategies continued until 2005, a turning point in Andhra Pradesh politics transformed the rules of the game both in the horizontal and vertical game model interactions in 1995. The emergence of Chandrababu Naidu as the new leader of the TDP and the chief minister of Andhra Pradesh can be seen as a turning point. Naidu's strategic choices to adopt the reform-oriented policies in Andhra Pradesh when Lalu Yadav was insisting on rejecting all reform agenda, recommended by the Center, is the key explanatory variable to explain the divergence between two States' economic performance after the 1990s.

Chandrababu Naidu dismissed his father-in-law, N.T. Rama Rao, through a 'Palace coup' in the TDP in 1995. Since its formation, the TDP had relied mostly on the charisma of NTR, which was rooted in his cinematic career and personal characteristics. Chandrababu Naidu neither had NTR's charisma, which attracted the attention of constituents to him and mobilized people based on identity politics and anti-centrism, nor enough financial resources to pursue populist welfare policies to convince masses to support him. While the TDP under the leadership of N.T. Rama Rao was supported mainly by the coalition between Kamma caste (Rao belonged to this caste), other backward castes, Muslims especially after Babri Masjid dispute, and all masses who were inspired by his NTR's charismatic character or his populist schemes; Chandrababu Naidu had several challenges to get support from party's traditional supporters. As a rational actor, Naidu confronted the leadership dispute and legitimacy vacuum at the State level, the change in power relations with the Center, which created more autonomy for the State, and development paradigm shift both at national and international level; as a result, he had new potential choices. He realized that possessing political power in Andhra Pradesh is not possible anymore through populism and confrontation with the Center. In the new institutional setting, Naidu should compete with other States to attract both Central financial allocation and private investments. He perceived the success in the completion as a way for attracting voters in the State. The strategic choice of Naidu to shift from the economic populism to the liberalization not only displayed a progressive image from TDP government and the new leadership, but also could attract votes and supports from the emerging urban middle class, the youth and women, and Kamma entrepreneurs. Chandrababu Naidu tried to create a dynamic, progressive and trustworthy image for the TDP leadership as an alternative to the charismatic image of NTR.

Moreover, Naidu realized that implantation of reform-oriented policies and developmental activities needed more central transfers and private investments. While NTR considered the Center as a 'conceptual myth' and confronted it, Naidu identified the pragmatic gains from cooperation with the Center in the age of inter-States rivalries. NTR's confrontation with the Center could be because the Congress, the main competitor of the TDP in AP, also was in power at the Center. However, the rise of NDA as a new political coalition at the Center paved the path for reconstruction of the relationship between the TDP and the Center. Chandrababu Naidu recognized that the TDP government could get maximum benefit from the Center by sustaining a constructive and friendly relation with it. As a result, despite the initial conflicts with the BJP, Naidu accepted finally to be a key partner in the ruling NDA government.

My findings indicate that although the Central transfers for development expenditures increased in the late 1990s, Naidu realized that he could not remain dependent on State's own income or the Central transfers for enhancing the economic growth. Although Naidu tried to improve the relations between the Center and State to convince the Union Government and the Planning Commission to allocate more financial resources to the State, he understood that the private sector's investments (by domestic or international companies) and international financial organizations' aid and loans would enhance economic growth in the State. Therefore, one of the most significant goals of the policy reforms in Andhra Pradesh was to create a business-friendly environment for attracting national and international companies to invest in the State. Naidu comprehended the new rules of the game in which State–Center confrontation transmuted to inter-States competition. Also, Naidu was aware of the consequences of the collapse of License Raj at the Center and its impact on the political economy of India; as a result, he believed that States should compete to attract private investments in the post-reform era.

While Andhra Pradesh transformed into a subnational developmental state with the leadership of Naidu, Lalu Yadav's strategic choices in the vertical and horizontal interactions led to stagnation of Bihar's economy as well as a decline in law and order. Table 8.3 compares the critical features of the Naidu and Yadav regimes in terms of leadership and their strategic choices in the vertical and horizontal interactions.

Both political leaders with these strategic choices reached the records of the most extended term that a chief minister in their State ever served. However, the results of these choices on economic performance in both States are dissimilar. Figure 8.3

Table 8.3 Main characteristics of the Naidu and Yadav regimes in term of leadership and their strategic choices

	Andhra Pradesh	*Bihar*
Background of the ruling party	Subnational identity (Telugu identity) against the Center and their representatives in the State	Caste identity (mainly the OBC castes) against upper castes
Leadership	Pragmatist and technocrat (Naidu, 1995–2004)	Charismatic with the populist policies (Yadav, 1991–2005)
The keywords of dominant discourse of the regional leader	Development Neo-liberal economy Good governance Information technology	Lower caste empowerment Social justice *Izzat*
Vertical strategies of leaders toward the Center	Cooperation	Conflicts
Strategy to attract private domestic/international investments	Yes	No
Strategy to cooperate with international aid agencies	Yes	No
Horizontal strategies toward regional institution	Improvement of current institution and creation of new institutions for enhancing development	Deinstitutionalization in the name of fighting against upper caste domination
Economic choices of the regional leaders	Neo-liberal economic reforms and investment in the infrastructure, attraction of the FDI and development of the IT sector	Pro the OBC populist policies without developmental vision

Source: Drawn by the author.

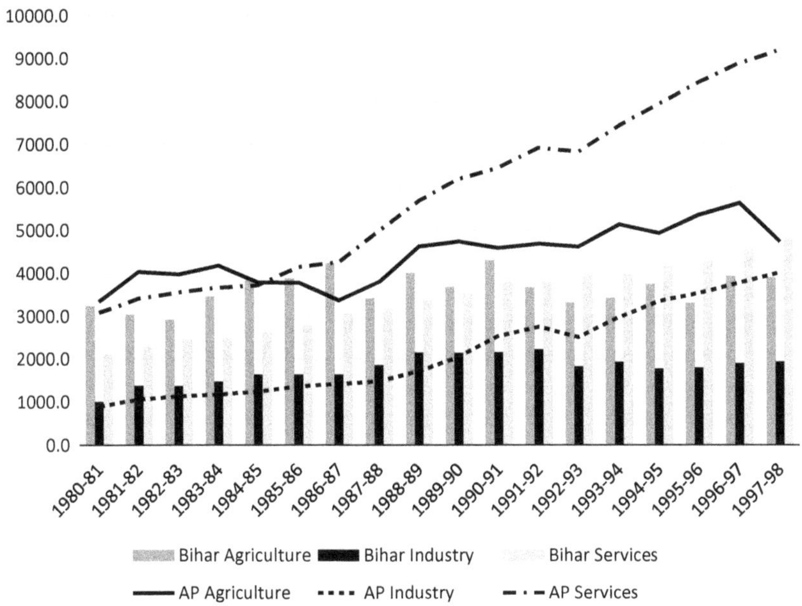

Figure 8.3 Components of NSDP at factor cost by industry of origin in Andhra Pradesh and Bihar.

Source: *Handbook of Statistics on Indian Economy 2005–06* (2006), drawn by the author.

compares components of net state domestic product at factor cost by industry of origin in both States between the 1980–1981 and 1997–1998 financial years.

As this figure reveals, although the size and value of the Service sector in Andhra Pradesh was higher than Bihar, the Agriculture and Industry sectors in both State had a relatively similar condition. Not surprisingly, after introducing the liberalization by the Center and implementation of economic reforms in Andhra Pradesh by the Congress government and subsequently by the TDP government, the rate of growth in all three sectors has been accelerated. Contrariwise, although there is a minor growth in the service sector in Bihar, the industry and agriculture sectors had remained stagnated without a significant change.

Finally, the end of 'Lalu Raj' and the emergence of Nitish Kumar as the new chief minister of Bihar (the 2005 election) paved the path for a cooperationist and growth-enhancing strategic choices in the vertical and horizontal interactions, which enhanced the State–Center cooperation and economic growth. In the horizontal game, Nitish Kumar, as a rational actor, confronted the solid caste/community vote banks of Lalu (MY and other lower castes), rewarding him for his *Izzat* promises, despite his poor performance at the State level. Moreover, Lalu Yadav with his humor, theatricality, and rustic oratory was a charismatic leader for the rural masses. Lalu Yadav was a professional leader who could use the caste politics weapon against his opponents; as a result, Nitish Kumar required another tool to challenge the RJD in the State. Nitish Kumar used 'development' and 'law and order' as an instrument for political mobilization against Lalu. Nitish Kumar recognized that securing the political power in Bihar is not possible anymore through populism, polarization, and confrontation with the Center in the name of fighting against the upper caste's domination. Accordingly, the constituents such as the forward caste elites as well as the OBS, EBCs, Dalits, and lower class Muslims would reward him if he demonstrates his performance for delivering better services and enforcing the rule of law. Therefore, development of the State became the central goal of his government.

Unlike the 'Lalu Raj' era, subjugated by the economic and financial consequences of confrontation with the Center and caste polarization, Nitish Kumar realized that confrontation with the Center and caste politics cannot enhance economic development; as a result, he tried with the reconstruction of bureaucracy, restoration of law and order and creating a business-friendly environment to attract private domestic and foreign investments. Under Nitish Kumar's government, Bihar transformed from one of the slowest-growing States to a fast-growing State, whose rate of growth could be compared with Gujarat. Figure 8.4 illustrates the game model behavior of a 'regional developmental leaders' at the State level such as Chandrababu Naidu and Nitish Kumar.

In the horizontal interactions, the leader offers the benefits of rapid economic growth and some targeted welfare schemes to the constituents and they reward him by reelection and political support. Moreover, the regional leader improves the capacity and effectiveness of the regional institutions such as State bureaucracy, which can enhance the service delivery to constituents. By advocating a unifying subnational identity, the regional leader attempts to provide a context for creating a socio-political consensus to refrain sub-regionalism or caste polarization. In the vertical game, the chief minister provides political support for the Center and implements economic policies based on the Center's agenda. Therefore, the Center provides political support to the State, as well as central transfers in the form of approved plan outlays and other means. However, the Center is not the only source for investment to enhance the economic development in the State. By adopting business-friendly measures and promoting reform agenda, the regional leader tries to attract the international and national private companies to invest in the State. Andhra Pradesh has emerged as a subnational developmental state with the leadership of Chandrababu Naidu, who provided a developmental vision for Andhra Pradesh, improved the current institutions in State, and implemented new policies to enhance economic growth. Similarly, Bihar after a long-term stagnation and lawlessness has emerged as a new subnational developmental state under the leadership of Nitish Kumar. He also reconstructed and improved the institutions in State, increased the level of the rule of law and order, and implemented new policies to enhance economic growth in the State.

While India's political economy in the 1950s and 1960s cannot be analyzed without studying the central role of Jawaharlal Nehru, his ideas, and management style, understanding the role, ideas and the strategic choices of the chief ministers such as Chandrababu Naidu and Nitish Kumar is vital in analyzing the post-1990s economic liberalization.

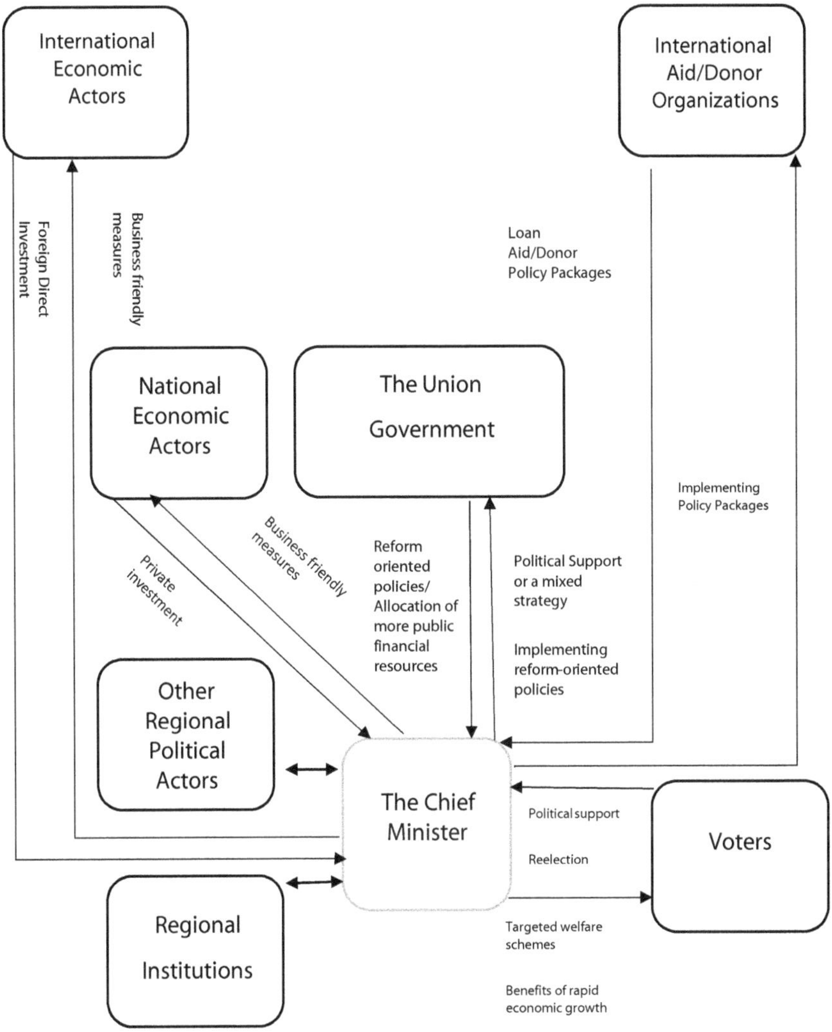

Figure 8.4 Multi-level and development enhancing model, the post-liberalization era.

Source: Drawn by the author.

Central transfers as a tool for reward and punishment

H4: *If regional political leaders opt for confrontational rhetoric and behavior against the Central Government, the share of State in financial transfers from the Center (such as approved plan outlay) will decrease. On the other hand, if regional political leaders opt for cooperationist rhetoric and behavior toward the Central Government and implement the reform agenda of the Central*

Government, the share of State in financial transfers from the Center (such as approved plan outlay) will increase.

It is a tough task to establish the causes for the rate of growth of States within India conclusively. There are several economic and non-economic independent variables; therefore, it is difficult to pin down and explore all of them. Therefore, this study instead of analyzing all causes of the growth has focused on the divergence in the post-reform economic performance of States.

Most of the development theories regard investment as a crucial factor for the rate of growth. In the previous sections, the current study elaborated how the strategic choices of regional leaders in a complex multilevel game are a significant variable that can explain the amount and pattern of private investment. However, more than the private investments, the pattern of public developmental expenditure can be seen as a critical factor to explicate the divergence in the economic performances of the States. Notably, the subnational states with a considerable need to invest in the infrastructures are more dependent on this kind of public developmental expenditures. Therefore, this study also focused on the developmental expenditures of States.

One of most significant sources of State Government for developmental expenditures is the money that had been paid by the Planning Commission. These Center–State transfers play a significant role in the development of infrastructures in State. The Planning Commission devoted these transfers for developmental purposes including project-specific expenditures. Although the Planning Commission presented a formula for distributing the State plan, including elements such as per capita income, fiscal performance or particular problems, the findings of the current study suggest that the State–Center relations are a significant informal variable that should be considered. As Figure 8.5 depicts, both States in the early 1990s had a relatively similar share in the approved Plan Outlays. Both States had confrontational attitudes toward the Congress government of P.V. Narasimha Rao.

Fascinatingly, the share of Andhra Pradesh increased after the 1997–1998 financial year, which is coincided with Naidu's decision to join the NDA, and became the partner of Central power. However, as the Figure 8.5 illustrates while the Center rewarded Andhra Pradesh's reform agenda through increasing Center-State transfers via approved Plan Outlays, punished Bihar, who rejected the all economic reforms and launched several attacks against the ruling coalition.

However, the 2005 election for Bihar was a turning point. Although Nitish Kumar belonged to the NDA alliance, he did not adopt an anti-Center strategy against the UPA government. On the contrary, based on neo-liberal consensus, he engaged actively in the economic reform agenda, pursued by the Center. From the 2006–2007 financial year onward, the Bihar Government resources for development expenditures have begun to benefit from a massive increase in plan transfers from Delhi. Inspired by his obligation to the development of State and his attitude toward the Center, the Central Government rewarded the Nitish Kumar Government with a more substantial amount of approved plan outlays.

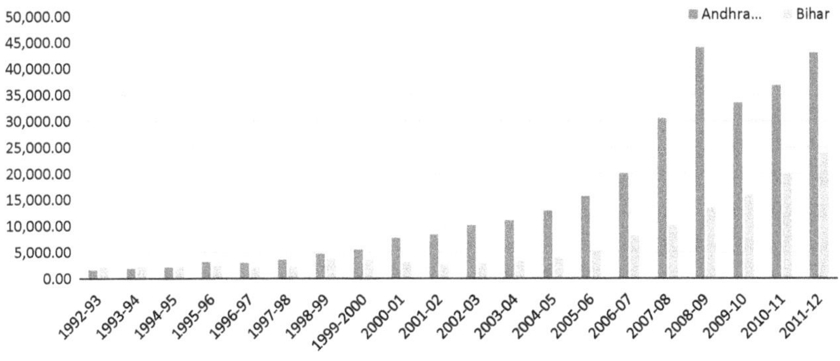

Figure 8.5 Annual approved plan outlays of Andhra Pradesh and Bihar between 1992–1993 and 2011–2012.

Source: *State Finances: A Study of Budgets* (Reserve Bank of India 2015), drawn by the author.

The growth rate of a share of Andhra Pradesh in the approved plan outlays accelerated after the election of Y.S. Reddy, the Congress leader in the 2004 election. Andhra Pradesh under the rule of the Congress received more central transfers than the past for YSR's developmental expenditure in the State. These expenditures could sustain the success of AP in terms of development. These Center–State transfers were accompanied with some expenditures in welfare schemes to form a balance between the rate of growth and poverty reduction and improvement in HDI. The findings of this study confirm there is an overall tendency for the Central Government to reward or punish subnational states based on their relations with the Center and their willingness to implement Center's recommended policies by developmental transfers to the States.

Final remarks

Most recent works on the relations between governance and development have focused on the interconnections between good governance and economic performance. The neo-statist studies with a neo-institutional approach have emphasized the role of the state (regardless of its democratic characteristic), and institutions such as the bureaucracy or military in making (under)development happen. The main contribution of this book is to suggest that democratic regime cannot automatically be translated into development. Moreover, the result of this study takes a stand against explanations of both supporters and opponents of state-centric theories. This book illustrated that core concepts, derived from both good governance and a neo-statist approach, cannot be adequate for understanding subnational interaction across the federal system in India.

This book does not consider the state as an aggregate entity; rather, it disaggregates the state relationally and spatially. Unlike the majority of comparative political economy theories, constructed based on a unitary and top-down notion of state, this book argues that analyzing development in India as a federal and multilevel political system is not possible with a mere aggregate notion of state.

The book does not suggest a simplified executive agency explanation, assuming development is the result of the will of political leaders. On the contrary, the book highlights the institutional change and explicates the altered patterns of interactions between rational actors within different levels of the state. My findings suggest that the post-liberalization divergences among subnational states in India have not originated from state or market-based action. Rather, this divergence is the result of different types of state-led strategies that are the consequence of strategic choices of rational regional leaders in the game model interactions. The book delineates how in the post one dominant party system and post liberalization era, in the framework of India's federal institutions, the regional leaders as the rational actors confirm or rebel against the policies and decisions of the Center (mainly economic reforms). The varied responses within India suggest that the post-liberalization institutional transformation paved the path for the development of room to maneuver for the regional leaders. Although the previous studies confirmed the increase in the role of regional leaders after the end of the centrally planned economy model and the emergence of the federal market economy, the dynamics and patterns of chief minister's strategic choices remained unstudied. The current study proposes a multilevel polycentric model to analyze the strategic choices of regional leaders, especially their economic policy choices after the liberalization. This model enables us to analyze the strategic choices of regional leaders to cooperate or confront the Center via analysis of horizontal and vertical interactions in a multilevel system.

My historical and empirical data have validated this argument that the spatial or central-regional dynamics affect regional developmental patterns. The subnational states in India are not the passive devotees of policies, introduced and pursued by New Delhi. These regional development trajectories are a complex aggregation of strategic choices of local elites based on the State-Centre relations and the regional institutional variations. By looking at these variations, the study shed lights on the roots of diversities of developmental trajectories within a democratic nation-state. This study delineates how the regional institutional variations and strategic choices of local elites can even engender anti-development tendencies in a democratic political system (the case of Bihar during Lalu Yadav).

My findings suggest that the post-1990s new institutional set up in the economic arena (abolishment of 'licence-permit raj' and Centrally planned economy) and political arena (transformation of one dominant party system to a regionalized multiparty coalition government system) paved the path for birth of a 'determined developmental leader' at the State level, whose strategic choices to implement reform agenda is based on their interest in the horizontal and vertical games. Therefore, the regional leaders as rational actors follow development-enhancing policies in the region if, and only if, they see such policies can improve their position in the regional politics in terms of reelection.

Finally, this book argues that the mono-causal explanation of development such as causality between democratic regime and development or political stability and economic development is too simple for analyzing the dynamics of development within the Indian States. The result of this comparative study confirms that despite the similarities in initial institutional arrangement and economic condition between two cases, the strategic choices of regional leaders in the vertical and horizontal games based on the regional institutional variations and local context caused a different reception to economic reforms and liberalization; consequently, it led to divergence in their economic performance.

Glossary

Adivasi Forest-dwelling aboriginal tribes

Bandh Collective cessation of public activities

Boycott A form of strike action where all contact is broken off

Brahmin Member of the first *varna;* the priestly class

Dalit Literally, oppressed; often refers to the scheduled castes

emerging markets Less developed countries where new markets for global trade and services are emerging

garibi hatao Quit poverty; a slogan popularized by Mrs. Gandhi during the 1971 parliamentary election campaign

Izzat Dignity, honor

Kshatriya Member of the second *varna*; the warrior, governing or princely class

Lok Sabha Lower house of Indian Parliament

mixed economy A core principle of India's developmental model based on public private partnership

Panchayat Village council

Panchayati Raj Local self-government at the village, sub-district and the district level (literally, the rule of the five)

Partition The territorial division of British India in 1947 into the independent states of India and Pakistan

President's rule Direct rule by the central government in a federal state (under Article 356 of the Indian constitution)

Quota Permit Raj Literally, a regime based on the grant of quotas, permits and licenses – an expression used to indicate patronage as a part of the politics of the Indian National Congress, during the period of one-party dominance

Raj Literally, rule; hence, British Raj or *Panchayati Raj*

reservation policy The policy of setting aside a quota of jobs in public services and places in educational institutions for under privileged social groups

riots Criminal uprising of five or more people

scheduled castes Formerly untouchable communities grouped together by the government under Article 341 of the Indian constitution, which entitles them to special privileges under the policy of reservation

scheduled tribes Forest-dwelling tribes grouped together by the government under Article 342 of the Indian constitution, which entitles them to special privileges under the policy of reservation

Sudras The lowest stratum (*varna*) of the Hindu caste system

Suhasan Good governance in Hindi

Untouchables Lower orders of the Hindu caste system who are considered ritually polluted

varna Classical social division, of which there are four, referred to in Hindu holy texts

vote bank A group of voters whose votes are controlled by a local leader

Zamindari From the Hindi–Persian *Zamindar* (landlord); *zamindari* denotes a practice introduced by the British colonial government

Bibliography

Government publications, party documents, and official statistical data

1991. *Census of India*. New Delhi: Office of the Registrar General & Census Commissioner, India (ORGI).

2001. *Census of India*. New Delhi: Office of the Registrar General & Census Commissioner, India (ORGI).

2006. *Handbook of Statistics on Indian Economy 2005–06*. Department of Statistics and Information Management. Mumbai: The Reserve Bank of India.

2007. *Bihar's Exposure to Innovative Governance Practices. Report of Special Task Force on Bihar*. New Delhi: Government of India. Accessed 22 June 2018. http://planningcommission.gov.in/aboutus/taskforce/tsk_binnotv.pdf.

2008. *Eleventh Five-Year Plan 2007–2012*. New Delhi: Planning Commission (Government of India).

2010. *Handbook of Statistics on Indian Economy 2009–10*. Department of Statistics and Information Management. Mumbai: Reserve Bank of India.

2011. *Census of India*. New Delhi: Office of the Registrar General & Census Commissioner, India (ORGI).

2014 *Handbook of Statistics on Indian Economy 2013–14*. Department of Statistics and Information Management. Mumbai: Reserve Bank of India.

2015. *Economic Survey 2014–15, Statistical Appendix*. New Delhi: Ministry of Finance, Department of Economic Affairs, Economic Division.

2015. *Handbook of Statistics on Indian Economy 2014–15*. Reserve Bank of India Department of Statistics and Information Management. Mumbai: The Reserve Bank of India.

Election Commission of India. 1951–2014. *Election Results, Full Statistical Reports*. Accessed 2 March 2015. http://eci.nic.in/eci_main1/ElectionStatistics.aspx.

Government of Andhra Pradesh. 1999. *Swarna Andhra Pradesh Vision 2020*. The State Secretariat. Hyderabad: Government of Andhra Pradesh.

Government of Andhra Pradesh. 2002. *ICT Policy 2002–2005*. Hyderabad: Information Technology and Communications Department.

Government of Andhra Pradesh. 2005. *Information & Communications Technology (ICT) Policy of the Government of Andhra Pradesh – ICT Policy 2005–2010*. Hyderabad: Information Technology and Communications Department.

Government of Bihar. 2006. *White Paper on State Finances and Development*. Patna: Finance Department.

Government of Bihar. 2007. *Economic Survey, 2006–07*. Patna: Department of Finance.

Government of Bihar. 2010. *Economic Survey, 2009–10*. Patna: Department of Finance.

Government of Bihar. 2012. *Economic Survey, 2011–12*. Patna: Department of Finance.

Government of Bihar. 2015. *Economic Survey, 2014–15*. Patna: Department of Finance.

Government of India. 1951–2013. *Crime in India*. New Delhi: Ministry of Home Affairs. Accessed 2 March 2015. http://ncrb.gov.in/.

Naidu, Chandrababu. 1995. *Speech of Sri N. Chandrababu Naidu, Hon'ble Finance Minister While Presenting the Budget for 1995–96 to the Andhra Pradesh Legislative Assembly*. Hyderabad: Andhra Pradesh Finance Department. Accessed 6 August 2017. www.apfinance.gov.in/Finance-Min-Speech-html/pbs-1995-middle.html.

Planning Commission (Government of India). 2002. *Tenth Five-Year Plan 2002–2007*. New Delhi: Oxford University Press.

Planning Commission (Government of India). 2008. *Eleventh Five Year Plan 2007–2012*. New Delhi: Oxford University Press.

Planning Commission (Government of India). 2014. *Data-Book Compiled for the Use of Planning Commission*. New Delhi: Planning Commission, Government of India. Accessed 22 July 2015. http://planningcommission.nic.in/data/datatable/data_2312/comp_data2312.pdf.

Reserve Bank of India. 2015. *State Finances: A Study of Budgets*. Mumbai: Government of India.

Srikrishna, B.N., Vinod Kumar Duggal, Ranbir Singh, Abusaleh Shariff, and Ravinder Kaur. 2010. *Report, Committee for Consultations on the Situation in Andhra Pradesh*. New Delhi: The Inter-State Council Secretariat (ISCS), Government of India.

Telugu Desam Party. 1983. *TDP's Election Manifesto*. Hyderabad: Telugu Desam Party.

Documents of international organizations

ADRI. 2007. "Documenting Reforms in Bihar: Recent Government of Bihar Initiatives and Their Impact." In *Working Paper*. Patna: Asian Development Research Institute.

DFID. 2006. "Making Governance Work for the Poor." Department for International Development. Accessed 2 March 2015. www.gov.uk/government/uploads/system/uploads/attachment_data/file/272330/6876.pdf.

European Commission. 2001. "White Paper on Governance." Accessed 20 February 2015. http://europa.eu/rapid/press-release_DOC-01-10_en.htm.

European Commission. 2003. "Governance and Development. Brussels." Accessed 25 April 2015. http://ec.europa.eu/governance/docs/comm_rapport_en.pdf.

International Monetary Fund. 1997. "Good Governance, The IMF's Role." International Monetary Fund. Accessed 20 February 2015. www.imf.org/external/pubs/ft/exrp/govern/govern.pdf.

Millennium Challenge Corporation. 2013. "Lesotho: Water Supply, Health Systems and Private Sector Development." Millennium Challenge Corporation. Accessed 20 February 2015. https://assets.mcc.gov/reports/countrybrief-2013002144701-lesotho.pdf.

UNDP. 1997. "Governance for Sustainable Human Development." UNDP. Accessed 15 August 2015. www.pogar.org/publications/other/undp/governance/undppolicydoc97-e.pdf.

UNDP. 2011. "Remarks by Helen Clark on Good Governance at all Levels." Accessed 20 February 2015. www.co.undp.org/content/turkey/en/home/presscenter/articles/2011/05/11/remarks-by-helen-clark-on-good-governance-at-all-levels.html.

United Nations. 2009. "Governance." Accessed 25 February 2015. www.un.org/en/globalissues/governance/.

World Bank. 1989. *Sub-Saharan Africa: From Crisis to Sustainable Growth*. Washington DC: The World Bank.

World Bank. 1992. *Governance and Development*. The World Bank. Accessed 10 December 2014. http://documents.worldbank.org/curated/en/1992/04/440582/governance-development.

World Bank. 1994. *Governance: The World Bank's Experience*. Washington, DC: The World Bank Publication.

World Bank. 1997a. *Andhra Pradesh: Agenda for Economic Reforms*. Washington, DC: The World Bank Publication.

World Bank. 1997b. *World Development Report 1997: The State in a Changing World*. New York: Oxford University Press.

World Bank. 2002. *World Development Report 2002: Building Institutions for Markets*. New York: Oxford University Press.

World Bank. 2005. "Bihar: Towards a Development Strategy." The World Bank. Accessed 10 December 2014. http://go.worldbank.org/0DK3NTTT70.

World Bank. 2012. "Structural Adjustment in India." The World Bank. Accessed 26 June 2015. http://lnweb90.worldbank.org/oed/oeddoclib.nsf/DocUNIDViewForJavaSearch/0586CC45A28A2749852567F5005D8C89.

World Bank. 2015. World Development Indicators. Accessed 29 August 2015. http://databank.worldbank.org/data/reports.aspx?source=world-development-indicators.

Newspapers, news websites and magazines (articles, news, and interviews)

2009. "India Shining, India Scraping, RBI Buys 200 Tonnes of IMF Gold; Alert on Rice." *Telegraph* 4 November 2009. Accessed 27 July 2015. www.telegraphindia.com/1091104/jsp/frontpage/story_11697358.jsp.

2010. "India's Surprising Economic Miracle." *The Economist*. 30 September 2010. Accessed 7 December 2014. www.economist.com/node/17147648.

2011. "Comparing Indian States and Territories with Countries an Indian Summary." In *The Economist*. Accessed 15 August 2015. www.economist.com/content/indian-summary.

2012. "How Nitish Kumar Led Bihar towards Its Double-digit Growth." *The Economic Times*. Accessed 17 March 2018. https://economictimes.indiatimes.com/slideshows/economy/how-nitish-kumar-led-bihar-towards-its-double-digit-growth/nitish-kumar-tooks-charge-to-turnaround-bihar/slideshow/11698209.cms.

Ahmed, Farzand. 1996. "Elections 1996: Laloo Prasad Yadav's Social Justice Campaign Given a Careful Spin." *India Today*, 15 May 1996. www.indiatoday.in/magazine/cover-story/story/19960515-elections-1996-laloo-prasad-yadav-social-justice-campaign-given-a-careful-spin-833165-1996-05-15.

Balasubrahmanyam, K. 2004. "Khammas of AP Have Money Power, So They Just Go Get It." *The Economic Times*, 5 March 2005. http://articles.economictimes.indiatimes.com/2004-03-05/news/27380540_1_film-studios-kammas-tdp.

Kumar, Nitish. 2006. "I Will Give any Concession for Money." In *Rediff*. Interviewer: Aditi Phadnis. Accessed 8 April 2015. www.rediff.com/money/2006/jan/18inter.htm.

Kumar, Nitish. 2013a. "For Their Interests, Corporates Speaking in Favour of One Individual: Nitish Kumar." In *The Hindu*. Interviewer: Prashant Jha. Accessed 16 February 2014. www.thehindu.com/opinion/interview/for-their-interests-corporates-speaking-in-favour-of-one-individual-nitish-kumar/article5175826.ece.

Lim, Edwin R. 2002. "Transcript of Interview with Edwin R. Lim." In *Oral History Program*. Interviewer: William H. Becker and Marie T. Zenni. Washington, DC: The World Bank Group.

Naidu, Chandrababu. 1998. "We Believe in Doing." In *Business Today*. Interviewer: Dilip Maitra. Accessed 19 September 2014. http://archives.digitaltoday.in/business today/22121998/cover4.html.

Naidu, Chandrababu. 2000a. "I Have Left Politics Behind in the Last Millennium." In *Rediff.* Interviewer: George Iype. Accessed 28 March 2014. www.rediff.com/news/2000/feb/08naidu.htm. Change 2013b to a in text.

Naidu, Chandrababu. 2004a. "Confident of Comming back to Power." In *Rediff.* Accessed 19 September 2014. www.rediff.com/election/2004/may/11einter.htm.

Naidu, Chandrababu. 2004b. "The Defeat Has Been an Eye Opener." In *Rediff.* Interviewer: George Iype. Accessed 2 February 2015. www.rediff.com/news/report/inter/20041111.htm.

Rao, K. Chandrasekhar. 2001. "No Force on the Earth Can Stop us from Achieving Telangana." In *Rediff.* Interviewer: Syed Amin Jafri. Accessed 13 March 2015. http://m.rediff.com/news/2001/may/29inter.htm.

Reddy, Y.S. Rajasekhara. 2004. "I Don't Want be Another Chandrababu Naidu." In *Rediff.* Interviewer: George Iype. Accessed 2 February 2015. www.rediff.com/news/2004/nov/10inter.htm.

Yadav, Lalu Prasad. 1997. "Always, I Get the Blame." In *Outlook India*. Accessed 21 January 2015. www.outlookindia.com/magazine/story/always-i-get-the-blame/203328.

Yadav, Lalu Prasad. 1998a. "Yeh garib dukhiare Laloo Yadav ko bhool nahi sakte, kyonki Laloo hi unka masiha hai. Baki sab bilkul bakwaas." In *Rediff*, Interviewer: Tara Shankar Sahay. Accessed 27 December 2014. www.rediff.com/news/1998/feb/13laloo.htm.

Yadav, Lalu Prasad. 1998b. "The Rediff Election Interview." In *Rediff.* Interviewer: Tara Shankar Sahay. www.rediff.com/news/1998/feb/13laloo.htm.

Yadav, Lalu Prasad. 1999. "If Laloo Goes, Naxals Will Surround the Cities." In *Outlook India*. Interviewer: Rajesh Joshi. Accessed 17 April 2015 www.outlookindia.com/article/if-laloo-goes-naxals-will-surround-the-cities/207162.

Yadav, Lalu Prasad. 2003. "Lathis against Trishuls." In *Frontline*. Interviewer: V. Krishna Ananth. Accessed 2 August 2015. www.frontline.in/static/html/fl2010/stories/20030523008300600.htm.

Yadav, Lalu Prasad. 2003. "Why Biharis?" In *Outlook India*. Interviewer: Nagendar Sharma. Accessed 17 April 2015 www.outlookindia.com/website/story/why-biharis/222293.

Books, book chapters, and journal articles

Ahluwalia, Isher Judge. 1985. *Industrial Growth in India: Stagnation since the Mid-sixties*. New York: Oxford University Press.

Ahluwalia, Montek S. 2002. "State Level Performance under Economic Reforms in India." *Economic Policy Reforms and the Indian Economy*, edited by Anne O. Krueger, 91–128. Chicago, IL: University of Chicago Press.

Ahrens, Joachim. 2002. *Governance and Economic Development: A Comparative Institutional Approach*. Cheltenham and Northampton: Edward Elgar Publishing.

Ahrens, Joachim. 2011. "Governance, Development, and Institutional Change in Time of Globalization." In *Good Governance in the 21st Century: Conflict, Institutional*

Change, and Development in the Era of Globalization, edited by Joachim Ahrens, Rolf Caspers and Janina Weingarth, 1–24. Cheltenham and Northampton: Edward Elgar Publishing.

Aiyar, Swaminathan S. Anklesaria. 2013. "Bihar: How the Poorest, Worst-Governed State Attained Double-Digit Growth and Became a Role Model." In *Economic Freedom of the States of India 2013*, edited by Bibek Debroy, Laveesh Bhandari, and Swaminathan S. Anklesaria Aiyar, 41–69. New Delhi: Academic Foundation.

Alakh, N. Sharma. 1995. "Political Economy of Poverty in Bihar." *Economic and Political Weekly* 30 (41/42): 2587–2602.

Alkire, Sabina and Suman Seth. 2015. "Multidimensional Poverty Reduction in India between 1999 and 2006: Where and How?" *World Development* 72 (0): 93–108.

Alkire, Sabina, James Foster, Suman Seth, Maria Emma Santos, José Manuel Roche, and Paola Ballon. 2015. *Multidimensional Poverty Measurement and Analysis*. Oxford: Oxford University Press.

Ananth, V.K. Krishna. 2005. "Shifting Alliances in Bihar." *Economic and Political Weekly* 40 (1): 13–14.

Andrews, Matt. 2010. "Good Government Means Different Things in Different Countries." *Governance* 23 (1): 7–35.

Baird, Ryan G. 2012. "Unpacking Democracy and Governance: Conceptualizing Governance Infrastructure." *Social Science Information* 51 (2): 263–279.

Balasubramanyam, V.N. and Ahalya Balasubramanyam. 2012. "Karnataka and Andhra Pradesh: The Disparate Twins." In *Growth, Development, and Diversity: India's Record since Liberalization*, edited by Kesavan Pushpangadan and V.N. Balasubramanyam, 23–54. Oxford: Oxford University Press.

Bandyopadhyay, D. 2001. "Andhra Pradesh: Looking beyond 'Vision 2020.'" *Economic and Political Weekly* 36 (11): 900–903.

Banerjee, Arpita and Pravat Kumar Kuri. 2015. "Regional Development in India." In *Development Disparities in India*, 21–34. London and Heidelberg: Springer.

Bang, Henrik P. 2003. "Governance as Political Communication." In *Governance as Social and Political Communication*, edited by Henrik P. Bang, 7–26. Manchester: Manchester University Press.

Bardhan, Pranab Kumar. 1984. *The Political Economy of Development in India*. Oxford: Oxford University Press.

Bardhan, Pranab and Dilip Mookherjee. 2012. *Political Clientelism and Capture: Theory and Evidence from West Bengal, India*. London: WIDER Working Paper.

Barkey, Karen and Sunita Parikh. 1991. "Comparative Perspectives on the State." *Annual Review of Sociology* 17: 523–549.

Bates, Robert H., Avner Greif, Margaret Levi, Jean-Laurent Rosenthal, and Barry R. Weingast, eds. 1998. *Analytic Narratives*. Princeton, NJ: Princeton University Press.

Bates, Robert H., Avner Greif, Margaret Levi, Jean-Laurent Rosenthal, and Barry R. Weingast. 2000. "Analytic Narratives Revisited." *Social Science History* 24 (4): 685–696.

Bell, Stephen and Andrew Hindmoor. 2009. *Rethinking Governance: The Centrality of the State in Modern Society*. Cambridge: Cambridge University Press.

Bernstorff, Dagmar. 1973. "Eclipse of 'Reddy-Raj'? The Attempted Restructuring of the Congress Party Leadership in Andhra Pradesh." *Asian Survey* 13 (10): 959–979.

Bernstorff, Dagmar. 1998a. "The Kingmakers of Andhra Pradesh." In *The Kingmakers: Politicians and Politics in Andhra Pradesh*, edited by Dagmar Bernstorff and Hugh Gray, 11–20. New Delhi: Har-Anand Publications.

Bernstorff, Dagmar. 1998b. "Political Leadership in Andhra Pradesh 1956–1973." In *The Kingmakers: Politicians and Politics in Andhra Pradesh*, edited by Dagmar Bernstorff and Hugh Gray, 80–108. New Delhi: Har-Anand Publications.

Bevir, Mark. 2009. *Key Concepts in Governance*. SAGE Key Concepts. Los Angeles and London: SAGE.

Bevir, Mark. 2011. "Governance as Theory, Practice, and Dilemma." In *The Sage Handbook of Governance*, edited by Mark Bevir, 1–16. London: Sage.

Bevir, Mark. 2012. *Governance, a Very Short Introduction*. Oxford: Oxford University Press.

Bhagwati, Jagdish N. 1993. *India in Transition: Freeing the Economy*. Oxford: University Press.

Bhandari, Laveesh and Swaminathan S. Anklesaria Aiyar. 2011. *Economic Freedom of the States of India 2011*. New Delhi: Academic Foundation.

Bhandari, Jitender, Manmohan Rahul, and Shalini Rahul Tiwari. 2015. "Regional Economic Imbalances: Business and Foreign Direct Investment in India." In *Promoting Socio-Economic Development through Business Integration*, edited by Kalia Shalini, Bhalla Bhavna, Das Lipi and Awasthy Neeraj, 1–16. Hershey, PA: IGI Global.

Bharadwaj, Krishna. 1982. "Regional Differentiation in India: A Note." *Economic and Political Weekly*: 605–614.

Bhattacharya, Mohit. 2008. "Conceptualizing Governance and Development." In *The Governance Discourse: A Reader*, edited by Bidyut Chakrabarty and Mohit Bhattacharya, 79–102. New Delhi: Oxford University Press.

Blair, Harry W. 1972. "Ethnicity and Democratic Politics in India: Caste as a Differential Mobilizer in Bihar." *Comparative Politics* 5 (1): 107–127.

Börzel, Tanja A. and Thomas Risse. 2010. "Governance without a State: Can it Work?" *Regulation & Governance* 4 (2): 113–134.

Börzel, Tanja A., Yasemin Pamuk, and Andreas Stahn. 2008. "Good Governance in the European Union." In *Berliner Arbeitspapier zur Europäischen Integration*. Berlin: Freie Universität Berlin.

Boyer, William W. 1990. "Political Science and the 21st Century: From Government to Governance." *PS: Political Science & Politics* 23 (1): 50–54.

Brass, P. 1994. *The Politics of India since Independence* (The New Cambridge History of India). Cambridge: Cambridge University Press.

Brinkerhoff, Derick W. 2007. "Introduction – Governance Challenges in Fragile States, Re-Establishing Security, Rebuilding Effectiveness, and Reconstituting Legitimacy." In *Governance in Post-Conflict Societies: Rebuilding Fragile States*, edited by Derick W Brinkerhoff, 1–21. New York: Routledge.

Brinkerhoff, Derick W. and Arthur A. Goldsmith. 2005. "Institutional Dualism and International Development: A Revisionist Interpretation of Good Governance." *Administration and Society* 37 (2): 199–224.

Calvert, Randall L. 1995. "Rational Actors, Equilibrium, and Social Institutions." In *Explaining Social Institutions*, edited by Jack Knight and Itai Sened, 57–93. Ann Arbor: University of Michigan Press.

Cerra, Valerie and Sweta Chaman Saxena. 2002. "What Caused the 1991 Currency Crisis in India?" *IMF Staff Papers*: 395–425.

Chakrabarty, Bidyut and Mohit Bhattacharya. 2008. "Introduction." In *The Governance Discourse: A Reader*, edited by Bidyut Chakrabarty and Mohit Bhattacharya, 1–75. New Delhi: Oxford Univ. Press.

Chandra, Kanchan. 2007. *Why Ethnic Parties Succeed: Patronage and Ethnic Headcounts in India*. Cambridge: Cambridge University Press.

Chang, Ha-Joon. 2002. "Breaking the Mould: an Institutionalist Political Economy Alternative to the Neo-Liberal Theory of the Market and the State." *Cambridge Journal of Economics* 26 (5): 539–559.

Chazan, Naomi. 1992. "Liberalization, Governance, and Political Space in Ghana." In *Governance and Politics in Africa*, edited by Göran Hyden and Michael Bratton, 121–142. Boulder: Lynne Rienner Publishers.

Chhibber, Pradeep K. 2001. *Democracy without Associations: Transformation of the Party System and Social Cleavages in India*. Ann Arbor, MI: University of Michigan Press.

Chhibber, P. and I. Nooruddin. 2004. "Do Party Systems Count? The Number of Parties and Government Performance in the Indian States." *Comparative Political Studies*, 37 (2): 152–187.

Chhotray, Vasudha and David Hulme. 2009. "Contrasting Visions for Aid and Governance in the 21st Century: The White House Millennium Challenge Account and DFID's Drivers of Change." *World Development* 37 (1): 36.

Chhotray, Vasudha and Gerry Stoker. 2009. *Governance Theory and Practice: A Cross-Disciplinary Approach*. New York: Palgrave Macmillan.

Choudhary, Kameshwar, ed. 2007. *Globalisation, Governance Reforms, and Development in India*. New Delhi: SAGE Publications India.

Cleveland, Harlan. 1972. *The Future Executive: A Guide for Tomorrow's Managers*. New York: Harper & Row.

Corbridge, Stuart, Glyn Williams, Manoj Srivastava, and Rene Veron. 2005. *Seeing the State: Governance and Governmentality in India*. Cambridge: Cambridge University Press.

Daly, Mary. 2003. "Governance and Social Policy." *Journal of Social Policy* 32 (1): 113–128.

Deshpande, Rajeshwari, K.K. Kailash, and Louise Tillin. 2017. "States as Laboratories: The Politics of Social Welfare Policies in India." *India Review* 16 (1): 85–105.

Doornbos, Martin R. 2001. "Good Governance: The Rise and Decline of a Policy Metaphor?" *The Journal of Development Studies* 37 (6): 93–108.

Dreze, Jean and Amartya Sen. 1997. *Indian Development: Selected Regional Perspectives*. New York: Oxford University Press.

Ebner, Alexander. 2009. "Governance, Institutions and Collective Action." In *International Encyclopedia of Public Policy – Governance in a Global Age*, edited by Phillip Anthony O'Hara, 218–231. Perth: GPERU.

Elliott, Carolyn. 2011. "Moving from Clientelist Politics toward a Welfare Regime: Evidence from the 2009 Assembly Election in Andhra Pradesh." *Commonwealth & Comparative Politics* 49 (1): 48–79.

Elliott, Carolyn. 2016. "Clientelism and the Democratic Deficit." *Studies in Indian Politics* 4 (1): 22–36.

Elsner, Wolfram and Werner Schoenig. 2009. "Governance." In *International Encyclopedia of Public Policy – Governance in a Global Age*, edited by Phillip Anthony O'Hara, 204–217. Perth: GPERU.

Epstein, Gil S. and Ira N. Gang. 2009. "Good Governance and Good Aid Allocation." *Journal of Development Economics* 89 (1): 12–18.

Evans, Peter B., Dietrich Rueschemeyer, and Theda Skocpol. 1985. *Bringing the State Back in*. Cambridge: Cambridge University Press.

Fickett, Lewis P., Jr. 1993. "The Rise and Fall of the Janata Dal." *Asian Survey* 33 (12): 1151–1162.

Forrester, Duncan B. 1970. "Subregionalism in India: The Case of Telangana." *Pacific Affairs* 43 (1): 5–21.

Frederickson, H George. 2007. "Whatever Happened to Public Administration? Governance, Governance Everywhere." In *The Oxford Handbook of Public Management* edited by Ewan Ferlie, E. Lynn Jr. Laurence, and Christopher Polli, 281–304. Oxford: Oxford University Press.

Frischtak, Leila L. 1994. *Governance Capacity and Economic Reform in Developing Countries*. Vol. 254: World Bank Publications. Washington DC: The World Bank.

Fukuyama, F. 2013. "What Is Governance?" *Governance* 26 (3): 347–368.

Fukuyama, F. 2014. *Political Order and Political Decay: From the Industrial Revolution to the Globalization of Democracy*. London: Profile Books.

Gamble, Andrew. 2001. "Neo-liberalism." *Capital & Class* (75): 127–134.

Gamble, Andrew. 2006. "Economic Governance." In *Debating Governance: Authority, Steering, and Democracy*, edited by Jon Pierre, 110–137. Oxford: Oxford University Press.

Gangadharan, K., ed. 2007. *Economic Reforms and Regional In-Equality in India*. New Delhi: Serials Publ.

Ganguly, Sumit and Rahul Mukherji. 2011. *India since 1980*. Cambridge: Cambridge University Press.

Ghosh, R.N., Rony Gabbay, and Abu Siddique. 1999. *Good Governance Issues and Sustainable Development: The Indian Ocean Region*. New Delhi: Atlantic Publishers and Dist.

Goodin, R.E. and H.D. Klingemann. 1996. "Political Science: The Discipline." In *A New Handbook of Political Science*, edited by R.E. Goodin and H.D. Klingemann, 3–49. Oxford: Oxford University Press.

Gopal, B. 1994. "Dynamics of Center-State Relations, Experience of Andhra Pradesh Since 1983." In *State Politics in India, Reflection on Andhra Pradesh*, edited by Agarala Esawara Reddi and D. Sundar Ram, 149–167. New Delhi: MD Publication.

Graham, John, Bruce Amos, and Tim Plumptre. 2003. "Principles for Good Governance in the 21st Century." In *Policy Brief*. Ottawa: Institute on Governance.

Gregory, Robert 2014. "Assessing Good Governance: Scientific Measurement and Political Discourse." *Policy Quarterly* 10 (1): 15–25.

Grindle, Merilee S. 2004. "Good Enough Governance: Poverty Reduction and Reform in Developing Countries." *Governance* 17 (4): 525–548.

Grindle, Merilee. 2007. "Good Enough Governance Revisited." *Development Policy Review* 25 (5): 533–574.

Grindle, Merilee. 2012. "Good Governance: The Inflation of an Idea." In *Planning Ideas that Matter*, edited by Bishwapriya Sanyal, Lawrence J. Vale, and Christina Rosan, 259–282. Cambridge, MA: The MIT Press.

Gulati, Rajinder Kumar. 1999. *Regional Disparities in Economic Development: Policies and Prospects for Balanced Regional Development*. New Delhi: Deep & Deep.

Gupta, Chirashree Das. 2013. "Fiscal Responsibility and Development Dilemma under Global Recession, a Perspective on Resurgent Bihar." In *Resurrection of the State: A Saga of Bihar; Essays in Memory of Papiya Ghosh*, edited by Sunita Loll and Shaibal Gupta, 168–208. New Delhi: Manak Publication.

Gupta, Tilak D. 1992. "Yadav Ascendancy in Bihar Politics." *Economic and Political Weekly* 27 (26): 1304–1306.

Gurr, Ted Robert. 1970. *Why Men Rebel*. Princeton, NJ: Princeton University Press.

Hall, Peter A. 1986. *Governing the Economy: The Politics of State Intervention in Britain and France*. Cambridge: Polity Press.

Hanumantha Rao, Chennameni H. 2010. *Regional Disparities, Smaller States, and Statehood for Telangana*. New Delhi: Academic Foundation.

Haragopal, G. 2010. "The Telangana People's Movement: The Unfolding Political Culture." *Economic and Political Weekly* 45 (42): 51–60.

Harriss, John. 1999. "Comparing Political Regimes across Indian States: A Preliminary Essay." *Economic and Political Weekly* 34 (48): 3367–3377.

Harriss, John. 2005. "Do Political Regimes Matter? Poverty Reduction and Regime Differences across India." In *Changing Paths: International Development and the New Politics of Inclusion*, edited by P. Houtzager and M. Moore, 204. Ann Arbor, MI: University of Michigan Press.

Hasan, Zoya. 2002. "Representation and Redistribution: The New Lower Caste Politics of North India." In *Parties and Party Politics in India*, edited by Zoya Hasan, 370–396. New Delhi: Oxford University Press.

Héritier, Adrienne. 2002. "New Modes of Governance in Europe: Policy-Making without Legislating." In *Common Goods: Reinventing European and International Governance*, edited by Adrienne Héritier, 185–206. Lanham: Rowman and Littlefield.

Herring, Ronald J. 1999. "Embedded Particularism: India's Failed Developmental State." In *The Developmental State*, edited by Meredith Woo-Cumings. Ithaca, NY: Cornell University Press.

Hirst, Paul. 2000. "Democracy and Governance." In *Debating Governance: Authority, Steering, and Democracy* edited by Jan Pierre. Oxford: Oxford University Press.

Holmberg, Sören, Bo Rothstein, and Naghmeh Nasiritousi. 2009. "Quality of Government: What You Get." *Annual Review of Political Science* 12 (1): 135–161.

Hughes, Owen. 2010. "Does Governance Exist?" In *The New Public Governance: Emerging Perspectives on the Theory and Practice of Public Governance*, edited by Stephen P. Osborne, 87–104. London and New York: Routledge.

Huntington, Samuel P. 1968. *Political Order in Changing Societies*. New Haven, CT: Yale University Press.

Huther, Jeff and Anwar Shah. 1998. *Applying a Simple Measure of Good Governance to the Debate on Fiscal Decentralization*. Policy Research Working Paper. Washington DC: Operations Evaluations Department.

Hyden, Goran. 1999. "Governance and the Reconstitution of Political Order." In *State, Conflict, and Democracy in Africa*, edited by Richard Joseph. Boulder, CO: Lynne Rienner Publishers.

Hyden, Göran, Kenneth Mease, and Julius Court. 2004. *Making Sense of Governance: Empirical Evidence from Sixteen Developing Countries*. Boulder, CO: Lynne Rienner Publishers.

Jaffrelot, Christophe. 2003. *India's Silent Revolution: The Rise of the Lower Castes in North India*. London: Hurst and Company.

Jain, R.B. 2003. *Corruption-Free Sustainable Development: Challenges and Strategies for Good Governance*. New Delhi: Mittal Publications.

Jenkins, Rob. 1999. *Democratic Politics and Economic Reform in India*. Cambridge: Cambridge University Press.

Jenkins, Rob. 2002. "The Emergence of the Governance Agenda: Sovereignty, Neoliberal Bias and the Politics of International Development." In *The Companion to Development Studies*, edited by V. Desai and R. Potter. London: Edward Arnold.

Jenkins, Rob. 2003. "How Federalism Influences India's Domestic Politics of WTO Engagement (and Is Itself Affected in the Process)." *Asian Survey* 43 (4): 598–621.

Jenkins, Rob. 2004. *Regional Reflections: Comparing Politics across India's States*. New Delhi: Oxford University Press.

Jessop, Bob. 1995. "The Regulation Approach, Governance, and Post-Fordism: Alternative Perspectives on Economic and Political Change?" *Economy and Society* 24 (3): 307–333.

Jha, Manish K. and Pushpendra. 2015. "Governing Caste and Managing Conflicts Bihar, 1990–2011." In *Government of Peace: Social Governance, Security and the Problematic of Peace*, edited by Ranabir Samaddar, 167–202. Farnham and Burlington: Ashgate Publishing, Ltd.

Jha, Shree Nagesh. 1970. "Caste in Bihar Politics." *Economic and Political Weekly* 5 (7): 341–344.

Johnson, Chalmers. 1982. *MITI and the Japanese Miracle: The Growth of Industrial Policy: 1925–1975*. Redwood City, CA: Stanford University Press.

Johnson, Chalmers. 1987. "Political Institutions and Economic Performance: The Government–Business Relationship in Japan, South Korea, and Taiwan." In *The Political Economy of the New Asian Industrialism*, edited by Frederic C. Deyo, 136–164. Ithaca, NY: Cornell University Press.

Johnson, Isabelle. 1997. *Redefining the Concept of Governance*. Gatineau: Canadian International Development Agency.

Jordan, Andrew, Rüdiger K.W. Wurzel, and Anthony Zito. 2005. "The Rise of 'New' Policy Instruments in Comparative Perspective: Has Governance Eclipsed Government?" *Political Studies* 53 (3): 477–496.

Jose, Jim. 2004. "Exploring the Genealogy of 'Governance' within Australian Political Discourse." Australasian Political Studies Association Conference, University of Adelaide.

Jose, Jim. 2009. "Concepts, Damned Concepts, and Governance." Newcastle Symposium on Governance, Faculty of Business & Law University of Newcastle.

Kailash, K.K. 2011. "Varieties of Comparative State Politics Research in India." States in Transition: A Symposium on Democracy, Politics and the Forthcoming State Elections. Accessed 10 December 2015. www.india-seminar.com/2011/620/620_k_k_kailash.htm.

Kalaiyarasan, A. 2017. "Populism and Party-Society Developmental Regimes in Tamil Nadu and West Bengal." In *Political Economy of Contemporary India*, edited by Nagaraj, Rayaprolu, and Sripad Motiram, 98–124. Cambridge: Cambridge University Press.

Kapoor, Mudit and Rahul Ahluwalia. 2015. "Andhra Pradesh." In *The Making of Miracles in Indian States: Andhra Pradesh, Bihar, and Gujarat*, edited by Arvind Panagariya and M. Govinda Rao, 21–119. New York: Oxford University Press.

Kaufmann, Daniel and Aart Kraay. 2008. "Governance Indicators: Where Are We, Where Should We Be Going?" *The World Bank Research Observer* 23 (1): 1–30.

Kaufmann, Daniel, Aart Kraay, and Massimo Mastruzzi. 2011. "The Worldwide Governance Indicators: Methodology and Analytical Issues." *Hague Journal on the Rule of Law* 3 (02): 220–246.

Keiko, Yamada. 2008. "Politics and Representation of Caste Identity in Regional Historiography: A Case Study of Kammas in Andhra." *Indian Economic & Social History Review* 45 (3): 353–380.

Kennedy, Loraine. 2004. "The Political Determinants of Reform Packaging: Contrasting Responses to Economic Liberalization in Andhra Pradesh and Tamil Nadu." In *Regional Reflections: Comparing Politics across India's State*, edited by Rob Jenkins, 29–65. Oxford: Oxford University Press.

Kennedy, Loraine. 2014. *The Politics of Economic Restructuring in India: Economic Governance and State Spatial Rescaling*. London and New York: Routledge.

Keohane, Robert O. and Joseph S. Nye Jr. 2002. "Governance in a Globalizing World." In *Power and Governance in a Partially Globalized World*, edited by Robert O. Keohane, 193–218. London: Routledge.

Khan, Amir Ullah and Harsh Vivek. 2007. *States of the Indian Economy: Towards a Larger Constituency for Second Generation Economic Reforms*. New Delhi and London: Sage Publications.

Khan, Mushtaq. 2012. "Governance and Growth: History, Ideology, and Methods of Proof." In *Good Growth and Governance in Africa: Rethinking Development Strategies*, edited by Akbar Noman, Kwesi Botchwey, Howard Stein, and Joseph Stiglitz, 51–79. Oxford: Oxford University Press.

Kirk, Jason. A. 2011. *India and the World Bank, the Politics of Aid and Influence*. London: Anthem Press.

Kjær, Anne Mette. 2004. *Governance*. London: Polity.

Kjær, Anne Mette. 2014a. "Debate on Governance in Africa: An Emerging Political Economy Paradigm." In *Challenges to Democratic Governance in Developing Countries*, edited by Gedeon M. Mudacumura and Morcöl Göktug, 19–35. London and Heidelberg: Springer.

Kjær, Anne Mette. 2014b. "From 'Good' to 'Growth-Enhancing' Governance: Emerging Research Agendas on Africa's Political-Economy." *Governance in Africa* 1 (1): 1–10.

Knack, Stephen and Philip Keefer. 1995. "Institutions and Economic Performance: Cross-country Tests Using Alternative Institutional Measures." Economics & Politics 7 (3): 207–227.

Knoll, Martin and Petra Zloczysti. 2012. "The Good Governance Indicators of the Millennium Challenge Account: How Many Dimensions are Really Being Measured?" *World Development* 40 (5): 900–915.

Kodandaram, M. 2007. "Movement for Telangana State: A Struggle for Autonomy." *Economic and Political Weekly* 42 (2): 90–94.

Kohler-Koch, Beate. 1999. "The Evolution and Transformation of European Governance." In *the Transformation of Governance in the European Union*, edited by Beate Kohler-Koch and Rainer Eising, 13–34. London: Routledge.

Kohli, Atul. 1987. *The State and Poverty in India: The Politics of Reform*. Cambridge: Cambridge University Press.

Kohli, Atul. 1988. "The NTR Phenomenon in Andhra Pradesh: Political Change in a South Indian State." *Asian Survey* 28 (10): 991–1017.

Kohli, Atul. 1990. *Democracy and Discontent: India's Growing Crisis of Governability*. Cambridge: Cambridge University Press.

Kohli, Atul. 2009. *Democracy and Development in India: From Socialism to Pro-business*. New Delhi: Oxford University Press.

Kohli, Atul. 2012. *Poverty amid Plenty in the New India*. Cambridge: Cambridge University Press.

Kohli, Atul and Prerna Singh. 2013. Introduction in *Routledge Handbook of Indian Politics*, edited by Atul Kohli and Prerna Singh, 1–18. London: Routledge.

Kooiman, Jan. 1993. "Social-Political Governance: An Introduction." In *Modern Governance: New Government–Society Interactions*, edited by Jan Kooiman, 1–8. London: Sage.

Kooiman, Jan. 1999. "Social-Political Governance: Overview, Reflections and Design." *Public Management an International Journal of Research and Theory* 1 (1): 67–92.

Kooiman, Jan. 2003. *Governing as Governance*. London: Sage.

Kothari, Rajni. 1964. "The Congress 'System' in India." *Asian Survey* 4 (12): 1161–1173.

Krishna, Ananth V. 2011. *India since Independence: Making Sense of Indian Politics*. New Delhi: Pearson.

Kuhn, Thomas S. 1970. *The Structure of Scientific Revolutions*. 2nd ed. Chicago, IL: University of Chicago Press.

Kulke, Hermann and Dietmar Rothermund. 2004. *A History of India*. New York: Routledge.

Kumar, Ashutosh. 2013b. "Development Focus and Electoral Success at State Level: Nitish Kumar as Bihar's Leader." *South Asia Research* 33 (2): 101–121.

Kumar, Ashwani. 2008a. *Community Warriors: State, Peasants and Caste Armies in Bihar*. New Delhi: Anthem Press.

Kumar, Niraj. 2008b. "India: A Failed Democratic Developmental State?" In *Democracy, Development and Discontent in South Asia*, edited by Veena Kukreja and Mahendra Prasad Singh, 148–170. New Delhi: Sage.

Kumar, Nitish. 2007. "Plans for Change." In *Frontline*. Interviewer: V. Sridhar. Accessed 8 April 2015. www.frontline.in/static/html/fl2403/stories/20070223003011900.htm.

Kumar, Sanjay. 1999. "New Phase in Backward Caste Politics in Bihar: Janata Dal on the Decline." *Economic and Political Weekly* 34 (34/35): 2472–2480.

Kumar, Sanjay. 2004. "Janata Regionalized, Contrasting Bases of Electoral Support in Bihar and Orissa." In *Regional Reflections: Comparing Politics across India's State*, edited by Rob Jenkins, 111–138. Oxford: Oxford University Press.

Kumar, Sanjay and Rakesh Ranjan. 2009. "Bihar: Development Matters." *Economic and Political Weekly*: 141–144.

Kurtz, Marcus J. and Andrew Schrank. 2007. "Growth and Governance: Models, Measures, and Mechanisms." *The Journal of Politics* 69 (02): 538–554.

Leftwich, Adrian. 1993. "Governance, Democracy, and Development in the Third World." *Third World Quarterly* 14 (3): 605–624.

Leftwich, Adrian. 1995. "Bringing Politics Back in: Towards a Model of the Developmental State." *The Journal of Development Studies* 31 (3): 400–427.

Leftwich, Adrian. 1996. "On the Primacy of Politics in Development." In *Democracy and Development: Theory and Practice*, edited by Adrian Leftwich, 3–24. Cambridge: Polity Press.

Leftwich, Adrian. 2000. *States of Development: On the Primacy of Politics in Development*. Cambridge: Polity Press.

Levi, Margaret. 2004. "An Analytic Narrative Approach to Puzzles and Problems." In *Problems and Methods in the Study of Politics*, edited by Tarek E. Masoud, 201–226. Cambridge: Cambridge University Press.

Levi-Faur, David. 2012. "From Big Government to Big Governance?" In *The Oxford Handbook of Governance*, edited by David Levi-Faur, 3–15. Oxford: Oxford University Press.

Lijphart, Arend. 1971. "Comparative Politics and the Comparative Method." *American Political Science Review* 65 (3): 682–693.

Lim, Edwin R. 2005. "Learning and Working with the Giants." In *At the Frontline of Development, Reflections from the World Bank*, edited by Indermit S. Gill and Todd Pugatch, 89–121. Washington DC: The World Bank.

Lipset, Seymor Martin. 1959. "Some Social Requisites of Democracy: Economic Development and Political Legitimacy." *American Political Science Review*, 69–105.

Luther, Narendra. 2006. *Hyderabad: A Biography*. Oxford: Oxford University Press.

Lynn, Laurence. 2012. "The Many Faces of Governance: Adaptation? Transformation? Both? Neither?" In *Oxford Handbook of Governance*, edited by David Levi-Faur, 49–64. Oxford: Oxford University Press.

Lynn, Laurence E., Carolyn J. Heinrich, and Carolyn J. Hill. 2000. "Studying Governance and Public Management: Challenges and Prospects." *Journal of Public Administration Research and Theory* 10 (2): 233–262.

Manor, James. 2002. "Democratic Decentralisation in Two Indian States: Past and Present." *The Indian Journal of Political Science* 63 (1): 51–71.

Manzetti, Luigi. 2009. *Neoliberalism, Accountability, and Reform Failures in Emerging Markets: Eastern Europe, Russia, Argentina, and Chile in Comparative Perspective*. University Park, PA: Pennsylvania State University Press.

March, James G. and Johan P. Olsen. 1983. "The New Institutionalism: Organizational Factors in Political Life." *American Political Science Review* 78 (03): 734–749.

March, James G. and Johan P. Olsen. 1989. *Rediscovering Institutions: The Organizational Basis for Politics*. New York: Simon and Schuster.

March, James G. and Johan P. Olsen. 1995. *Democratic Governance*. New York: Free Press.

Marinetto, Mike. 2003. "Governing beyond the Centre: A Critique of the Anglo-Governance School." *Political Studies* 51 (3): 592–608.

Markussen, Thomas. 2011. "Inequality and Political Clientelism: Evidence from South India." *Journal of Development Studies* 47 (11): 1721–1738.

Mathew, Santhosh and Mick Moore. 2011. "State Incapacity by Design: Understanding the Bihar." In *IDS Working Paper*. Brighton Institute of Development Studies, University of Sussex.

Mathew, Santhosh and Mick Moore. 2015. "The Purposeful Destruction of State Capacity in Bihar, India." In *Governance in South, Southeast, and East Asia: Trends, Issues, and Challenges*, edited by Ishtiaq Jamil, Salahuddin M. Aminuzzaman, and Sk. Tawfique M. Haque, 229–244. Heidelberg and London: Springer.

Mauro, Paolo. 1995. "Corruption and Growth." *The Quarterly Journal of Economics* 110 (3): 681–712.

Mayntz, Renate. 1993. "Governing Failures and the Problem of Governability: Some Comments on a Theoretical Paradigm." In *Modern Governance: New Government–Society Interactions*, edited by Jan Kooiman, 9–20. London: Sage.

Mayntz, Renate. 2004. "Governance Theory als fortentwickelte Steuerungstheorie?" In *MPIfG Working Paper*. Köln: Max-Planck-Institut für Gesellschaftsforschung.

McCarney, Patricia L. 2000. "Thinking about Governance in Global and Local Perspective." *Urban Forum* 11 (1): 1–30.

McCartney, Matthew. 2010. *Political Economy, Growth, and Liberalisation in India, 1991–2008*. London and New York: Routledge.

McGuigan, Jim. 2005. "Neo-Liberalism, Culture and Policy." *International Journal of Cultural Policy* 11 (3): 229–241.

Misra, Baidyanath, ed. 2000. *Economic Liberalisation and Regional Disparities in India*. New Delhi: A.P.H. Pub. Corp.

Mitra, Roma. 2007. "Role and Impact of Caste and Political Parties and Elections in Bihar." In *Role of Regional Political Parties in India*, edited by Dasarathi Bhuyan, 29–52. New Delhi: A Mittal Publication.

Mitra, Subrata Kumar. 1991. "Room to Maneuver in the Middle: Local Elites, Political Action, and the State in India." *World Politics* 43 (3): 390–413.

Mitra, Subrata Kumar. 1992. *Power, Protest, and Participation: Local Elites and Development in India*. London: Routledge.

Mitra, Subrata Kumar. 2006. *The Puzzle of India's Governance: Culture, Context, and Comparative Theory*. London and New York: Routledge.

Mitra, Subrata Kumar. 2008. "Elite Agency and Governance in Changing Societies: India in Comparative Perspective." *Asian Journal of Political Science* 16 (1): 1–23.

Mitra, Subrata Kumar. 2011. *Politics in India: Structure, Process, and Policy*. London and New York: Routledge.

Mitra, Subrata. 2012. "Sub-National Movements, Cultural Flow, the Modern State, and the Malleability of Political Space: From Rational Choice to Transcultural Perspective and Back Again." *Transcultural Studies* (2): 8–47.

Mitra, Subrata Kumar and Mike Enskat. 2004. "Introduction." In *Political Parties in South Asia*, edited by Subrata Kumar Mitra, Mike Enskat, and Clemens Speiß, 1–30. Westport, Conn: Praeger.

Mitra, Subrata Kumar and Vir B. Singh. 1999. *Democracy and Social Change in India: a Cross-Sectional Analysis of the National Electorate*. New Delhi: Sage.

Mitra, Subrata Kumar and Vir B. Singh. 2009. *When Rebels Become Stakeholders: Democracy, Agency and Social Change in India*. Los Angeles, CA: Sage.

Mohanty, P.K. 2003. "Andhra Pradesh: Improving Governance through Performance Management." In *CGG Collected Working Papers*: Centre for Good Governance.

Mooij, Jos. 2003. "Smart Governance? Politics in the Policy Process in Andhra Pradesh, India." In *Working Paper*. London: Overseas Development Institute.

Mooij, Jos. 2013. "Hype, Skill and Class, Politics of Reforms in Andhra Pradesh, 1995–2004 and Beyond." In *Handbook of Politics in Indian States: Regions, Parties, and Economic Reforms*, edited by Sudha Pai, 401–418. New Delhi: Oxford University Press.

Mukherjee, Rohan. 2010. "Reviving the Administration: Bihar State, India, 2005–2009." Princeton University. Accessed 28 July. http://successfulsocieties.princeton.edu/sites/successfulsocieties/files/Policy_Note_ID115.pdf.

Mukherji, Arnab and Anjan Mukherji. 2015. "Bihar." In *The Making of Miracles in Indian States: Andhra Pradesh, Bihar, and Gujarat* edited by Arvind Panagariya and M. Govinda Rao, 123–226. New York: Oxford University Press.

Mukherji, Rahul. 2008. "The Political Economy of India's Economic Reforms." *Asian Economic Policy Review* 3 (2): 315–331.

Mukherji, Rahul. 2009. "The State, Economic Growth, and Development in India." *India Review* 8 (1): 81–106.

Mukherji, Rahul. 2014. *Globalization and Deregulation: Ideas, Interests, and Institutional Change in India*. New Delhi: Oxford University Press.

Nachimuthu, V. 2009. *Regional Economic Disparities in India*. New Delhi, India: New Century Publ.

Nag, Kingshuk. 2011. *Battleground Telangana: Chronicle of an Agitation*. New Delhi: Harper Collins.

Naidu, Chandrababu. 2000b. *Plain Speaking*, edited by Sevanti Ninan. New Delhi: Viking.

Nanda, Ved P. 2006. "The 'Good Governance' Concept Revisited." *ANNALS of the American Academy of Political and Social Science* 603: 269–292.

Narisetti, Innaiah. 2002. *A Century of Politics in Andhra Pradesh: (Ethnicity & Regionalism in Indian State)*. Hyderabad: Rationalist Voice Publications.

Naseemullah, Adnan. 2017. *Development after Statism: Industrial Firms and the Political Economy of South Asia*. Cambridge: Cambridge University Press.

Neuss, Juergen. 1998. "The NTR Phenomenon Reconsidered." *Internationales Asienforum* 29 (1–2): 23–45.

North, Douglass C. 1990. *Institutions, Institutional Change and Economic Performance*. Cambridge: Cambridge University Press.

Ojha, Anil. 2006. "Alliances, Castes and Personalities: 14th Lok Sabha Elections in Bihar." *The Indian Journal of Political Science* 67 (4): 717–732.

Osborne, David and Ted Gaebler. 1992. *Reinventing Government: How the Entrepreneurial Spirit is Transforming Government*. Reading, MA: Addison Wesley.

Panagariya, Arvind and M. Govinda Rao. 2015. *The Making of Miracles in Indian States: Andhra Pradesh, Bihar, and Gujarat, Studies in Indian Economic Policies*. New York: Oxford University Press.

Panagariya, Arvind, Pinaki Chakraborti, and Marapalli Govinda Rao. 2014. *State Level Reforms, Growth, and Development in Indian States, Studies in Indian economic policies*. New York: Oxford University Press.

Pankaj, Ashok. 2009. "Toward Changing Institutions for Governance and Development of Bihar." In *Crisis of Governance, the Case of Bihar*, edited by Sachchidananda and B.B. Mandal, 13–42. New Delhi: Serials Publication.

Partridge, Eric. 1966. *Origins, a Short Etymological Dictionary of Modern English*. London and New York: Routledge.

Paul, Samuel and Kala Seetharam Sridhar. 2015. *The Paradox of India's North–South Divide: Lessons From the States and Regions*. New Delhi: SAGE.

Peters, B. Guy. 1999. *Institutional Theory in Political Science: The "New Institutionalism."* London: Pinter.

Peters, B. Guy. 2000. "Governance and Comparative Politics." In *Debating Governance. Authority, Steering, and Democracy*, edited by Jon. Pierre, 36–53. Oxford: Oxford University Press.

Peters, B. Guy. 2011. "Institutional Theory." In *The SAGE Handbook of Governance*, edited by Mark Bevir, 78–90. Los Angeles, CA: SAGE.

Peters, B. Guy. 2012. "Governance as Political Theory." In *The Oxford Handbook of Governance*, edited by David Levi-Faur, 19–32. Oxford: Oxford University Press.

Peters, B. Guy and Jon Pierre. 2006. "Governance, Accountability and Democratic Legitimacy." In *Governance and Democracy: Comparing National, European and International Experiences*, edited by Arthur Benz and Yannis Papadopoulos, 29–43. London and New York: Routledge.

Pierre, J. and B.G. Peters. 2000. *Governance, Politics and the State*. New York: St. Marin.

Pierre, Jon. 2000. "Introduction: Understanding Governance." In *Debating Governance: Authority, Steering, and Democracy*, edited by Jon Pierre, 1–10. Oxford: Oxford University Press. Original edition, 2006.

Platteau, Jean-Philippe. 1995. "An Indian Model of Aristocratic Patronage." *Oxford Economic Papers*: 636–662.

Plattner, Marc F. 2013. "Reflections on Governance." *Journal of Democracy* 24 (4): 17–28.

Pomerantz, Phyllis R. 2011. "Development Theory." In *The SAGE Handbook of Governance*, edited by Mark Bevir, 160–178. London: Sage Publications.

Powell, Walter W. and Paul J. DiMaggio. 2012. *The New Institutionalism in Organizational Analysis*. Chicago, IL: University of Chicago Press.

Prasad, Binoy S. 1997. "General Elections, 1996: Major Role of Caste and Social Factions in Bihar." *Economic and Political Weekly* 32 (47): 3021–3028.

Prasad, G. Koteswara. 1994. "Politics in a Former Non-Congress (I) State." In *State Politics in India, Reflection on Andhra Pradesh*, edited by Agarala Esawara Reddi and D. Sundar Ram, 301–308. New Delhi: MD Publication.

Prasad, Pradhan H. 1979. "Caste and Class in Bihar." *Economic and Political Weekly* 14 (7/8): 481–484.

Price, Pamela and Dusi Srinvas. 2014. "Patronage and Autonomy in India's Deepening Democracy." In *Patronage as Politics in South Asia*, edited by Anastasia Piliavsky, 217–236. New Delhi: Cambridge University Press.

Putnam, Robert D. 1988. "Diplomacy and Domestic Politics: The Logic of Two-Level Games." *International Organization* 42 (3) (1988): 427–460.

Rajendra Prasad, R.J. 2004. *Emergence of Telugu Desam: And an Overview of Political Movements in Andhra*. Hyderabad: Master Minds.

Raju, B. Yerram and N.G.P. Rao, eds. 2001. *Andhra Pradesh Vision 2020, Strategy for Sustainable Agricultural Growth*. New Delhi: New Age International.

Ram Reddy, G. 1976. "Andhra Pradesh: The Citadel of the Congress." In *State Politics in India*, edited by Iqbal Narian, 1–29. New Delhi: Meenakshi Prakashan.

Ram Reddy, G. 1989. "The Politics of Accommodation: Caste, Class, and Dominance in Andhra Pradesh." In *Dominance and State Power in Modern India: Decline of a Social Order*, edited by Francine R. Frankel and Rao Madhugiri Shamarao Ananthapadmanabha, 265–321. Oxford: Oxford University Press.

Ramachandraiah, C. and Arun Kumar Patnaik. 2005. "State versus Public Sector Profitability: Andhra Pradesh State Road Transport Corporation." In *The Politics of Economic Reforms in India*, edited by Jos Mooij, 227–263. New Delhi: Sage.

Rao, K.V. Narayana. 1994. "N.T. Rama Rao in Power in Andhra Pradesh 1983–1989 – A Review." In *State Politics in India, Reflection on Andhra Pradesh*, edited by Agarala Esawara Reddi and D. Sundar Ram, 75–115. New Delhi: MD Publication.

Rao, S.K. 1973. "A Note on Measuring Economic Distances between Regions in India." *Economic and Political Weekly* 8 (17): 793–800.

Rapoport, A. and A.M. Chammah. 1965. "*Prisoner's Dilemma: A Study in Conflict and Cooperation*." Ann Arbor, MI: University of Michigan Press.

Ravi Yadav, Ramendra Kumar, ed. 2004. *Bihar: Myth and Reality*. Gurgaon: Hope India Publications.

Reddi, A. Reddepa. 1994. "From Neelam Sanjiva Reddy to Nedurumalli Janardhana Reddy (A Study of Party Politics in Andhra Pradesh)." In *State Politics in India, Reflection on Andhra Pradesh*, edited by Agarala Esawara Reddi and D. Sundar Ram, 191–207. New Delhi: MD Publications.

Reddi, Agarala Esawara and D. Sundar Ram. 1994. "The Era of One-Party Dominance System in Andhra Pradesh: A Study of the Congress Party Politics." In *State Politics in India* edited by Agarala Esawara Reddi and D. Sundar Ram, 15–47. New Delhi: MD Publications.

Reddy, G. Krishna. 2002. "New Populism and Liberalisation: Regime Shift under Chandrababu Naidu in AP." *Economic and Political Weekly* 37 (9): 871–883.

Reddy, G. Krishna. 2007. "Governance Reforms in Andhra Pradesh: Viewing through Rural Prism." In *Globalisation, Governance Reforms and Development in India*, edited by Kameshwar Choudhary, 161–180. New Delhi: SAGE.

Rhodes, Roderick Arthur William. 1994. "The Hollowing out of The State: The Changing Nature of the Public Service in Britain." *The Political Quarterly* 65 (2): 138–151.

Rhodes, Roderick Arthur William. 1996. "The New Governance: Governing without Government." *Political Studies* 44 (4): 652–667.

Rhodes, Roderick Arthur William. 1997. *Understanding Governance*. Buckingham and Philadelphia: Open University Press.

Rhodes, Roderick Arthur William. 2000. "Governance and Public Administration." In *Debating Governance, Authority, Steering, and Democracy*, edited by Jon Pierre, 54–90. Oxford: Oxford University Press.

Rhodes, Roderick Arthur William. 2007. "Understanding Governance: Ten Years On." *Organization Studies* 28: 1243–1264.

Rhodes, Roderick Arthur William. 2012. "Waves of Governance." In *The Oxford Handbook of Governance*, edited by David Levi-Faur, 34–48. New York: Oxford University Press.

Richards, David and Martin J. Smith. 2002. *Governance and Public Policy in the United Kingdom*. Oxford: Oxford University Press.

Robichau, Robbie Waters. 2011. "The Mosaic of Governance: Creating a Picture with Definitions, Theories, and Debates." *Policy Studies Journal* 39 (1): 113–131.

Robin, Cyril. 2009. "Bihar: New Stronghold of OBC Politics." In *Rise of the Plebeians?: The Changing Face of the Indian Legislative Assemblies*, edited by Christophe Jaffrelot and Sanjay Kumar, 65–102. New Delhi: Routledge.

Rodrik, Dani. 1990. "How Should Structural Adjustment Programs be Designed?" *World Development* 18 (7): 933–947.

Rosenau, James N. 1995. "Governance in the Twenty-First Century." *Global Governance*: 13–43.

Rotberg, R.I. 2014. "Good Governance Means Performance and Results." *Governance – An International Journal of Policy Administration and Institutions* 27 (3): 511–518.

Rothermund, Dietmar. 2008. *India: The Rise of an Asian Giant*. New Haven, CT: Yale University Press.

Rothermund, Dietmar. 2013. *Contemporary India: Political, Economic and Social Development Since 1947*. New Delhi: Pearson.

Rothstein, Bo and Jan Teorell. 2012. "Defining and Measuring Quality of Government." In *Good Government: The Relevance of Political Science*, edited by Bo Rothstein and Sören Holmberg, 6–26. Cheltenham: Edward Elgar Publishing.

Roy, Ramashray. 1966. "Intra-Party Conflict in the Bihar Congress." *Asian Survey* 6 (12): 706–715.

Roy, Ramashray. 1994. "Bihar Politics." *The Indian Journal of Political Science* 55 (3): 221–230.

Rudolph, Lloyd I. and Susanne Hoeber Rudolph. 1987. *In Pursuit of Lakshmi: The Political Economy of the Indian State*. Chicago, IL: University of Chicago Press.

Rudolph, Lloyd I. and Susanne Hoeber Rudolph. 2013. "The Iconization of Chandrababu: Sharing Sovereignty in India's Federal Market Economy." In *Handbook of Politics in Indian States: Regions, Parties, and Economic Reforms*, edited by Sudha Pai, 315–338. New Delhi: Oxford University Press.

Rueschemeyer, D. and Evans, P. 1985. "The State and Economic Transformation: Toward an Analysis of the Conditions Underlying Effective Intervention." In *Bringing the State Back In*, edited by P. Evans, D. Rueschemeyer, and T. Skocpol, 44–77. Cambridge: Cambridge University.

Sankaran, S.R. 1996. "Introduction." In *Land Reforms in India, Andhra Pradesh – People's Pressure and Administrative Innovations*, edited by B.N. Yugandhar, 17–27. New Delhi: Sage.

Santiso, Carlos. 2001. "World Bank and Good Governance: Good Governance and Aid Effectiveness: The World Bank and Conditionality." *The Georgetown Public Policy Review* 7 (1): 1–22.

Sarangi, Prakash. 2004. "Telugu Desam Party: The Dialectics of Regional Identity and National Politics " In *Political Parties in South Asia*, edited by Subrata Kumar Mitra, Mike Enskat, and Clemens Speiß, 366. S. Westport, CT: Praeger.

Satyanarayana, Adapa. 2007. *Society, Economy, and Polity in Modern Andhra*. New Delhi: Kanishka Publ.

Scharpf, Fritz W. 1997. *Games Real Actors Play: Actor-Centered Institutionalism in Policy Research*. Boulder, CO: Oxford: Westview Press.

Schneider, Volker and Dirk Hyner. 2006. "Security in Cyberspace: Governance by Transnational Policy Networks." In *New Modes of Governance in the Global System:*

Exploring Publicness, Delegation, and Inclusiveness, edited by M. Koenig Archibugi and M. Zürn, 154–176. New York: Palgrave.

Sen, Amartya. 1993. "Capability and Well-Being." In *The Philosophy of Economics, an Anthology*, edited by Daniel M. Hausman, 270–294. Cambridge: Cambridge University Press.

Seshadri, K. 1970. "The Telangana Agitation and the Politics of Andhra Pradesh." *The Indian Journal of Political Science* 31 (1): 60–81.

Sharma, B.A.V. and K. Madhusuhan Reddy. 1979. "Electoral Politics and Voting Behaviour." In *State Government and Politics*, edited by G. Ram Reddy and B.A.V. Sharma. New Delhi: Sterling.

Shepsle, Kenneth A. 1989. "Studying Institutions: Some Lessons from the Rational Choice Approach." *Journal of Theoretical Politics* 1 (2): 131–147.

Shepsle, Kenneth. 2008. "Rational Choice Institutionalism." *The Oxford Handbook of Political Institutions*, edited by R.A.W. Rhodes, S.A. Binder, and B.A. Rockman, 23–38. Oxford: Oxford University Press.

Sills, David L., ed. 1968. *International Encyclopedia of the Social Sciences*. New York: Macmillan and Free Press.

Sinha, Arun. 2011. *Nitish Kumar and the Rise of Bihar*. New Delhi: Penguin Books India.

Sinha, Aseema. 2003. "Rethinking the Developmental State Model: Divided Leviathan and Subnational Comparisons in India." *Comparative Politics* 35 (4): 459–476.

Sinha, Aseema. 2005. *The Regional Roots of Developmental Politics in India: A Divided Leviathan*. Bloomington, IN: Indiana University Press.

Sitapati, Vinay. 2016. *Half-Lion: How PV Narasimha Rao Transformed India*. New Delhi: Penguin.

Skocpol, Theda. 1985. "Bringing the State Back in Strategies of Analysis in Current Research." In *Bringing the State Back in*, edited by Theda Skocpol, Peter B. Evans and Dietrich Rueschemeye, 3–37. Cambridge: Cambridge University Press.

Snyder, Richard. 2001. "Scaling Down: The Subnational Comparative Method." *Studies in Comparative International Development* 36 (1): 93–110.

Sørensen, Eva. 2002. "Democratic Theory and Network Governance." *Administrative Theory & Praxis* 24 (4): 693–720.

Srikanth, H. 2013. "Construction and Consolidation of the Telangana Identity." *Economic & Political Weekly* XLVIII (45–46): 39–45.

Srinivas, S.V. 2009. *Megastar: Chiranjeevi and Telugu Cinema after N.T. Rama Rao. South Asian cinema*. New Delhi: Oxford University Press.

Srinivasulu, Karli. 1999. "Party Competition and Strategies of Mobilisation: An Analysis of Social Coalitions in the 1999 Elections in Andhra Pradesh." In *India's 1999 Elections and 20th Century Politics*, edited by Paul Wallace and Ramashray Roy, 141–166. New Delhi: Sage Publication.

Srinivasulu, Karli. 2002. "Caste, Class, and Social Articulation in Andhra Pradesh: Mapping Differential Regional Trajectories." In *Working Paper*. London: Overseas Development Institute.

Srinivasulu, Karli. 2004. "Political Articulation and Policy, Discourse in the 2004 Election in Andhra Pradesh." In *GAPS Series*. Hyderabad: Centre for Economic and Social Studies.

Srinivasulu, K. and Hari Prasad. 1987. "Emergence of Telugu Desam Party." In *Parliamentary Democracy in India*, edited by V. Bhaskara Rao and Borra Venkateswarlu, 144–153. New Delhi: Mittal Publications.

Srivastava, Sumit Saurabh. 2017. "Aspiring Modernity, Lingering Traditionalism: Explorations of Clientele & Patronage Politics in India." *The Eastern Anthropologist* 70 (1): 21–38.

Stein, Howard. 2006. "Structural Adjustment." In *The Elgar Companion to Development Studies*, edited by David Clark, 596–601. Cheltenham: Edward Elgar Publishing.

Stivers, Camilla. 2008. "The Ontology of Public Space: Grounding Governance in Social Reality." *American Behavioral Scientist* 52 (7): 1095–1108.

Stockemer, Daniel. 2012. "Regime Type and Good Governance in Low and High Income States: What Is the Empirical Link?" *Democratization* 21 (1): 118–136.

Stoker, Gerry. 1998. "Governance as Theory: Five Propositions." *International Social Science Journal* 50: 17–28.

Subramanyam, P. 2007. "Regional Political Party in Andhra Pradesh: Telugu Desam – A Study." In *Role of Regional Parties in India*, edited by Dasarathi Bhuyan, 65–78. New Delhi: Mittal Publication.

Suleiman, Ezra N. 2005. *Dismantling Democratic States*. Princeton, NJ: Princeton University Press.

Suri, K.C. 2002. *Democratic Process and Electoral Politics in Andhra Pradesh, India*. London: Overseas Development Institute.

Suri, K.C. 2004a. "Andhra Pradesh: Fall of the CEO in Arena of Democracy." *Economic and Political Weekly* 39 (51): 5493–5497.

Suri, K.C. 2004b. "Telugu Desam Party: Rise and Prospects for Future." *Economic and Political Weekly* 39 (14/15): 1481–1490.

Suri, K.C. 2005. "The Dilemma of Democracy: Economic Reforms and Electoral Politics in Andhra Pradesh." In *The Politics of Economic Reforms in India*, edited by Jos Mooij, 130–169. New Delhi: Sage Publications.

Suri, K.C. 2013. "From Dominance to Disarray, the Telugu Desam Party in Andhra Pradesh." In *Handbook of Politics in Indian States: Regions, Parties, and Economic Reforms*, edited by Sudha Pai, 166–179. New Delhi: Oxford University Press.

Thakur, Sankarshan. 2000. *The Making of Laloo Yadav: the Unmaking of Bihar*. Noida: Harper Collins.

Thakur, Sankarshan. 2014. *Single Man: The Life and Times of Nitish Kumar of Bihar*. Noida: Harper Collins.

Thirumali, Inukonda. 2013. *Telangana-Andhra: Castes, Regions, and Politics in Andhra Pradesh*. Delhi: Aakar Books.

Tillin, Louise. 2013. "National and Subnational Comparative Politics: Why What and How." *Studies in Indian Politics* 1 (2): 235–240.

Tollefson, Chris, Anthony R. Zito, and Fred Gale. 2012. "Symposium Overview: Conceptualizing New Governance Arrangements." *Public Administration* 90 (1): 3–18.

Torfing, Jacob. 2010. "Governance." In *Encyclopedia of Political Theory*, edited by Mark Bevir, 563–567. Los Angeles, CA: Sage.

Torfing, Jacob, B. Guy Peters, Jon Pierre, and Eva Sørensen. 2012. *Interactive Governance: Advancing the Paradigm*. Oxford: Oxford University Press.

Treib, Oliver, Holger Bähr, and Gerda Falkner. 2007. "Modes of Governance: A Note towards Conceptual Clarification." *Journal of European Public Policy* 14 (1): 1–20.

Tsebelis, George. 1990. *Nested Games: Rational Choice in Comparative Politics*. Berkeley, CA: University of California Press.

V., R. 1999. "Sweet Dreams: Andhra's 'Vision 2020.'" *Economic and Political Weekly* 34 (7): 391–392.

Van Kersbergen, Kees and Frans Van Waarden. 2004. "'Governance' as a Bridge between Disciplines: Cross-Disciplinary Inspiration Regarding Shifts in Governance and Problems of Governability, Accountability, and Legitimacy." *European Journal of Political Research* 43 (2): 143–171.

Varma, Vishwanath Prasad. 1987. "The Political System of Bihar." *The Indian Journal of Political Science* 48 (4): 506–511.

Vayunandan, E. and Dolly Mathew. 2004. *Good Governance: Initiatives in India*. New Delhi: PHI Learning Pvt. Ltd.

Verma, Ravindra Kumar. 1991. "Caste and Bihar Politics." *Economic and Political Weekly* 26 (18): 1142–1144.

Von Fürer-Haimendorf, C. 1963. "Caste and Politics in South Asia." In *Politics and Society in India*, edited by C.H. Philips, 52–70. London: George Allen and Unwin.

Wachhaus, Aaron. 2014. "Governance beyond Government." *Administration & Society* 46 (5): 573–593.

Watts, Ronald L. 1998. "Federalism, Federal Political Systems, and Federations." *Annual Review of Political Science* 1 (1): 117–137.

Weeks, John and Howard Stein. 2006. "Washington Consensus." In *The Elgar Companion to Development Studies*, edited by David Alexander Clark, 676–680. Cheltenham: Edward Elgar Publ.

Weiner, Myron. 2001. "The Struggle for Equality: Caste in Indian Politics." In *The Success of India's Democracy*, edited by Atul Kohli, 193–225. Cambridge: Cambridge University Press.

Weingast, Barry. 1998. "Political Institutions: Rational Choice Perspectives." In *A New Handbook of Political Science*, edited by Robert E. Goodin and Hans-Dieter Klingemann. Oxford: Oxford University Press.

Weyland, Kurt. 2002. "Limitations of Rational-Choice Institutionalism or the Study of Latin American Politics." *Studies in Comparative International Development* 37 (1): 57–85.

Williamson, John, ed. 1990. Chapter 2: "What Washington Means by Policy Reform." In *Latin American Adjustment: How Much Has Happened?*, edited by John Williamson and Economics Institute for International. Washington, DC: Institute for International Economics.

Williamson, Oliver E. 2008. "Transaction Cost Economics." In *Handbook of New Institutional Economics*, edited by Mary M. Shirley, 41–65. Berlin: Springer.

Witsoe, Jeffrey. 2013. *Democracy against Development: Lower-Caste Politics and Political Modernity in Postcolonial India, South Asia across the Disciplines*. Chicago, London: University of Chicago Press.

Wyatt, Andrew. 2009. *Party System Change in South India: Political Entrepreneurs, Patterns, and Processes*. London and New York: Routledge.

Wyatt, Andrew. 2013. "Combining Clientelist and Programmatic Politics in Tamil Nadu, South India." *Commonwealth & Comparative Politics* 51 (1): 27–55.

Wyatt, Andrew. 2017. "Paradiplomacy of India's Chief Ministers." *India Review* 16 (1): 106–124.

Yadagiri, R. 1994. "Decline and Fall of Telugu Desam Party." In *State Politics in India, Reflection on Andhra Pradesh*, edited by Agarala Esawara Reddi and D. Sundar Ram, 301–308. New Delhi: MD Publication.

Yadav, Muneshwar. 2004. "Politics from Below." *Economic and Political Weekly* 39 (51): 5510–5513.

Zanotti, Laura. 2005. "Governmentalizing the Post–Cold War International Regime: The UN Debate on Democratization and Good Governance." *Alternatives: Global, Local, Political* 30 (4): 461–487.

Index

Page numbers in **bold** denote tables, those in *italics* denote figures.

www.ingramcontent.com/pod-product-compliance
Ingram Content Group UK Ltd.
Pitfield, Milton Keynes, MK11 3LW, UK
UKHW011002180926
475701UK00004B/522
* 9 7 8 0 3 6 7 5 8 6 7 6 8 *